Monetary Strategies for Joining the Euro

Monetary Strategies for Joining the Euro

Edited by

György Szapáry

Deputy Governor, Magyar Nemzeti Bank, Hungary

Jürgen von Hagen

Professor of Economics and Director, Center for European Integration Studies (ZEI), University of Bonn, Germany

Edward Elgar

Cheltenham, UK • Northampton, MA, USA

Published by
Edward Elgar Publishing Limited
Glensanda House
Montpellier Parade
Cheltenham
Glos GL50 1UA
UK

Edward Elgar Publishing, Inc.
136 West Street
Suite 202
Northampton
Massachusetts 01060
USA

A catalogue record for this book
is available from the British Library

Library of Congress Cataloguing in Publication Data

Monetary strategies for joining the euro/edited by György Szapáry,
Jürgen von Hagen.
p. cm.
Includes bibliographical references and index.
1. Monetary policy—Europe, Eastern—Congresses. 2. Monetary policy—Europe, Central—Congresses. 3. Economic and Monetary Union—Europe, Eastern—Congresses. 4. Economic and Monetary Union—Europe, Central—Congresses. 5. Monetary unions—European Union countries—Congresses. I. Szapáry, György. II. Hagen, Jürgen von.
HG930.7.M664 2004
332.4'94'0943—dc22

2003068783

ISBN 1 84376 689 2

Printed and bound in Great Britain by MPG Books Ltd, Bodmin, Cornwall

Contents

Figures

Tables

Contributors

Jorge Braga de Macedo, Special Adviser to the Secretary-General, OECD
Willem Buiter, Chief Economist, European Bank for Reconstruction and Development
Luís Campos e Cunha, Professor, School of Economics, Nova University
Jean-Philippe Cotis, Chief Economist and Head of Economics Department, OECD
Paul De Grauwe, Professor, Department of Economics, Centre for Economic Studies, Katholieke Universiteit Leuven
Gabriel Fagan, Head of Econometric Modelling Division, European Central Bank
Fiorella De Fiore, Economist, Directorate-General Research, European Central Bank
Nicholas C. Garganas, Governor, Bank of Greece
Vítor Gaspar, Director General, Research Department, European Central Bank
András Inotai, General Director, Institute for World Economics, Hungarian Academy of Sciences
Otmar Issing, Member of the Executive Board, European Central Bank
Zsigmond Járai, Governor, Magyar Nemzeti Bank
Mihály A. Kovács, Senior Economist, Magyar Nemzeti Bank
Alfredo Pereira, Thomas Arthur Vaughn Professor of Economics, Department of Economics, The College of William and Mary
Helmut Reisen, Head of Research Division, OECD Development Centre
Patrícia Silva, Economist, Bank of Portugal, Assistant Professor at School of Economics, Nova University
Pedro Solbes, Member, European Commission
Jürgen Stark, Vice-President, Deutsche Bundesbank
György Szapáry, Deputy Governor, Magyar Nemzeti Bank
Jürgen von Hagen, Director, Center for European Integration Studies (ZEI), University of Bonn, Indiana University Kelly School of Business, and CEPR
Jizhong Zhou, Senior Fellow, Center for European Integration Studies (ZEI), University of Bonn, Professor at School of Finance, Shanghai University of Finance and Economics

Foreword

In May 2004, ten new member states will join the European Union.[1] Eight of them are formerly centrally planned economies of Central and Eastern Europe. Following their accession to the EU, the focus of attention in the new member states will shift to the second step of the integration process: the adoption of the European single currency, the euro. Accession to monetary union is not an option but an obligation of the new members, which only have the freedom to choose the timing of their adoption of the euro. To enter EMU, a country must satisfy the Maastricht criteria on inflation, interest rate, exchange rate, fiscal deficit and public debt. What monetary and exchange rate strategy will be appropriate during the run-up to EMU to ensure both nominal and real convergence? How important will the Balassa-Samuelson effect be in the new member states and what will its implications be in terms of meeting the Maastricht inflation criterion? Under what conditions can membership in the new Exchange Rate Mechanism (ERM II) play the role of an anchor to guide expectations? What are the benefits and risks of joining EMU earlier rather than later? These and other questions related to the choice of monetary and exchange rate strategies in the new EU member states are discussed in this book.

The book includes the papers and contributions presented at a seminar on 'Monetary Strategies for Accession Countries' held in Budapest during February 27–28, 2003. The seminar was organized by the Magyar Nemzeti Bank (MNB, the central bank of Hungary), the Institute for World Economics of the Hungarian Academy of Sciences and the Center for European Integration Studies (ZEI), University of Bonn. The seminar benefited from the participation of high-level officials from the European Central Bank, the OECD, the EBRD, the EU Commission and the central banks of the Czech Republic, Estonia, Germany, Greece, Hungary, Poland and Slovakia, as well as officials from various Hungarian ministries and representatives of the European and the Hungarian academic community. The editors of this book are grateful for the financial and intellectual support of all who contributed to the success of the seminar.

NOTE

1. The new member countries are Cyprus, the Czech Republic, Estonia, Hungary, Latvia, Lithuania, Malta, Poland, Slovakia and Slovenia.

Acknowledgements

We would like to express our appreciation to the authors and the other contributors for the excellent papers, discussions and speeches included in this volume and for cooperating actively in preparing the material for publication. We are grateful to Leszek Balcerowicz, Mitja Gaspari, Alexandre Lamfalussy and Richard Portes for chairing the seminar sessions and for contributing to the discussion. We also thank the staff of the Magyar Nemzeti Bank, in particular Judit Krekó and Gergely Kiss who helped to produce the material for publication, and Éva Hörcsöki and Gábor Kerekes who helped to organize the seminar. Finally, we thank Hadya Eisfeld from the Center for European Integration Studies (ZEI), University of Bonn for her excellent assistance in preparing the manuscript.

György Szapáry
Jürgen von Hagen

Introduction and summary

György Szapáry and Jürgen von Hagen

The appropriate choice of the exchange rate regime and the associated monetary strategy is a topic that has been debated, researched and written about extensively in the economic literature. What brings this topic into the focus of policy debate in the new Central and East European EU member states is their commitment to join the Economic and Monetary Union (EMU) and adopt the euro. While there is no official deadline for adopting the euro, the expectation is that the new member states will adopt policies allowing them to enter the eurozone in the foreseeable future. These policies should ensure macroeconomic stability and sustainable growth, i.e. bring about both *nominal* and *real* convergence at the same time. The new members are also expected to adopt the new Exchange Rate Mechanism (ERM-II), the normal exchange rate arrangement for EU countries that have not yet adopted the euro.

A country must satisfy the well-known Maastricht requirements to be granted the right to adopt the euro. Three of these criteria, the inflation, the nominal interest rate, and exchange rate stability criterion, are directly relevant for the choice of a monetary policy strategy in these countries. The new member states are faced with the critical question of when to join the euro zone and what is the best monetary policy strategy in the run-up to EMU. The chapters in this volume address specific issues related to these questions and the choice of a monetary policy strategy in the new member states. The experiences of Greece and Portugal are discussed since they, too, are catching-up countries like the new members and in many ways faced similar challenges in the run-up to EMU.

HOW IMPORTANT IS THE BALASSA-SAMUELSON EFFECT?

One specific issue to be considered is the so called Balassa-Samuelson (B-S) effect. The B-S effect arises from the fact that the growth of productivity differs across sectors while wages tend to be less differentiated. Typically, productivity growth is faster in the traded goods sector than in the non-traded goods sector. To the extent that faster productivity growth in the traded goods sector pushes up wages in all sectors, the relative price of non-traded goods will have to rise. Since productivity growth is faster in a catching-up economy than in a more mature economy, the B-S effect implies that, *ceteris paribus*, the real exchange rate of the catching-up economy will appreciate. With fixed nominal exchange rates, consumer price inflation in the catching-up economy will exceed inflation in the mature economy. This is an equilibrium phenomenon, which nevertheless may create a conflict between the Maastricht criteria for inflation and for exchange rate stability, especially if the ERM-II is applied with narrow exchange rate bands.

This conflict might encourage the new member states to adopt an attitude which one might call the 'weighing-in' syndrome: like the boxer who refrains from eating for hours prior to the weighing-in only to consume a big meal once the weighing-in is over, the candidate country will pursue a very tight monetary policy and resort to all sorts of techniques (freezing of administered prices, lowering of consumption taxes, etc.) to squeeze inflation prior to the entry test for adopting the euro, only to shift back gears after it has joined the EMU.[1] The convergence of short-term interest rates to EMU levels will automatically mean a loosening of monetary policy after the country has become a member of the monetary union. That loosening will be reinforced if, in order to help to meet the inflation target, the country had previously allowed its exchange rate to appreciate against the euro and if that appreciation is then not fully validated in the final conversion rate. The result would be an inefficient stop-and-go cycle.

To deal with the conflict presented by the B-S effect, von Hagen and Zhou suggest softening either the inflation criterion or the exchange rate stability criterion to make them compatible with the situation of the new member countries. Gaspar, by contrast, argues that the procedures established in the EU Treaty offer sufficient flexibility and should be maintained. He argues that the ERM-II is compatible with equilibrium real exchange rate appreciations, because the possibility of revaluing the central parity is not ruled out. In his view, what is important is that the new members realistically assess their degree of convergence when adopting the ERM-II.

How important is the B-S effect in the new member countries? The chapter by Kovács reviews the literature and the empirical work done in this area and presents calculations for the Czech Republic, Hungary, Poland, Slovenia and Slovakia (CEC5). One of its merits is that its calculations are based on a simple but comprehensive accounting framework applied in a harmonized way, facilitating the comparison across countries. Kovács finds that the B-S effect on CPI inflation in the CEC5 countries has not exceeded 2 per cent per annum and is comparable in magnitude to the B-S effect experienced in the less developed eurozone members prior to their entry into the EMU. The implication is that the B-S effect should not endanger the fulfilment of the Maastricht inflation criterion. However, as pointed out by von Hagen and Zhou, empirical estimates of the B-S effect in the new member states reported in the literature display a wide range of variation.

Kovács emphasizes that the B-S effect is not the only source of possible inflation differentials. For example, traded real exchange rates have appreciated significantly in some countries. Moreover, other factors, such as sectoral wage and price setting behaviour, have also contributed to the development of the relative price of non-tradables. However, these other sources of inflation differentials seemed to be much less systematic than the B-S effect.

Cotis cautions that it would be dangerous to extrapolate the CEC5 pre-EMU experience to the period following EMU entry. EMU membership might speed up productivity catch-up and, therefore, increase the B-S effect. Furthermore, countries might experience a trend inflation due to strong capital inflows when exchange rate flexibility is not available anymore, a point also emphasized by von Hagen and Zhou.

Fagan, Gaspar and Pereira address the effects of structural changes on the real exchange rate. They investigate a package of stylized structural changes including changes in total factor productivity in the traded goods sector, financial integration and EU transfers of 'Structural Funds'. The authors conclude that such a package sets off a number of dynamic effects on the real exchange rate, which differ in important respects from the standard, static B-S effects. In particular, they find that there is significant 'front-loading' in the real exchange rate appreciation due to wealth effects on consumption and labour supply. Another conclusion is that a switch from a fixed to a floating exchange rate regime with the objective of ensuring domestic price stability does not significantly change the macroeconomic effects of structural change. The authors interpret this finding as illustrating the absence of a trade-off between nominal and real convergence.

IS ERM-II SUITABLE FOR THE NEW MEMBER STATES?

The new members from Central and Eastern Europe display practically the full range of possible exchange rate regimes: currency boards (Estonia, Lithuania), fixed rate (Latvia), free float (Poland), managed floats (the Czech Republic, Slovenia, Slovakia) and ERM-II-type arrangements with ±15 per cent fluctuation bands (Hungary). A common characteristic of these countries has been the appreciation of their real exchange rates, accompanied by an impressive decline in the initially high rates of inflation. The real appreciation has been the consequence of higher rates of inflation in these countries than in trading partners and in some cases has been accompanied by the nominal appreciation of the currencies. In countries with floating or wide-band regimes, nominal exchange rates have appreciated as a result of capital inflows in the form of FDI and portfolio investments. The latter were driven to a large extent by 'convergence plays', which had earlier characterized the less developed current EMU members in their run-up to EMU. In countries where inflation is above EU levels, nominal interest rates are higher, which attracts capital inflows when markets believe in the credibility of policies and the eventual convergence of interest rates to EU levels. As emphasized by von Hagen and Zhou, this convergence play makes the new members vulnerable to shifts in market sentiment that can trigger sudden reversals of capital flows.

What is the optimal exchange rate regime under such circumstances? One view expressed in the economic literature is that only corner solutions are viable in today's environment of free and rapid capital movements, i.e., either free floats or very hard pegs such as currency boards. Intermediate regimes would sooner or later come under speculative attacks. Is the ERM-II, a typical intermediate regime, a good solution for the new members? Von Hagen and Zhou reject the ERM-II and recommend instead that the small economies among the new member states should adopt currency boards or even be allowed to adopt the euro unilaterally, while the larger economies should opt for floating rates combined with a strategy of inflation targeting coordinated with the ECB's inflation target. By contrast, Braga de Macedo and Reisen argue that the prospect of regional integration eliminates the option of a free float as a non-cooperative strategy and that hard pegs are costly to exit. Garganas points out that the flexibility of the ERM-II regime is necessary to ensure nominal convergence and Stark emphasizes that, without the exchange rate as an adjustment tool in the catching-up process and as a correction mechanism for country-specific shocks, the donkey work has to be done by flexible labour and goods markets.

Braga de Macedo and Reisen, Garganas, and Stark emphasize the viability of the ERM-II as a *transitional* arrangement on the way to EMU – provided that it is accompanied by sound policies. However, not everybody agrees. Buiter and Grafe, like von Hagen and Zhou, warn that the requirement that a country spend at least two years in ERM-II before being allowed to join EMU exposes it to speculative attacks that can be costly and can occur even if governments pursue sound domestic policies. In their view, therefore, this requirement is pointless and resembles an 'ERM purgatory'. Buiter and Grafe advocate a derogation, waiver or flexible interpretation of the exchange rate criterion.[2]

WHEN IS THE RIGHT TIME TO JOIN EMU?

Joining EMU requires continuous efforts towards reducing the rate of inflation and the fiscal deficit to Maastricht levels in a *sustainable* way. It is not possible to meet the Maastricht requirements by 'ambush'; EMU membership must be built on broad public support and firm political commitment to the structural and fiscal adjustments needed. The chapter by Campos e Cunha and Silva describes Portugal's decision to enter the EMU as the beginning of a new economic policy regime, one that changed the rules guiding economic policies and transformed expectations and the behaviour of economic agents in ways that are desirable and long-lasting. But the authors also emphasize that political support was the crucial precondition for success of the new economic regime. Garganas reports that the Greek government's publicly stated objective of joining EMU provided powerful incentives for mobilizing public support for policy adjustments and that the ERM-II provided a regime shift that allowed Greece to orient its policies towards stability, fostering convergence.

Issing stresses the prerequisites of a successful strategy to join EMU. These are a clear mandate for the central bank to achieve price stability, central bank independence, transparent and accountable monetary policy design and implementations, and sound fiscal policy. Fiscal policy plays a key role, not just because it has to meet the Maastricht deficit criterion, but also because a sustainable fiscal adjustment is the foundation on which the credibility of the ERM-II regime is built. All contributors to this volume agreed that – as Járai emphasized – a proper monetary-fiscal policy mix is required. In this connection, Inotai draws attention to the paradoxical situation that the first years of EU membership are likely to generate additional budgetary pressures for the new members because of the need to comply fully with the EU's legal and institutional framework and because EU-funded projects will have to be prefinanced by the member governments.

De Grauwe raises an interesting question in this context. He argues that convergence in the Southern European countries took place not only because of the efforts of the authorities, but also because of the perception of the markets that there was a political will to accept these countries in the first wave of EMU membership. A virtuous circle of convergence emerged. Will the new member states be able to profit from a similar virtuous circle in the convergence process? De Grauwe thinks that this will very much depend on financial market perceptions of the political will to let the new member states enter quickly into EMU. The implication is that fulfilling the requirements for EMU would be easier, if the incumbent EMU members expressed their commitment to an early entry of the new member states clearly.

The point raised by De Grauwe is relevant, but the situation is more complex. There are also risks involved in a premature announcement of a target date for EMU membership, if there is no clear political support in the new member states for the policies required to meet the convergence criteria. The virtuous circle has to start at home. Even strong initial political support could vanish, however, if meeting the Maastricht criteria early entails too high costs. As Solbes points out, an early move towards fixed exchange rates combined with an unfavourable fiscal starting position may place an excessive burden on fiscal policy in case of external shocks.

Von Hagen and Zhou distinguish two possible strategies for joining EMU: the fast track and the slow track. The main advantage of the fast track scenario is that the instabilities created by the combination of an intermediate exchange rate system, high capital mobility and convergence plays can be overcome in a relatively short time. The main disadvantage is that the new EU members would have to make extra efforts to meet the Maastricht criteria and prepare for the adoption of the euro. To the extent that this requires solutions for inherited structural fiscal problems and further efforts at reducing inflation, the fast track eliminates the possibility of using monetary policy to ease the macroeconomic consequences of structural reforms. The main advantage of the slow-track scenario is that this possibility is maintained, since the exchange rate can still adjust.

Clearly, it is necessary for the authorities of the new members to carefully assess the possibilities and weigh the risks before entering ERM-II and announcing a target date for EMU entry. So far no country has ever missed a self-announced date of EMU membership. Doing so involves high risks, as it could lead to a reversal of market sentiment and capital flows that would undermine economic stability and make it harder to secure convergence.

LIFE AFTER EMU

Convergence to EMU may also hold some unpleasant surprises. In discussing the experience of Portugal, Campos e Cunha and Silva show that the decline in nominal and real interest rates may lead to overheating due to the loosening of liquidity constraints and positive wealth effects. The decline in nominal rates relaxes the liquidity constraints of households and firms by reducing the debt service burden. The decrease in real interest rates creates a sudden positive wealth effect for households by increasing the present value of future incomes. Whether these developments will lead to asset price bubbles and inflation will depend on how successfully fiscal policy can counterbalance the above expansionary effects. In this context, Cotis points out that the euro area has so far not performed as well as expected, as inflation has remained stubbornly above 2 per cent well into the economic slowdown. The outcome would have been much better had fiscal tightening in the overheating economies materialized over the past years. He warns that what applies today to EMU members could apply tomorrow to the new member states.

NOTES

1. See Szapáry, György (2000), 'Maastricht and the choice of exchange rate regime in transition countries during the run up to EMU', National Bank of Hungary Working Paper 2000/7.
2. See Buiter, Willem H. and Clemens Grafe (2002), 'Anchor, float or abandon ship: exchange rate regimes for the accession countries', *Banca Nazionale del Lavoro Quarterly Review*, No. 221, June, pp. 1–32.

1. Challenges faced by the accession countries

REMARKS

Zsigmond Járai

This book on the monetary strategies for joining the euro is very timely. The Copenhagen Summit, which sealed the agreement on the enlargement of the EU by ten new member countries, is just behind us. The EU referendums in the accession countries will be held in the coming weeks. Last but not least, in just 14 months, the accession countries will be full members of the EU. Questions regarding the effects of the accession, which heretofore had been merely theoretical in nature, have now become very real in all areas — from agriculture to education, from cohesion fund issues to European elections. This obviously also holds true in the area of monetary policy.

Compared to other areas affected by accession, monetary policy has a distinctive character. The process of monetary integration will not end with the accession to the Union. This will rather be simply the starting point for further steps, namely, the introduction of the ERM-II exchange rate system and the ultimate step of joining the EMU in subsequent years.

No doubt, monetary integration is one of the most significant economic challenges facing the accession countries. It is also an issue widely discussed in academic circles across Europe. Looking at the ten countries and the diversity of their current exchange rate regimes — which range from currency boards, through wide-band regimes, to free floats — it is clear that there is no straightforward uniform strategy followed in these countries. Considering that none of the accession countries was given an opt-out from the introduction of the euro, the main question that each country now faces is when to join the monetary union. Given the complexity of the issue, it is no surprise that most of the countries have yet to decide on the date of accession to the EMU.

The wide range of exchange rate regimes in the accession countries notwithstanding, these countries, particularly the five Central European countries, nonetheless experience similar macroeconomic developments and challenges. Among these are: the real appreciation of their currencies, the huge capital inflows associated mainly with the strengthening of the convergence play, expansionary fiscal policy and the success of disinflation. Let me elaborate on these issues briefly. The gradual appreciation of the real exchange rate in the catching-up countries is well established in economic theory. However, the real appreciation experienced by the accession countries in recent years was due, in various degrees, to nominal appreciations fuelled by strong capital inflows. Considering that the accession countries are small open economies, the strong appreciation inevitably weakened their competitiveness, putting a pressure on exports, at times of sluggish world demand. Its adverse impact on competitiveness notwithstanding, the influx of capital served to reduce long-term interest rates, as well as to ease the financing of the balance of payments. The inflows resulted from increased investor activity in the local markets, particularly on the long end of the yield curve. Let me mention the case of Hungary, where between May 2001 and the end of 2002, foreign holdings of forint-denominated government securities doubled, parallel with the almost doubling of the maturities of these securities.

Investor activity can, however, be driven by overoptimistic expectations. The recent events in Hungary, where in mid-January, within a few hours, €5.3 billion speculative capital inundated the country in the expectation of an appreciation of the exchange rate which we had successfully resisted, illustrate how investors, who pay little attention to the economy's fundamentals, could endanger the implementation of the optimal monetary policy of the central bank. It is thus of utmost importance to find the appropriate mix of monetary, fiscal and income policies to ensure the smooth development of the economy along the path leading to the EMU. In the area of fiscal policy, it is evident that the budget deficits in a number of accession countries are unsustainable in the medium term. Governments in these countries have tended to pay less attention to fiscal discipline, as they faced lighter constraints on financial equilibrium, not least because of the investors' appetite for local securities.

As a central banker, what I consider to be the most important macroeconomic phenomenon in the accession countries is the success of disinflation. The rate of disinflation in these countries during the last couple of years is remarkable. The results are even more impressive if we look back at the high double-digit inflation rates of the early 1990s. At the end of 2002, the average inflation rate in the five Central European countries stood lower than in the eurozone. This implies that, contrary to what economists had thought a few years ago, the inflation rate may not be the critical point in meeting the Maastricht criteria.

Apart from looking at recent events in the accession countries, it is equally important to analyse the experiences of the current members of the EMU.

There is, indeed, much to learn from our Portuguese and Greek colleagues. Soon, being members of the EU, the accession countries will face the same questions as the Mediterranean countries faced during the 1990s with regard to the fulfilment of the nominal convergence criteria, without endangering the pace of real convergence. I would like to cite three issues, in particular, that accession countries face.

The first is whether or not to join the ERM-II upon EU accession. As we know, in the ERM-II, the exchange rate is a matter of common interest to the national authorities and the ECB. An agreement should thus be reached on the central rate. This brings us to the second issue, that is, the choice of the central rate. This is far from being a purely technical one. As the ERM-II system is the anteroom to EMU membership, a decision on the central rate for ERM-II has strong implications for the final conversion rate. Finally, the accession countries should also form a view regarding the timing of entry into the EMU. Since adopting the euro will also have a permanent impact on economic growth, entering the monetary union is not merely a monetary step. The key question in this regard is whether the accession countries and the eurozone form an optimum currency area and whether the strictures of EMU membership are compatible with the optimal growth path. Monetary policy in the eurozone has to be capable of adequately substituting for the independent national monetary policies in smoothing out cyclical fluctuations and in responding to possible asymmetric shocks. Fiscal policy has to be aimed at meeting the Maastricht criteria prior to accession and, subsequently, at satisfying the conditions of the stability and growth pact. Clearly, the right monetary-fiscal policy mix is required.

REMARKS

András Inotai

Following the successful conclusion of official negotiations on accession, ten candidate countries are at the threshold of full membership in the EU. We all are interested in a successful membership. We do know that the degree of success depends on the implementation of the necessary reforms, both at the level of member states and at the EU level. It goes without saying that the success of the monetary union and its impact on reforms within the enlarged EU is a key element of the framework within which the new member states have to formulate and implement their economic policy objectives.

In the short run, accession countries face four clear challenges. First, they have to hold referenda on accession. Second, they have to devote the utmost attention to the adjustment tasks which result from the accession treaty and which have to be implemented, both in legal terms and in terms of institution-building, before the date of accession of May 1, 2004. Third, a broad dialogue has to be started with society in order to prepare the people for the chances and challenges of membership. The success of accession largely depends on the state of preparedness of societies, not just at the moment of joining the Union, but in many ways in the difficult first years of membership. Finally, each new member state has to clearly define its national strategy in all community policy areas. Only on this basis will they be able to develop their role as full members, defend their interests, enter into reasonable compromises and contribute to the shaping of a new Europe.

Preparing and eventually joining the EMU is a key element, or even more the crowning of a successful integration into Europe. As a representative of the Hungarian research community, I would like to make some observations, and address some questions and dilemmas. Each accession country is firmly committed to the objectives of the EMU, not only because this commitment is part of the fulfilment of the Copenhagen criteria (sharing the community policies in all aspects and areas), but also in order to be able to enjoy all the benefits of a large economic and monetary union in Europe in this age of globalization. In this context, we pay particular attention to two basic issues: the developments within the monetary union that will form the framework and shape the conditions of our entry into the EMU, and the domestic tasks of preparing for a successful participation in EMU.

Concerning the first set of questions, the future of the euro, both as a stable currency and an increasingly important international reserve asset, is of crucial importance. I am convinced that the sustainable success of the monetary union requires further steps towards deepening European integration. They include economic measures, mainly in the fiscal policy area, institutional reforms, mainly in the labour market, and most probably also enhanced political cooperation in all fields that may, directly or indirectly, affect the internal stability and the international standing of the euro. The ability to reform the members' domestic economies has become a key element of the success of the EMU. At the same time, the reforms are indispensable for ensuring the success of Europe as a growing global economy. To some extent, the successful integration of the new members may be influenced by the growth performance of their main trading partners, such as Germany, France or Italy. The sustainable fulfilment of the Maastricht criteria has been seriously challenged by the recent and, according to various signs, prolonged world economic recession, in particular the slowdown in the EMU economies. The higher than permissible budget deficits in some key member countries direct attention to the importance of having a balanced or surplus budget in years of high growth, which would create room for manoeuvre in more difficult times.

One of the basic questions is whether the common currency and the sound monetary policy of the European Central Bank will be a sufficient 'disciplinary' force to prevent some influential member countries from pursuing loose fiscal policies. How can national fiscal policies be efficiently influenced by the monetary policy of the ECB, considering national lobby interests and political pressures? In case differing economic and productivity growth rates resulting in different levels of international competitiveness cannot be rebalanced by the adequate flexibility of the labour market, wages and production costs, the sustainability of the EMU, as an unquestionable cornerstone achievement of the European integration, may require additional instruments, including the possibility of introducing a system of transfer payments. This, however, would fundamentally challenge the solidarity of the member countries. There is no doubt that such payments, if necessary, would be twice to three times higher than the present ceiling of the EU budget of 1.27 per cent of the GNP of the member countries. Such a development would be a much more crucial challenge to the common budget than the money available for the financing of the coming enlargement. With or without this possibility, the substantial restructuring of the present EU budget as of 2007 is anyhow a must for a sustainable European integration. Not only the accession countries, but also the current member states have a high degree of responsibility with respect to the successful EU enlargement and the subsequent accession of new members into the EMU.

Turning to the domestic tasks of the candidate countries, I would like to stress that the basic issue is not whether to join or not to join the EMU, but when to join without threatening the sustainability of a relatively high growth process. Since catching-up is a basic precondition of successful membership that needs a constant strengthening of competitiveness, monetary policies should not hamper this process. This challenge assumes particular importance in a period of slow world economic growth which weakens export-led growth, accompanied by partly understandable wage pressure on the eve of EU accession and substantial currency appreciations fuelled by capital inflows in anticipation of EMU membership.

There are differences in approach among countries regarding the appropriate timing of entering EMU and also differences in opinion among economists and politicians within the same country. Some people emphasize the evident benefits of becoming part of a currency union and consider the costs of early entry lower than the advantages. Others believe that a more cautious approach should be followed, and fear that a too early entry could seriously jeopardize the sustainability of growth and the continuous improvement of competitiveness.

The key policy issues are budget deficits and inflation. There is general agreement that budget deficit and inflation have to be substantially reduced and that, in due course, they have to satisfy the Maastricht criteria. The disagreement lies in the timing necessary and the policy mix to be applied to achieve the above goals without constraining growth. In my view, and from today's perspective, the achievement of the inflation target seems to be the easier objective to be achieved, even if we know that the catching-up process is accompanied by the so called Balassa-Samuelson effect which, for a certain period, results in higher inflation rates in the catching-up countries than in 'mature' economies. More problematic seems to be the budgetary deficit which, for various reasons, reached record levels in some candidate countries in 2002. Part of this deficit can and must be corrected in a rather short period of time. Another part, however, that is linked to the financing of the modernization process and the reforms in health, education, taxation, institutions, regional policies, etc. can hardly be implemented without a fundamental reform of the whole budget structure. The difficulties, which are not by any means only economic ones, are well known also in a number of EU member countries, and have been responsible for the large fiscal deficits in several EMU member countries in past years. Therefore, the main challenge of successfully preparing for membership in the EMU comes from the budgetary side. Since budgetary reforms need substantial time, all candidate countries would be well advised to start with these reforms as soon as possible in order to be able to join EMU at a relatively early time after accession to the EU.

Paradoxically, a special budgetary problem emerges in connection with the accession process. According to forecasts, the first years of membership in the EU are likely to generate additional budgetary constraints, particularly if the European economy is able to come back to a higher growth path by that time. The challenge partly comes from the still heavy financial burden of completing the adjustment process to the EU and complying with the legal and institutional criteria prior to accession and in the first period of membership. Another part of budgetary constraint stems from the direct payment to farmers (up to 55 per cent of the EU level) that the new members have to pay in advance of reimbursements and the cost of project cofinancing in order to have access to EU resources. Furthermore, a large part of project financing will be reimbursed by the EU in the last stages of implementation of a given project, meaning that the national budgets will have to prefinance these projects. Meanwhile, the new member countries will have to pay their full contribution to the EU budget right from the very start of membership, which implies that their net financial position vis-à-vis the EU could be negative in the beginning. One of the key issues is to find the right answers to this serious challenge, without curtailing those parts of the budget which are basic preconditions of a successful membership.

Contributions in this book deal with the relevant experience of some EMU member countries which, on the basis of their major economic indicators a few years prior to the adoption of the euro, had seemed to have little chance of entering the monetary union from the very beginning. Their experience will certainly be very helpful to the applicant countries. They were able to substantially improve their performance to fulfil the Maastricht criteria in a surprisingly short period of time. It would be interesting to know how they could perform so well, what were the economic and social costs and how sustainable they consider their present situation to be. Some differences in initial conditions should, however, not be forgotten when comparisons are made with the accession countries. First, the countries we are talking about had been members of the EU for a decade or more when they started preparations for the EMU. Second, the decisive part of their adjustment effort was accompanied by favourable world economic developments. Last but not least, they have been the beneficiaries of large net resource transfers from the EU, which substantially eased the budgetary burden of the financing of large projects that helped sustain growth and competitiveness. Precisely in the first and crucial period of successful membership of the EU and preparation for EMU, these favourable initial conditions are either missing or difficult to identify in the case of the newcomers.

2. Some thoughts on monetary strategy

EXCHANGE RATE POLICIES AND EMU PARTICIPATION OF ACCESSION COUNTRIES

Pedro Solbes

I would like to share some thoughts on the exchange rate strategies of accession countries on their road towards euro area participation. One year ago, we successfully completed the introduction of euro notes and coins, the largest currency changeover operation ever undertaken. This was an outstanding achievement and a major milestone of European monetary integration. A main challenge in the future will be to fully integrate the acceding countries in the EMU framework. With the successful conclusion of accession negotiations at the Copenhagen Summit and the prospect of EU accession in about a year, acceding countries are increasingly focusing their attention on the next step in the integration process: their participation in Economic and Monetary Union (EMU), leading to the adoption of the euro. In this context, a key issue arises: which exchange rate strategies should these countries follow for a smooth and successful entry in the euro area?

At present, acceding countries rely on a wide range of exchange rate arrangements, covering the full spectrum from currency boards to free floats. This diversity reflects the different approaches chosen by the acceding countries to manage their transition process, taking into consideration the economic conditions prevailing in each of them. It also reflects the fact that, from the EU side, there are no specific requirements on the exchange rate regime before accession to the Union. In general, the exchange rate arrangements of the acceding countries have served them well in the pursuit of macroeconomic stability and disinflation, as long as they were supported by an appropriate policy mix. If the starting points differ between accession countries, they all share the ultimate goal of adopting the euro. No opt-out clauses, such as those accorded to Denmark and the UK in the Maastricht Treaty, have been agreed for any of these.

In my presentation, I would like to discuss briefly three issues:

- first, the institutional framework for the adoption of the euro that should serve as the main reference of the acceding countries' strategies;
- second, the policy challenges ahead confronting these countries on the road to the adoption of the euro;
- third, the approach of the acceding countries to monetary integration as reflected in their pre-accession economic programmes.

The Economic Case for Adopting the Euro

Before dealing with the institutional framework, let me say a few words on the economic arguments for the adoption of the euro by new member states. There is, of course, a strong a priori economic case for EMU participation for the acceding countries. They are relatively small economies, highly integrated with the EU and have liberalized their financial markets. The theory of optimum currency areas tells us that the more open an economy is the greater the potential benefits from monetary unification. This situation characterizes many of the acceding countries. Therefore, the potential benefits from joining the euro area should in principle outweigh the cost of renouncing an independent monetary and exchange rate policy. The benefits would mainly stem from the elimination of the exchange rate risk, the reduction of transaction costs, lower interest rates due to imported credibility as well as from making their economies less vulnerable to external shocks. These conditions in turn will lead to an increase in trade, investment, employment and growth. However, there are also significant risks associated with a premature EMU participation for these countries, as countries lose their exchange rate flexibility, while the process of structural change, catching up and fiscal consolidation is not yet finished. But I will return to these issues later. This is the reason why the EU Treaty foresees a sequential approach to EMU membership.

The Institutional Path

The EU Treaty clearly defines the path for the full monetary integration of the acceding countries. These countries will not be able to adopt the euro immediately upon accession. They will first have to comply with the relevant Treaty requirements, including the exchange rate criterion, which foresees a minimum two-year participation in ERM-II. This institutional framework and its implications for the exchange rate strategies of candidate countries have been further clarified by the Economic and Financial Affairs (ECOFIN) Council in its report of November 2000 to the Nice European Council:

- Upon accession, the new member states will participate in EMU with the status of 'member states with a derogation' from adopting the euro. This is the same status that Greece had until 31 December 2000 and the status that Sweden still has now. This status will be confirmed in the Accession Treaty.
- New member states will have to treat their exchange rate policy as a matter of common concern. This implies that they should avoid rates that are inconsistent with economic fundamentals, excessive exchange rate fluctuations and competitive devaluations. They are expected to join the exchange rate mechanism, ERM-II, at some point after accession. Furthermore, new member states will have to regard their economic policies as a matter of common concern and hence will be subject to the policy coordination and multilateral surveillance procedures.
- For the next step, which is the adoption of the euro, the Treaty requires that new member states achieve a high degree of sustainable convergence. This achievement will be assessed against the convergence criteria laid down in the Treaty.

These convergence criteria have been the centre of much academic discussion. For example, it is sometimes argued that the inflation and exchange rate criteria should be adjusted to take into account the specific circumstances of accession countries and the potential trade-offs between nominal and real convergence they are likely to face. Let me stress here that new member states wishing to adopt the euro will have to comply with the same conditions set by the Treaty as the current euro area Members. The principle of equal treatment between the original and future participants in the euro area will thereby be fully honoured. The convergence criteria are meant to help assess whether a given country has achieved a high degree of sustainable convergence, that is whether its economy is sufficiently in tune with the rest of the euro area to adopt the common currency. In order to fulfil their purpose, these criteria need to be applied in a consistent way. This institutional path excludes the possibility of either an adoption of the euro immediately upon accession or the unilateral adoption of the euro before accession, sometimes referred to as 'euroization'. The logic behind this is simply that when a member state adopts the euro, it joins the euro area club with a 'voice and vote' and the decision obviously belongs also to the club, and has to be taken on the basis of the criteria set out in the Treaty.

As I have already mentioned, new member states are expected to join ERM-II some time after accession. This framework is sufficiently flexible to accommodate different exchange rate regimes in the run-up to the adoption of the euro. The only clear incompatibilities with ERM-II identified so far are fully floating exchange rates, crawling pegs and pegs against anchors other than the euro. Countries with currency board arrangements have, in principle, the possibility of keeping their euro-based currency board until the adoption of the euro. Although currency board arrangements are not a substitute for participation in ERM-II, they can constitute a unilateral commitment of the new member state to a greater degree of fixity against the euro within ERM-II. However, the new member state wishing to keep the currency board will be subject to the common procedure established by the European Council Resolution of June 1997 on the establishment of ERM-II, which means that the central rate parity will have to be agreed multilaterally.

Key Policy Challenges Facing Accession Countries

In the run-up to full EMU membership, acceding countries will face several challenges which will have a bearing on their strategy for monetary integration. In my view, three principal policy challenges confront the acceding countries:

- First, in the run-up to accession these countries must focus on preparing their economies for integration into the EU and pursue policies favouring real convergence; structural reforms, in particular, will improve the flexibility of the economy and will lessen the impact of shocks to income and employment.
- Second, given their present degree of real convergence and in a context of full capital account liberalization, it might be desirable for some of these countries to have some exchange rate flexibility. In this respect, the ERM-II mechanism could provide them with the required degree of flexibility, while providing a means to anchor market expectations.
- Third, the acceding countries need to reform and consolidate their public finances and create the necessary margin for manoeuvre so that fiscal policy can serve as an adjustment instrument when the exchange rate instrument is no longer available.

The Copenhagen economic criteria

As I mentioned already, the priority of accession countries in the period before accession should be to prepare their economies for integration into the EU. In this period, they should focus on furthering the process of structural and economic reform in order to enhance their status as functioning market economies and be able to cope with competitive pressure and market forces within the Union. Acceding countries should not endeavour to meet the nominal convergence criteria prematurely. Prior to accession, progress towards real convergence should take precedence over nominal convergence, even though the two can be mutually supportive. In a sense, the Copenhagen economic criteria could also be viewed as a measure of achieved real convergence. Of course, even once the Copenhagen economic criteria is fulfilled, continued reforms in order to increase the flexibility of the economy will still be needed so as to further enhance both nominal and real convergence.

The Commission's Regular Reports review progress towards the fulfilment of the Copenhagen criteria every year. What do they tell us? The progress made by the accession countries in this respect has been impressive. The ten acceding countries are now considered functioning market economies and are expected to be sufficiently able to meet competitive pressures by the date of accession, provided they continue on their reform path. However, progress in terms of real income convergence, the principal measure of real convergence, has only been modest. In 2001, GDP per capita measured in purchasing power terms reached around 45% of the EU average for the ten acceding countries, against around 41% in 1995. For most of them, closing the income gap with the current member states will require reaching and sustaining growth rates well above the EU average over the coming years. But what is also essential in view of EMU membership is the convergence of economic structures towards those of current member states. Such structural convergence with the euro area is desirable before the adoption of the euro in order to reduce the adverse effects of asymmetric shocks and increase the degree of correlation of business cycles.

With regard to progress in the pursuit of real convergence, let me stress that a vigorous and determined implementation of the structural reform agenda is crucial. In particular, in most accession countries, further reforms of labour, product and financial markets are needed to strengthen the supply side of the economy and enhance their growth potential.

Exchange rate regimes in accession countries and ERM-II

A wide variety of exchange rate regimes currently exists in accession countries. These regimes have evolved over time to adapt to macroeconomic and structural changes. In particular, in recent years, several accession countries have moved towards more flexible exchange rate arrangements, usually augmented by an inflation-targeting framework. When considering moving towards greater fixity against the euro, three factors need to be taken into consideration:

- The first is the possible costs associated with asymmetric shocks. Small open economies with high import dependence benefit from stable or fixed exchange rates as the literature on optimal currency areas suggests. Yet, if markets are not sufficiently flexible, adjusting to an adverse shock through output and employment changes can be more costly and disruptive than if assisted by changes in the exchange rate.

- Second, the acceding countries ought to pay attention to their vulnerability to reversals in capital flows. Capital flows to accession countries might be strong and volatile especially in a context of rapid growth and full liberalisation of the capital account and, therefore, could make the defence of a pegged exchange rate difficult. This is particularly so if structural reforms are not pursued with vigour and the prospective productivity gains initially forecast do not materialise. Here, I cannot stress enough the importance of policy credibility for supporting stable capital flows in this context.
- Third, some upward pressures on prices are likely to result from the so-called Balassa-Samuelson effect and continued price liberalisation, resulting in a trend real exchange rate appreciation which could create challenges to the simultaneous pursuit of nominal exchange rate stability and low inflation. For instance, structural reforms leading to an increase in productivity growth are likely to cause an incipient appreciation of the real exchange rate. This can happen either through an appreciation of the nominal exchange rate or through increased inflation or a combination of both. Clearly, there will be circumstances where nominal exchange stability, low inflation and reforming the domestic economy will be more difficult to achieve simultaneously.

In view of these factors, I am convinced that the ERM-II constitutes a useful framework for accession countries as it combines stability with flexibility and credibility. It provides a degree of exchange rate stability and an incentive for macroeconomic policy discipline while leaving the possibility of adjusting to shocks and market developments, even by changing the central rate. It provides an anchor to guide inflationary expectations, and its multilateral nature increases its credibility. It is also a framework for pursuing real and nominal convergence in parallel, provided that an appropriate policy mix exists. In this context, the moment of entry and the length of ERM-II participation should be determined according to what serves best the transition and macroeconomic needs of each individual country.

Fiscal policy and the transition to EMU

When designing their strategy for monetary integration, countries should also take into account the numerous goals that fiscal policy will need to pursue in the run-up to the adoption of the euro and beyond. This is an issue of crucial importance. Fiscal policy will be called upon to play an enhanced role in stabilizing the economy in an environment marked by continued current account deficits, the independence of monetary authorities and the progressive abandoning of the exchange rate instrument. It will need to support the catching-up efforts of the acceding countries. It will have to cope with substantial expenditure pressures stemming from the completion of transition reforms, compliance with the Community acquis and the need for extensive investments in transport and environmental infrastructure. Additional constraints will be placed on fiscal policy under the EMU's policy framework applying to 'member states with a derogation'. The burden put on fiscal policy will not only depend on the present situation of public finances but also on the degree of exchange rate flexibility in the respective countries. In the event of an early move towards fixed exchange rates combined with an unfavourable fiscal starting position, fiscal policy could become unduly restrictive while still having to bear the burden of any adjustment needed in case of external imbalances, external shocks or a reversal in capital inflows.

All this underscores the need for these countries to use the remaining years before EMU membership to consolidate public finances. Reaching sound public finances will require substantial efforts in some countries. In particular, they will need to implement reforms in order to reorient the structure of government expenditures and to cut the currently high levels of mandatory and quasi-mandatory expenditures.

Pre-accession Economic Programmes

In order to prepare for future membership, acceding countries have engaged in a multilateral economic policy dialogue with the EU. In this context, they participate in a voluntary initiative called the Pre-accession Fiscal Surveillance Procedure. This includes the establishment of annual pre-accession economic programmes (PEPs). The programmes submitted to the Commission in 2002 give a good indication of the challenges ahead and the accession strategies pursued. With regard to monetary and exchange rate policies, the PEPs envisage on the whole a continuation of the current monetary and exchange rate regimes up to accession. However, Malta and Romania indicate their intention to link their currencies closer to the euro. Malta has done so since then by increasing the share of the euro in its reference basket. Romania envisages switching to the euro as the reference currency in 2003–04.

The PEPs, however, remain vague about the strategies and the timing for ERM-II participation and the subsequent adoption of the euro, even though many acceding countries have already signalled their intention to join ERM-

II and to adopt the euro as soon as possible. The only exception is the Polish PEP that sets as an objective to comply with the convergence criteria by 2005. I welcome the fact that accession countries have opted not to be too specific at this stage in their strategies for monetary integration. The time will come to develop further these strategies and probably the next round of PEPs will provide us with more information in this regard.

Let me say a few words to conclude. For any acceding country, the choice of exchange rate policy in the run-up to the adoption of the euro is a difficult exercise. Acceding countries must take into account a number of economic and institutional factors and choose a policy path that makes possible both a rise in the standards of living while respecting the relevant EU acquis. In view of these countries' different present exchange rate regimes and different degrees of convergence with the EU, there is a priori a case for a diversity of approaches. This applies as much to the choice of monetary and exchange rate policies as to the timing and length of ERM-II membership and of the subsequent adoption of the euro. The current Treaty framework provides the needed flexibility to accommodate these different approaches. In particular, I see no need to envisage an adaptation of the convergence criteria, as is sometimes suggested. However, what is required in most accession countries in the period up to the adoption of the euro is renewed efforts to implement structural reforms and consolidate public finances in order to further reduce the need for the exchange rate as an adjustment instrument. Provided that the right sequencing is followed, and as long as economic policies in accession countries are consistent with their exchange rate strategies, we will all benefit from the enlargement of the euro area.

CONSIDERATIONS ON MONETARY POLICY STRATEGIES FOR ACCESSION COUNTRIES

Otmar Issing

I would like to start by reminding us all of the difficulties that central banks in accession countries face when taking monetary policy decisions. Their biggest challenge today — uncertainty — is also the main challenge the European Central Bank (ECB) faced at its establishment. In my remarks, I will discuss the implications of uncertainty for the design of monetary policy. I will also highlight some desirable principles for a monetary policy strategy aimed at achieving price stability in economies characterized by structural reforms, rapid growth, developing financial markets and vulnerability to external factors. A main conclusion I will draw is that monetary policy is effective in fostering welfare only if complemented by a sound macroeconomic environment and by an efficient microeconomic structure.

Monetary Policy Under Uncertainty

The difficulties of policy-making under uncertainty are well known to all central banks. They have nonetheless been a particular challenge for the ECB at its establishment, due to the new and rapidly changing environment induced by the creation of EMU. During the initial phase of EMU, it was particularly important for the ECB to ensure effective policy actions and to foster credibility in an environment characterized by pervasive uncertainty. The choice of the ECB monetary policy strategy was helpful in this respect. On the one hand, the strategy ensures effective policy actions by allowing the ECB to base its decisions upon a sufficiently large information set. On the other hand, it fosters credibility by avoiding pure discretion. Indeed, the ECB strategy provides commitment to a medium-term objective — price stability — and a structural framework to analyse the changing environment and to take monetary policy decisions that are consistent with this objective.

In order to reduce discretion and to enhance credibility, academics often recommend central banks to commit to *monetary policy rules*. In its strict formulation, a monetary policy rule prescribes how the policy instrument should be set as a function of a limited number of variables. Some proponents suggest the use of simple rules. These include unconditional rules (such as constant money growth rules) and conditional rules (such as McCallum base-money and Taylor interest-rate rules). One main criticism of simple rules is that the information set upon which monetary policy decisions have to be taken is too narrow. Consequently, other proponents have suggested the use of optimizing rules which allows the central bank to react to a larger information set. The popular inflation targeting adopted by a number of countries in recent years finds a theoretical formulation within this approach. The reaction of the policy instrument is derived optimally over time, starting from a given objective of the central bank and a simple 'model' of the economy.

In my view, the presence of uncertainty severely limits the usefulness of simple and fully specified reaction functions for guiding monetary policy decisions. One reason is that policy-makers face a very limited knowledge of the precise structure of the economy (the 'model' and its parameters). Therefore, they also imperfectly observe the channels of monetary policy transmission at work and the precise lags at which monetary policy impulses are transmitted to the economy. This limited knowledge constrains the ability of policy-makers to derive optimizing rules within a given model and it emphasizes the need to complement the criterion of optimality with that of robustness to alternative model specifications. This uncertainty also reduces the desirability of rules that prescribe the central bank to reach its target at fixed horizons, as this may require undertaking costly counteracting actions later on.

A further reason why rules may not perform well in uncertain environments is that central banks imperfectly observe the state of the economy, the realization of current and future shocks and their underlying nature (whether affecting demand or supply, and whether being transitory or long-lasting). It becomes then difficult to correctly represent future inflation at a given horizon with the model-based inflation forecast, as required by the theoretical inflation targeting approach. An imperfect knowledge of the state of the economy also affects the performance of simple conditional rules, such as the Taylor rule. Variables appearing in these rules — such as the output gap and the equilibrium real interest rate — can only be estimated with high uncertainty. Recent academic literature has shown that sizeable and persistent measurement errors arise in estimates of these indicators based on real-time data, and that such errors typically lead to a significant deterioration of the performance of simple conditional rules.

In complex and uncertain environments, a mechanical use of rules is too restrictive to approximate the optimal policy. This should not lead to the conclusion that monetary policy should be purely discretionary. In economies where the lags of monetary transmission are long and uncertain, discretionary policy actions can exacerbate economic fluctuations and postpone the achievement of the central bank's objective. Moreover, monetary policy needs to behave in a predictable and systematic way in order to stabilize expectations and to increase the effectiveness of policy actions. For these reasons, the ECB has committed itself to a monetary policy strategy. A *monetary policy strategy* provides a systematic framework for the analysis of information and a set of procedures designed to achieve the central bank's main objective. As such, it differs from the strict formulation of a rule because it is contingent on all relevant information and it does not have a simple analytical representation. Committing to a strategy is particularly appropriate when the central bank has limited knowledge of the structure of the economy and when structural changes occur frequently. Indeed, a strategy should allow policy-makers to take into account all relevant information and to translate it into effective policy actions.

The ECB Monetary Policy Strategy: Does One Size Fit All?

Let me now turn to the characterizing elements of the *ECB monetary policy strategy*. This latter specifies how information is systematically organized and translated into policy actions aimed at achieving price stability — the ECB primary objective as stipulated in Article 105 of the EU Treaty. I would like to briefly describe the main features of the strategy and to discuss how they enhance the performance of the ECB monetary policy under uncertainty.

One important element of the ECB strategy is the definition of *price stability* as an annual increase in the Harmonised Index of Consumer Prices (HICP) in the euro area of below 2%. By providing a clear benchmark against which to evaluate the performance of the ECB, this definition promotes transparency and accountability of its monetary policy decisions. It also facilitates the achievement of high credibility — although this latter will be determined in the end by the ECB's own performance. It might be surprising to find a definition of price stability as part of the ECB strategy.[1] The objective of price stability and its overriding nature is the core of the mandate of the ECB. It is enshrined in the Treaty and as such it cannot be subject to revisions at the initiative of the governing council. However, when devising its monetary policy strategy the ECB recognized that a quantitative definition of price stability was useful as a yardstick for accountability and to anchor inflation expectations — particularly for a new institution without a track record.

To reflect the long and uncertain lags of monetary policy transmission, the strategy adopts a *medium-term orientation*. Recent research by Eurosystem economists has confirmed that relevant lags in the transmission of monetary policy impulses in the euro area are two years or longer. Therefore, policy decisions need to be taken in a forward-looking and pre-emptive way. The medium-term orientation also allows for measured responses to unforeseen shocks, thus avoiding the introduction of unnecessary volatility in output, employment and interest rates. Furthermore, the ECB commitment to achieve and maintain low inflation over the medium term ensures credibility of future policy intentions. By anchoring the private sector expectations of future variables, this allows us to maximize the benefits of price stability. The strategy's diversified approach based on *two pillars* provides robustness to model and parameters uncertainty. This approach ensures that all elements in the ECB's information set are taken into account and organized in a coherent way when taking monetary policy decisions. The first pillar assigns a prominent role to money, recognizing the stable relationship between money and prices in the euro area and the fundamental monetary nature of inflation in the long run. The second pillar complements the analysis of money with a broad assessment of non-monetary indicators. Both pillars provide input into policy decisions aimed at price stability. Therefore, the two-pillar strategy ensures that the analysis produced under each of the two perspectives is confronted and cross-checked.

Today, central banks in accession countries face a challenge similar — if not greater — to the one faced by the ECB at its establishment, as their convergence process contributes to create an uncertain and rapidly changing environment. In this context, it is worthwile to recall that despite all the potential uncertainty the start of EMU became a reality after many years of preparation — one might say even decades — and after a gradual process of economic convergence towards stability in Western Europe. This provided the necessary basis for the successful launch of the monetary policy of the ECB. Just as the ECB did not start out of the blue, accession countries need not leap in the dark. In this respect, the ECB monetary policy framework and its implementation provides a valuable benchmark and an anchor for the end point of the accession countries' own paths to convergence and stability. Several elements characterizing the ECB monetary policy strategy could already now be useful for accession countries. Nonetheless, any general guideline for the design of a monetary policy framework needs to be tailored to country-specific considerations. For instance, the one-to-one relationship between money and prices in the long run has been found to be empirically robust across countries, periods and policy regimes, as well as across estimation methodologies and definitions of the monetary aggregate. Therefore, any strategy aimed at price stability must monitor long-term monetary developments. However, the precise role of money in a strategy over a shorter horizon should reflect country-specific considerations. Accession countries are small open economies and, as such, they are vulnerable to international factors. In particular, they are exposed to capital flows, which are a potential source of high volatility in domestic monetary and credit aggregates. Moreover, the presence of recurrent structural changes in the financial sector of accession countries may induce instability of the money demand along the convergence process.

Before discussing monetary policy strategy issues for accession countries, I would like to delineate some contours within which the choice of a suitable strategy can be made. I will first identify some general prerequisites for any successful monetary policy strategy. Some relate to the strategy itself, others to the prevailing institutional arrangements and others to the underlying macroeconomic environment or microeconomic structure. I will then point to additional prerequisites, which need to be satisfied by central banks aiming at price stability in accession countries.

Prerequisites for a Successful Monetary Policy Strategy

The first general prerequisite for a successful strategy is the existence of a clear objective to be achieved by the monetary authorities. There is widespread consensus today on the importance of *price stability*. Through its achievement, monetary policy can make its best contribution to economic growth and prosperity by reducing the social cost of holding money, by allowing for an efficient adjustment of relative prices and by maintaining low risk premia on interest rates. It is therefore important that institutional arrangements provide central banks with *a clear mandate* to achieve price stability. This ensures commitment of the central bank in pursuing its main objective, thus enhancing credibility. A key additional prerequisite is *central bank independence*. This institutional feature isolates the central bank from political pressures and it ensures that monetary policy actions are taken with the unique objective of pursuing the central bank's mandate. Only a central bank that is mandated to refuse to fund budget deficits by money creation can be credibly committed to the achievement of stable prices over the medium term. The assignment of an important public policy to an independent institution needs to be accompanied by *transparent and accountable* policy design and implementation. By enhancing central bank discipline and communication with the public, transparency and accountability help to improve credibility and to generate low inflation expectations. It is also crucial that the achievement of price stability is supported by sound *fiscal policies* because this enhances the credibility of the goal of price stability and helps maintain low inflation expectations. Irresponsible fiscal policies can jeopardize credibility, as higher inflation becomes desirable to reduce the real value of government debt.

Accession countries should ensure that these general prerequisites are satisfied. Indeed, some of these requirements will have to be met for membership in EU. Article 4 of the EU Treaty states that the activities of EU member states should entail compliance with the guiding principle of stable prices. The Treaty also foresees an assessment of each EU member state's convergence process that comprises an examination of its national legislation, including the statute of its national central bank. An important point of this examination relates to the independence of member states' central banks. The successful implementation of a monetary policy strategy in accession countries requires that additional prerequisites be satisfied. The most important is for central banks to achieve and *maintain high credibility of the disinflation process*. Several accession countries have made remarkable progress in reducing inflation over the last years. To be able to continue this process until the achievement of price stability, central banks need to preserve their credibility. By ensuring that low inflation expectations become entrenched, credibility contributes to achieving and to maintaining price stability. In fact, low inflation expectations have a beneficial effect on economic decisions that are relevant for inflation developments, such as wage and price setting.

It is also crucial that accession countries implement structural reforms to facilitate the *smooth functioning of goods, labour and capital markets*. When goods and labour markets are rigid, inflation and inflation expectations may remain high even in the presence of monetary regimes committed to the achievement of price stability. The existence of liquid and well-functioning capital markets is also important, as it allows for an efficient conduct of monetary policy through the use of market-based instruments. A further requisite for a successful strategy in accession countries is *consistency with the ongoing process of nominal and real convergence*. Monetary and exchange rate policies should aim at generating a stable environment that enables us to anchor expectations while providing enough flexibility to allow for adjustments in the case of unforeseen shocks. To ensure such a stable environment, it is important to create a sound institutional setting for *regulation and supervision of the financial sector*. An inadequate structure of public incentives for the corporate and banking sector may induce us to overlook economic risk, leading to low profitable investments and to insufficiently performing bank loans. In economies exposed to external shocks and large capital flows, this may add to the financial vulnerability and increase the probability of occurrence of a currency crisis.

What Monetary Policy Strategy after EU Accession?

The question to answer at this point is what monetary policy strategy is suitable for accession countries after EU accession. It is impossible to envisage one strategy that shares the same elements across countries and over time. Some elements are common — such as the desirability of price stability. Other elements depend on specific features — such as the appropriate choice of the exchange rate regime. For instance, fixed exchange rates may be appropriate during the initial phase of a disinflation process for small open economies with little rigiditiy in goods and labour markets and with an economic structure similar to the one of the anchor country. Under such circumstances, wage and price flexibility can be used as a substitute for exchange rate flexibility to absorb the shocks hitting the economy, while a common economic structure limits the probability of frequent asymmetric shocks.

At present, monetary policy strategies in accession countries diverge considerably. The exchange rate regimes vary from completely fixed arrangements to pure floats. In the early stages of the transition process, most accession countries have relied on pegging the exchange rate to a highly stable currency, as a way to import credibility from abroad and to reduce the inflation rate from high levels. Since the mid-1990s, a number of countries have gradually softened their pegs and moved towards a greater role for monetary policy. Several among them have adopted inflation targeting as a monetary policy framework. The overall success in anchoring expectations and in reducing inflation suggests that alternative strategies can be adopted. Nonetheless, it is important to ensure that current strategies are able to maintain a credible disinflation process and to achieve price stability consistent with a sustainable process of nominal and real convergence. Therefore, the assessment of alternative strategies needs to take into account two characterizing features of the convergence process in accession countries, namely the trend appreciation of the real exchange rate and the exposure to large capital flows.

Over the recent past, most accession countries have experienced an *appreciation of the real exchange rate*. Several factors can explain this real appreciation as an equilibrium phenomenon. One common explanation relies on the higher productivity growth experienced for tradables than for non-tradables in fast-growing economies (the so-called Balassa-Samuelson effect). When labour is mobile domestically and the law of one price holds, high productivity growth for tradables increases the overall level of real wages and the relative price of non-tradables to tradables. If the productivity growth differential with the euro area is larger for tradables than for non-tradables, the price level of accession countries increases relative to that of the euro area, inducing a real exchange rate appreciation. Other features of the convergence process in accession countries can generate an equilibrium appreciation — such as the increasing demand of non-tradables relative to tradables along the transition path and the capital inflows induced by initial disparities in capital to labour ratios.

Accession countries have also experienced large and volatile *capital flows*, which expose them to the risk of sudden speculative attacks. The size of accession countries is small relative to the global capital markets. Minor shifts in international portfolio allocations can have large effects on the amount of capital flows directed to these countries and thus on their economic conditions. The presence of high capital mobility and pegged exchange rates has often been regarded in the literature as the main cause of the financial crises experienced in emerging markets during the 1990s. A large initial capital inflow may induce booms and generate large current account deficits. If, for any reason, capital flows reverse, this may lead to increases in the degree of country risk, further capital outflows and pressures on the exchange rate up to the point where the peg has to be abandoned. Provided that a *hard peg* ensures credibility, this exchange rate regime will limit the risk of speculative attacks. This choice can also be useful to steer inflation expectations and thus to reduce inflation. However, the presence of a fixed exchange rate inevitably shifts the burden of international relative price adjustments towards domestic prices. This can potentially endanger the convergence to the euro area inflation rate and the achievement of price stability, although this would require large and persistent shifts in relative prices.

A regime of *flexible exchange rates* offers some protection against speculative attacks while providing ample room to accommodate the adjustment in relative prices through an appreciation of the nominal exchange rate. To anchor inflation expectations, this regime requires that monetary policy is credibly committed to achieve low inflation. The choice of many accession countries to combine flexible exchange rates with inflation targeting may reflect this need. It is important that each country decides its inflation targets in accordance with the degree of sustainable convergence already achieved. For economies currently experiencing higher inflation rates, it may be appropriate to pre-announce a disinflation path as a way to steer inflation expectations and wage developments. However, the credibility of such pre-announcements would require that disinflation should not be artificially supported by short-term developments in indirect taxes or administrative prices. For countries already experiencing low rates of inflation, it may be appropriate to consider the definition of price stability adopted by the ECB as a benchmark against which to set their own inflation targets. The alternative choice for accession countries is to adopt an *intermediate exchange rate regime* such as ERM-II. Intermediate regimes provide some anchor to expectations, while countries retain the flexibility to adjust the parity in case of asymmetric shocks and exchange rate pressures. The main difficulty with this option is that it leaves the country exposed to changing conditions in the global capital markets. It becomes then even more crucial for the monetary and fiscal authorities to credibly commit to stability-oriented policies.

An essential task of any monetary policy strategy after EU accession will be to guide the choice of the timing of entry into ERM-II and later into EMU. EU accession does not necessarily imply immediate entry into ERM-II, although this may be an option for some countries. It is important that any decision to join ERM-II is consistent with an adequate level of nominal and real convergence with the euro area. This would reduce the risk of currency crises and of choosing an inappropriate parity for the exchange rate. Once in ERM-II, countries will be expected to continue their convergence process until the sustainable achievement of the Maastricht criteria. ERM-II could provide a suitable environment to accommodate this process. On the one hand, currency stability is ensured by the commitment of domestic policies to achieve price stability. On the other hand, the wide band of ±15% provides enough flexibility to accommodate necessary movements in relative prices.

The decision of the timing of the adoption of the euro will also become part of the country's overall monetary policy framework. To adopt the euro, countries will have to satisfy the Maastricht criteria and the requisites for sustainable convergence. These include a minimum participation in ERM-II of two years. The period necessary to satisfy the requirements, however, may vary considerably among countries. More importantly, the optimal timing of adoption of the euro from the perspective of each accession country may differ, depending on the structural and institutional features prevailing after the required two years in ERM-II. The adoption of the euro will benefit accession countries by reducing interest rate premia, real interest rates and the risk of speculative attacks. Nonetheless, for some countries the benefits of staying longer in ERM-II could more than offset the opportunity costs. A longer stay would allow using some exchange rate flexibility to adapt remaining differences in productivity gains, wage growth and inflation relative to the euro area. Once the euro is adopted, differences will translate into costly changes in competitiveness and in economic activity. Therefore, optimally choosing the timing of adoption of the euro also implies reducing the differences in per capita income levels.

Concluding Remarks

To conclude, I think that central banks in accession countries can do a lot to facilitate a smooth and sustainable accession process. Their main contribution is to establish a framework for monetary and exchange rate policy that is at the same time stable and flexible. This can facilitate the achievement of a credible disinflation path and later the maintenance of price stability, in the respect of a sustainable process of nominal and real convergence. Price stability and satisfying results for employment and growth can only be achieved if the central bank is not left alone. Monetary policy needs to be complemented by a sound macroeconomic environment and a well-functioning microeconomic structure. Achieving a stable and efficient environment may impose significant constraints on accession countries. Nonetheless, this effort is necessary for a sustainable convergence process and therefore for EU and EMU accession. We should not forget that the rewards in terms of economic activity and overall welfare for accession countries would be large and long-lasting.

EXCHANGE RATE REGIMES ON THE ROAD TO EMU: LESSONS FROM GREECE'S EXPERIENCE

Nicholas C. Garganas[2]

In contemplating the subject of this seminar, one is struck by how dramatically things have changed in the course of a decade. In 1992 and 1993, when the Exchange Rate Mechanism — or ERM — underwent a series of speculative attacks, the prospects of a European monetary union were viewed, by many observers, with considerable scepticism. This scepticism was not without foundation. After all, hadn't there been previous false starts on the road to EMU? Hadn't the Werner Report prescribed a European monetary union by the end of 1970s? Yet, here we are today, having fulfilled the dreams of Pierre Werner and his colleagues and having celebrated the fourth anniversary of EMU.

I would like to discuss some of the lessons from the experience of Greece, the newest member of the euro area, in its quest for EMU membership. I will address what appears to be a dilemma. Much of the economics profession appears to have been converted to the 'hypothesis of the vanishing middle': for economies well integrated into world capital markets, there is little, if any, middle ground between floating exchange rates and monetary unification. Effectively, this hypothesis rules out intermediate regimes. Yet, a requirement for entering the euro area is participation in ERM-II, which is, after all, an intermediate regime. How can this dilemma be resolved?

The Retreat from Intermediate Regimes

Before I discuss Greece's experience, let me address the reasons underlying the retreat from intermediate regimes. What has caused this retreat? First, an explosive increase in capital flows during the 1990s has made the operation of intermediate regimes problematic. According to the thesis of the Impossible Trinity, developed in the 1980s, it is not possible to pursue an independent monetary policy on a sustained basis under a system of pegged exchange rates and free capital mobility. Eventually, current account disequilibria and changes in reserves will provoke an attack on the exchange rate.

The enormous increase in capital flows has been accompanied by abrupt reversals of these flows. Whereas the logic of the thesis of the Impossible Trinity suggests that exchange rate attacks typically originate in response to current account disequilibria and build up gradually, recent speculative attacks in fact have often originated in the capital account, have been sudden and difficult to predict, and have included the currencies of countries without substantial current account imbalances. Capital flow reversals have involved a series of speculative attacks, mostly against pegged exchange rate arrangements. These reversals of capital flows and resulting exchange rate depreciations have often been accompanied by sharp contractions in economic activity and have, at times, entailed 'twin crises' — crises in both the foreign exchange market and the banking system. Finally, there has been a tendency for instability in foreign exchange markets to be transmitted from one pegged exchange rate regime to another in a process that has come to be known as 'contagion'. The victims of contagion have seemingly included innocent bystanders, i.e. economies with sound fundamentals whose currencies might not have been attacked had they adopted one of the corner solutions. This triad of factors — (1) the difficulty of conducting an independent monetary policy when the exchange rate is pegged and the capital account is open, (2) the sudden capital flow reversals and (3) contagion — have profoundly affected the way we think about exchange rate regimes.

The Experience of Greece: Pre-ERM

The foregoing factors significantly affected the Greek economy in the 1990s. Through 1994, the performance of the Greek economy was pretty dismal. Growth was almost flat, and inflation and the fiscal deficit as a percentage of GDP were in the double digit levels throughout the period. Other EU countries were moving forward in their quests to become members of EMU while Greece was falling farther and farther behind. Clearly, a regime change was called for. It came in 1995. The signing of the Maastricht Treaty in 1992 and the government's publicly stated objective of joining the euro area provided powerful incentives for mobilizing broad public support for policy adjustment. Among the policy measures undertaken were the following:

- Fiscal policy was progressively tightened. The fiscal deficit, as a percentage of GDP, fell from over 10 per cent in 1995 to around 4 per cent in 1997.
- Financial deregulation, which had begun in the late 1980s, was completed and the capital account was opened in 1994. The deregulated financial system facilitated the use of indirect instruments of monetary policy so that small, frequent changes in the instruments became feasible, enabling rapid policy responses.
- The Greek Parliament approved the independence of the Bank of Greece and provided the Bank with a mandate to achieve price stability.

For its part, beginning in 1995, the Bank of Greece adopted what became known as a 'hard drachma policy', under which the exchange rate was used as a nominal anchor. For the first time, the Bank announced a specific exchange rate target. Underlying this policy was the belief, both in Greece and elsewhere during the 1990s, that the adoption of a visible exchange rate anchor could enhance the credibility of the disinflationary effort, because the traded goods component of the price level could be stabilized and wage-settling and price-setting behaviour would be restrained.

I will not go into details of the operation of the hard drachma policy. Suffice it to say that, during the years 1995–97, real interest rates at the short end were kept in the vicinity of 5 per cent. Fairly specific targets for the exchange rate were announced in each of the three years and were achieved. Importantly, inflation fell from about 11 per cent in 1994 to under 5 per cent at the end of 1997 while, in the first three years of the hard drachma policy, the real growth rate almost tripled compared with the rate recorded in 1991–94. Yet, as is typically the case with all nominal anchor exchange rate pegs, this regime produced difficulties. As predicted under the thesis of the Impossible Trinity, the ability to conduct an independent monetary policy under an exchange rate peg and open capital account became increasingly demanding. The wide interest rate differentials in favour of drachma-denominated financial instruments led to a capital inflows problem. The Bank of Greece responded by sterilizing these inflows, limiting the appreciation of the nominal exchange rate, reducing the impact of the inflows on the monetary base, and buying time for other policies to adjust. Still, the sterilization entailed quasi-fiscal costs and, by preventing domestic interest rates from falling, tended to maintain the yield differential that had given rise to the inflows. Additionally, the Greek economy experienced a fundamental problem associated with all exchange rate nominal anchor pegs during the move to lower inflation; the real exchange rate appreciated significantly, contributing, along with strong domestic demand, to a widening current account deficit.

This brings me to the second and third of the triad of factors – sudden capital flow reversals and contagion. The widening current account deficit, combined with rapid wage growth, fed market expectations that the drachma was overvalued and provided the basis for contagion from Asia, which commenced with the devaluation of the Thai baht in July 1997. The sharp rise in interest rates required to support the drachma increasingly undermined growth and fiscal targets. A further regime shift was needed. That regime shift was provided by the ERM. Effective March 16, 1998, the drachma joined the ERM at a central rate that implied a 12.3 per cent devaluation against the ECU. Entry into the ERM allowed Greece to orient its policies to stability, fostering convergence. Because participation in the ERM without severe tensions plays a role in the convergence criteria for joining the euro area, it acts as a testing phase for the central rate, as well as for the sustainability of convergence in general.

Lessons from the ERM

Before I discuss the drachma's experience in the ERM, let me pose a question: what kind of an intermediate exchange rate regime do we have in mind when we refer to the ERM? In my view, the present ERM system is the result of an evolutionary process. Like all Darwinian evolutions, several distinct versions of the species can be distinguished. I think it useful to distinguish the following:

ERM Mark 1

This species lasted from the inception of the EMS, in 1979, to 1987. Compared with the 2 per cent wide band under the Bretton Woods system, the ERM fluctuation band of 4.5 per cent was fairly wide and the system was supported by capital controls. For some currencies, the band was even wider, at 12 per cent. Small realignments occurred frequently. Between March 1979, when the system started, and January 1987, realignments occurred on eleven occasions. The system allowed France, for example, to devalue the franc by shifting the upper and lower limits of its band without affecting the market exchange rate, helping to forestall the possibility of large profit opportunities that give rise to speculative attacks.

ERM Mark 2

What has been dubbed the 'new EMS' began to take shape in 1987. Increasingly, the Deutsche Mark was used as a nominal anchor, with the Bundesbank's reputation as a stalwart inflation fighter supporting the monetary authorities of some participating countries in their efforts to attain anti-inflation credibility. Except for an implicit devaluation of the Italian lira in January 1990, when that currency moved from the wide band to the narrow band, realignments ceased to be a characteristic of the system. In 1990, the remaining capital controls were eliminated by participating countries. German reunification required a tight monetary policy to counterbalance the large fiscal deficits generated by reunification. With other ERM countries in recession and requiring a loosening of monetary policy, the ERM was confronted with a classic (n – 1) problem. Specifically, in a pegged exchange rate system consisting of n currencies there is only one degree of freedom. In the ERM, that degree of freedom was used by the Bundesbank to set monetary policy for the remaining (i.e. n – 1) participants of the system. The

Bundesbank's tight policy stance, however, was incompatible with the requirements of many of the other members of the ERM.

ERM Mark 3

Beginning in September 1992, many of the currencies participating in the ERM were subject to attacks, leading to a series of devaluations and the suspension of the pound sterling and the Italian lira from the system. These attacks were sudden and massive. Thus, they were different from the currency realignments of the 1980s, which were mainly the result of pressures that had build up gradually in response to current account disequilibria. With the lifting of capital controls, the attacks in 1992–93 originated from the capital account and sometimes infected the currencies of countries with seemingly sound fundamentals, such as France. Several new terms made their way into the lexicon of economists: capital account-driven crises, sudden stops and contagion.

ERM Mark 4

In a last ditch effort to rescue the system, the ERM band was widened to ±15 per cent in August 1993. As things turned out, this move helped salvage the system. It provided necessary breathing space for nominal convergence to occur.

ERM Mark 5, or formally, ERM-I

Under the present arrangement, exchange rate stability is explicitly subordinated to the primary objective of price stability for all participating currencies, and obligations under the system are deliberately more asymmetric than under the previous ERM. The notion of asymmetry is particularly important in underlining the principle that the country whose currency comes under pressure has to undertake the necessary policy adjustments.

Let me now return to the case of the drachma and the ERM. By the time the drachma entered the ERM in March 1998, the participating countries had demonstrated their determination to form a monetary union by attaining considerable nominal convergence, as specified in the Maastricht criteria. This convergence took place under conditions of market-based economies that could compete effectively in an open economic and financial system. As a result, the system built up a considerable amount of trust. As Otmar Issing pointed out in several recent papers, the trust generated by governments, including in their ability to deliver credible, non-inflationary policies, is a prerequisite for the existence of a stable currency, both internally and externally.[3]

When the drachma entered the ERM, it became a beneficiary of the credibility established in the system over the previous years. It also benefited from the market's knowledge of the availability of the system's mutual support facilities, such as the Very Short-Term Financing Facility. However, Greece's participation was not a free ticket. The other participants in the system did not wish to endanger the credibility that had taken so long to achieve. They rightly asked for an entry fee. This fee included the following elements:

- The new central rate — which, as I have noted, involved a 12.3 per cent devaluation — had been agreed by all members.
- The devaluation of the drachma was both backward-looking and forward-looking. The magnitude of the devaluation took account of both past inflation differentials between Greece and other EU countries and prospective differentials in the period leading up to Greece's expected entry into the euro area. Thus, the new central rate was meant to be sustainable.
- A package of supportive fiscal and structural measures was announced. Efforts to restructure public enterprises were stepped up. The aim of the measures was to ensure the sustainability of the drachma's new central rate. In other words, the ERM was meant to be a testing phase for EMU participation, not a free pass into the euro area.

Unlike many other devaluations of the mid- and late 1990s, the drachma's devaluation was not followed by further rounds of speculative attacks, nor by a financial crisis. Unlike other devaluations, it was not followed by contraction in economic activity, but by an acceleration. Moreover, and again by contrast with the other devaluations of this period, the impact of the drachma's devaluation on inflation was strictly contained. What accounts for the drachma's successful move from one central rate to another? In my view, the key ingredients of the successful devaluation were the following:

- Unlike other currencies that were devalued during the mid- and late 1990s, the drachma exited a unilateral peg and entered a systems' arrangement, benefiting from the credibility of the ERM.
- Fiscal tightening continued following the devaluation. The fiscal deficit, as a per cent of GDP, fell to about 1 per cent in 1999, from 4 per cent in 1997. Labour market policy gradually adjusted to the needs of fiscal discipline and of enhancing international competitiveness.
- Prudential regulation and supervision of the banking system had been strictly enforced and there was no net foreign exposure of the banking

> system. Thus, there was no currency mismatching problem — i.e. large, uncovered foreign currency positions which, under conditions of currency devaluations, raise the debt burden of domestic borrowers in foreign currency, resulting in bankruptcies and financial crises.

In addition to placing the Bank of Greece's disinflation strategy within a new institutional framework that gave it added credibility, the ERM provided another important advantage. Entry at the standard fluctuation band of ±15 per cent gave the Bank ample room for manoeuvre. Thus, when capital inflows resumed following ERM entry, the Bank allowed the exchange rate to appreciate relative to its central rate, helping to maintain the tight monetary policy stance and to contain the inflationary impact of the devaluation. The exchange rate remained appreciated relative to its central rate throughout the rest of 1998 and for all of 1999. In 1999, for example, the drachma traded (on average) 7.7 per cent above its central rate while, for most of that year, the three-month interbank rate stood about 700 basis points above the corresponding German rate. As a result of the tightened and consistent policy mix, inflation reached a low of 2 per cent during the second half of 1999. Then, in order to limit the degree of depreciation that would be required for the market rate to reach its central rate and to contain the resulting inflationary pressures, the central rate was revalued by 3.5 per cent in January 2000. The rest, as they say, is history; having fulfilled all the Maastricht criteria, Greece became the 12th member of the euro area on January 1, 2001.

Concluding Remarks

What are the key lessons that emerge from Greece's experience? The following points may be highlighted.

First, an intermediate exchange rate regime can be viable in today's world of high capital mobility, provided that (1) the participants adhere to sound and sustainable policies, including those that ensure the existence of a well-functioning market economy; and (2) the intermediate regime is used as a transitional arrangement on the road to the corner solution of a monetary union. There is no contradiction between the existence of ERM-II and the hypothesis of the vanishing middle regime.

Second, ERM-II provides the credibility of a systems' arrangement, built up in a Darwinian evolution, and the flexibility through the wide fluctuation bands that may be necessary to achieve nominal convergence. The credibility derived by participating in the ERM-II should not, however, be endangered by use of frequent adjustments of the central parity. As the ERM experiences of the 1980s and 1990s vividly demonstrated, frequent adjustments of central parities within a pegged regime are feasible only in the presence of capital controls. In today's world of high capital mobility, exchange rate changes are not instruments that policy-makers can use flexibly and costlessly. The more often they are used, the less can be the credibility of a pegged exchange rate system.

Third, the need of a consistent policy mix is crucial and has important implications in terms of how we need to view policy analysis. An implication of both the Mundell-Fleming model and Mundell's famous assignment problem is that monetary policy and fiscal policy constitute two separate policy instruments. However, the simple fact that government expenditure has to be financed by either taxation, borrowing and/or money creation implies that the conduct of monetary policy must make consistent assumptions about fiscal policy. In other words, monetary and fiscal policies are not independent policy instruments. They must work in tandem on the road to and in EMU.

Lastly, a credible exchange rate regime depends upon the trust generated by governments. A governance structure that enforces the rule of law and sanctity of contracts and a political system that delivers credible, non-inflationary policies are prerequisites for the existence of a stable exchange rate regime.

NOTES

1. See Issing, Otmar, Vitor Gaspar, Ignzio Angeloni and Oreste Tristani (2001), *Monetary Policy in the Euro Area*, Cambridge University Press, Chapter 4.
2. I am grateful to George Tavlas for helpful comments.
3. See, for example, Issing (2001).

REFERENCES

Eichengreen, Barry (2002), 'Lessons of the euro for the rest of the world', first annual Marshall Plan Lecture, Austrian Marshall Plan Foundation, Vienna, 4 December.

Issing, Otmar (2001), 'The Euro and the ECB: successful start-challenges ahead', address at Market News Seminar, London, 3 May.

Werner, Pierre (1970), 'Report to the council and the commission on the realisation by stages of economic and monetary union in the community', *Bulletin of the European Community*, Supplement, Vol. 3 (Werner Report).

3. Exchange rate policies on the last stretch*

Jürgen von Hagen and Jizhong Zhou**

1 INTRODUCTION

At the Copenhagen Summit on 12 and 13 December 2002, the European Council declared that accession negotiations had been successfully concluded with eight Central and Eastern European (CEE) accession countries — the Czech Republic, Estonia, Hungary, Latvia, Lithuania, Poland, the Slovak Republic and Slovenia — as well as Cyprus and Malta. These countries will join the European Union (EU) from 1 May 2004.[1] Now that the accession process has reached its final phase, the conduct of monetary and exchange rate policies in the accession countries are confronted with new challenges. EU membership requires that accession countries abolish any remaining controls to allow free cross-border movement of capital, a requirement that has already largely been implemented. As a result, these countries will be fully exposed to the whims of international financial markets and exchange rates are likely to be more volatile. However, according to Article 99 (1) of the *Treaty Establishing the European Community*, exchange rate policies are a matter of common concern once a country is admitted to the EU and the new members cannot treat their exchange rates with total neglect, even if they preferred to do so. This implies that exchange rate flexibility is constrained. As semi-fixed exchange rates tend to be less viable under free capital mobility,[2] the monetary authorities of the new EU members must find safe strategies to ensure exchange rate stability in an environment of high capital mobility.

Another challenge is related to the participation in Economic and Monetary Union (EMU). All accession countries aspire to an early EMU membership, and, therefore, must meet the convergence criteria as soon as possible. These criteria include price stability and exchange rate stability, which amounts effectively to the stipulation that real exchange rates must be stable too. However, since the new member countries are catching up to the income level of the existing EU members, their price levels relative to the EU will also rise, so that a real appreciation of their currencies is inevitable, especially in the long run.[3] This is likely to create conflicts between price stability and exchange rate stability.

This chapter addresses these challenges and analyses appropriate monetary and exchange rate policies for the eight CEE accession countries during the run-up to the EU and EMU. At the starting point, the existing exchange rate regimes vary across countries, ranging from rigid currency board arrangements to flexible floating regimes. Nevertheless, the end point is fixed for all these countries, namely the adoption of the common currency. Therefore, the transition strategies towards EMU are likely to differ across countries, despite the similarities of the catching-up process and the common ultimate goal. The chapter is organized as follows. Section 2 provides a brief review of current exchange rate policies and convergence performance by the accession countries. In Section 3, we analyse the implications for exchange rate policies of heightened capital mobility and trend real appreciations, two prominent issues that are likely to complicate the making of exchange rate policies. Section 4 discusses the standard route towards EMU via ERM-II regimes, while the non-standard approaches via currency boards or unilateral euroization are discussed in Section 5. Section 6 concludes.

2 THE CURRENT SCENARIO: AN ASSESSMENT

2.1 Current Exchange Rate Policies

Although all the eight CEE accession countries are aiming at the irrevocable pegging of their currencies to the euro in the medium-term future, their current exchange rate regimes are quite diverse, reflecting differences in economic fundamentals, such as economic openness, size of economy, level of economic development, and trade structure, as well as prevailing macroeconomic circumstances when these regime choices are made, including reserve adequacy and external competitiveness.[4]

The variety in the exchange rate regime choices also reflects different stabilization strategies and the availability of alternative monetary policy frameworks for this purpose. Achieving price stability still remains the main stabilization task.[5] For this purpose, the choice of a nominal anchor of monetary policy is important. Table 3.1 reports the exchange rate regimes and monetary policy frameworks currently adopted in the CEE accession countries. It shows that the countries use exchange rate targets, inflation targets or monetary targets for that purpose.

Table 3.1 Exchange rate regimes and monetary policy frameworks (as of November 2002)

Country	Exchange Rate Regime	Monetary Policy Framework(1)
Czech Republic	Independent float	Inflation target(2) (Jan. 1998)
Estonia	Currency board (euro)	Exchange rate target (Jun. 1992)
Hungary	Horizontal band (±15%, euro)	Inflation target (May 2001)
Latvia	Conventional fixed peg (SDR)	Exchange rate target (Feb. 1994)
Lithuania	Currency board (euro)(3)	Exchange rate target (Apr. 1994)
Poland	Independent float	Inflation target (Apr. 2000)
Slovak Republic	Managed float	Multiple targets (Oct. 1998)
Slovenia	Managed float	M3 target (Oct. 1991)

Notes:
(1) Starting dates in brackets.
(2) Net inflation targets for 1998–2001; headline inflation targets since 2002.
(3) On 2 February 2002 the anchor currency was switched from the US dollar to the euro.

Sources: IMF, *IFS*; updated based on information from national sources.

The exchange rate as a nominal anchor

Only the three Baltic states — Estonia, Latvia and Lithuania — currently maintain some type of exchange rate targeting framework for their monetary policies. Estonia and Lithuania have currency board arrangements (CBA), the most rigidly fixed exchange rate regime short of monetary union. It should be noted that both countries are among the smallest countries among the CEE candidates.[6] This conforms well to the international experiences to the effect that CBA tends to be adopted by small open economies.[7] Both CBAs now have the euro as the anchor currency.[8] Latvia has a less rigid exchange rate anchor: a conventional fixed peg vis-à-vis the Special Drawing Right (SDR). Although the Latvian peg has been stable since its introduction in April 1994, the commitment to a stable exchange rate is not protected by the same institutional arrangement we observe in a CBA: therefore, flexibility is still reserved to some extent. Moreover, pegging to a basket currency like the SDR can mitigate impacts on the home currency of exchange rate fluctuations among major international currencies. However, an immediate problem with this regime in the current accession scenario is that it is not tied to the euro, which is regarded as incompatible with the spirit of integration into EMU.

Inflation targeting with flexible exchange rate regimes

Inflation targeting has gained popularity in the CEE accession countries, especially in those more advanced in the transition process. The Czech Republic, Hungary and Poland have abandoned exchange rate targeting in favour of inflation targeting as the framework for monetary policies. While the Czech koruna and the Polish zloty float freely, the Hungarian forint fluctuates within an official band of ±15 per cent. Compared to exchange rate anchors, inflation targeting directly addresses the issue of price stability, which is explicitly stipulated as the primary objective of monetary policies. Stronger independence enables the central banks to devote the use of all available instruments to achieving the inflation targets, especially to counteract the excessive price rises due to expansionary fiscal policies.[9] Meanwhile, the exchange rates are flexible so as to absorb the impact of capital flows, which tends to be larger as the countries are further integrated into the international financial markets.

Table 3.2 Financial development and economic openness

Country	Index of Financial Development(1)		Economic Openness(2)	
	1999	2001	1999	2001
Czech Republic	73	78	50	62
Estonia	78	78	68	70
Hungary	85	90	55	62
Latvia	62	65	35	37
Lithuania	66	70	36	45
Poland	77	81	24	25
Slovak Republic	58	65	55	67
Slovenia	73	70	46	52

Notes:
(1) In per cent of the EU average.
(2) The average of export and import values in per cent of GDP.

Sources: Own calculations based on EBRD, *Transition Report*; IMF, *IFS*.

Implementing an inflation targeting strategy requires a functioning domestic financial sector to facilitate the transmission of interest rate policies, typically used to implement inflation targeting. Table 3.2 displays an index of financial development for the eight CEE accession countries. The index is based on the average values of the European Bank for Reconstruction and Development (EBRD) indices of banking and non-banking reforms, with higher index values denoting more advanced financial sector development. It is expressed as a percentage of the EU average.[10] The table shows that the Czech Republic, Hungary and Poland, whose index values are close to the EU standard, have indeed more developed financial sectors than the other accession countries.

Inflation targeting can be largely equivalent to exchange rate targeting, if the economy is very open to foreign trade. To see this, we can decompose an inflation target (π^{TARGET}) into a target for non-tradable goods inflation (π^N), which is not influenced by foreign trade, and a target for tradable goods inflation (π^T), which is influenced by foreign (tradable) inflation (π^*) and a targeted rate of home currency depreciation (Δe). That is,

$$\pi^{TARGET} = (1 - \alpha)\pi^N + \alpha\pi^T = (1 - \alpha)\pi^N + \alpha(\pi^* + \Delta e),$$

with α denoting the share of tradable goods in the consumer price index. The larger α, the more open an economy to foreign trade, the more important is the implicit exchange rate target for inflation targeting. Interestingly, Table 3.2 indicates that two of the three current inflation targeters, Hungary and the Czech Republic, are more open to foreign trade than Latvia and Lithuania. This suggests that, even with an inflation targeting framework in place, both countries need to pay great attention to exchange rate stability.

Note that the importance of exchange rate stability for inflation targeting is based on the assumption that the law of one price holds for tradable goods, which might be questionable if local currency pricing is pervasive. However, deviations from the law of one price due to local currency pricing are likely to be of a short-run nature. In the medium to long run, competition and arbitrage will realign domestic prices of tradables to the foreign counterparts corrected for exchange rate movements, all the more so, the more intensively are the accession countries involved in trade with EU member states. Given fast integration into the euro area economy, this is very likely true for the accession countries.[11]

Managed floating with a monetary target or multiple targets

Slovenia is the only country among the EU accession countries that currently uses a monetary target as the anchor for monetary policy. Its exchange rate regime is a managed float. In practice, Slovenia has used the monetary target pragmatically to take into account external competitiveness and sustainability.[12] While money growth targets are set to steer a disinflation process, the nominal exchange rate is heavily managed to avoid severe real exchange rate misalignment. As a result, Slovenia's de facto exchange rate regime has been among the most stable in the region. Similarly, the Slovak Republic pursues a managed floating exchange rate regime which allows sufficient room for policy manoeuvre. While monetary policy has been predominantly geared towards a core inflation goal, the monetary authority also considers exchange rate targets and intervenes in the foreign exchange market to restrain excessive exchange rate volatility.

In sum, although official descriptions of monetary policy regimes among the accession countries show some divergence, exchange rate considerations are likely to play a large role for all of them except, perhaps, Poland. This suggests that the exigencies implied by considering their exchange rate policies as a matter of common concern will not place overwhelming demands on them.

2.2 Convergence Performance

Roughly ten years into transition, the CEE accession countries have made considerable progress in the convergence towards EU standards. The upcoming EU accession is a recognition of these achievements and signifies that the accession criteria have been fulfilled.[13] However, since the accession countries aspire to EMU membership, they need to further meet the 'Maastricht Criteria'. In this subsection we will briefly assess the latest development in the real and nominal convergence of the eight CEE accession countries.

Real convergence

A common indicator of real convergence is the candidates' per capita GDP (in purchasing power standards) relative to the EU average, which reflects the alignment of economic welfare in the accession countries to the level prevailing in the EU.[14] Table 3.3 shows that the degree of convergence is rather diverse in the accession countries. At the lowest end of the scale, per capita GDP of Latvia and Lithuania is less than one third of the EU average in 2001. At the highest position, Slovenia's per capita GDP has risen to 69 per cent of the EU average, above some poorest EU countries around the time of accession.[15] On average, this group of accession countries have a per capita GDP of roughly 47 per cent of the EU level.[16]

Table 3.3 Real convergence

Country	GDP per capita[1] (% of EU average)		Productivity growth (% p.a.)	
	1997	2001	1996–2000[2]	2001
Czech Republic	63	57	2.0	3.5
Estonia	37	42	5.8	5.4
Hungary	47	51	3.1	3.5
Latvia	27	33	4.8	7.6
Lithuania	31	38	4.7	6.3
Poland	40	40	3.8[3]	3.2
Slovak Republic	47	48	6.3	2.2
Slovenia	68	69	7.1	2.5
EU-15	*100*	*100*	*2.2*	*0.4*

Notes:
(1) In Purchasing Power Standards.
(2) Average productivity growth rates over the period 1996–2000.
(3) Average over 1996–1999.

Sources: European Commission, *Strategy Paper* (2002) and *Regular Report* (1998); IMF, *IFS*; Buiter and Grafe (2001).

From a dynamic point of view, most of the accession countries have seen a rise in their per capita GDP relative to the EU average over the period 1997–2001, except for the Czech Republic, which had a 6 percentage point decline, and Poland, whose per capita GDP has been growing at exactly the same speed as that of a typical EU country. This catching-up process is mainly propelled by faster productivity growth in the accession countries than in the relatively richer EU countries. Table 3.3 shows that, over the period 1996–2000, only the Czech Republic had a productivity growth rate lower than that of the EU average, while the other countries were improving their labour productivity faster than the EU on average. In 2001, all the eight accession countries exhibited much faster productivity growth than a typical EU country.

Nominal convergence

The 'Maastricht Criteria' set the conditions for the nominal convergence for the accession into EMU. Although the accession countries will not join the euro earlier than 2006, it is worthwhile checking to what extent the Maastricht Criteria have already been met as well as in which areas further efforts are necessary. Table 3.4 provides an overview.

The Maastricht Treaty stipulates that inflation rates should not exceed the average inflation rate of the three best performing EMU member states by more than 1.5 per centage points. This leads to a reference inflation rate of 3.0% per annum in 2000 and 3.4% in 2001. It is clear from Table 3.4 that only Latvia and Lithuania fulfilled this criterion in 2001. The other countries need to make serious efforts to bring down their inflation rates to the level consistent with the Maastricht Criteria.[17]

Table 3.4 Nominal convergence

Country	Inflation rate (% p.a.)		Fiscal balance (% of GDP)		Public debt (% of GDP)		Exchange rate fluctuations (1)		Interest rate (% p.a.)
	2000	2001	2000	2001	2000	2001	(+)	(−)	2001
Czech Rep.	3.9	4.7	−4.2	−5.5	17.3	19.4	6.4	−12.2	5.3
Estonia	4.0	5.7	−0.7	−0.4	5.3	5.4	0.9	−0.9	6.8
Hungary	9.8	9.1	−3.1	−4.1	55.7	51.8	5.2	−4.8	7.0
Latvia	2.7	2.5	−2.7	−1.6	14.1	13.8	8.9	−7.0	10.2
Lithuania	1.0	1.2	−3.3	−1.9	23.7	29.1	5.6	−5.0	6.3
Poland	10.1	5.5	−3.5	−3.9	40.9	42.9	8.2	−9.4	8.8
Slovak Rep.	12.0	7.3	−6.7	−5.6	37.3	42.7	4.3	−3.8	7.7
Slovenia	8.9	9.4	−2.3	−2.5	25.8	28.4	4.5	−5.0	9.7
Reference	*3.0*	*3.4*	*−3.0*	*−3.0*	*60.0*	*60.0*	*15.0*	*−15.0*	*6.8*

Note: (1) Maximum percentage deviation in both directions of end-month exchange rates from central parities. Central parities are approximated by the average exchange rates over the two-year period (July 2000 to June 2002). The exchange rates are expressed in units of national currencies per euro, so positive (negative) deviations denote depreciation (appreciation) of the national currencies.

Sources: IMF, *IFS*; European Commission, *Strategy Paper* (2002).

On the fiscal front, the Maastricht Criteria set ceilings for general government budget deficits at 3% of GDP and for public debt stocks at 60% of GDP.[18] In 2000, five countries — the Czech Republic, Hungary, Lithuania, Poland and the Slovak Republic — reported fiscal deficits larger than 3% of GDP. Except for Lithuania, this group of countries failed to bring their deficits below the threshold in 2001. Hungary, Poland and the Slovak Republic have the largest debt stocks in this group. None of the eight CEE accession countries, however, exceeds the 60 per cent ceiling on public debt. The general tendency is that most accession countries have disciplined their fiscal policies in recent years, and fulfil or are close to fulfilling the related convergence criteria in 2002. It should nevertheless be noted that the approaching EU accession may actually weaken or worsen their fiscal positions. Although the phasing-out of subsidies, tax harmonization and transfers from the Cohesion Fund will have positive effects on the fiscal budget, they are insufficient to compensate the negative effects caused by contributions to the EU budget, preparation of matching funds for the projects supported by the EU funds and other infrastructure expenditures (Kopits and Székely, 2002). It is estimated that the overall direct impact of EU accession on the fiscal budget of these countries is to increase deficits (or reduce surpluses) by 3%–4.75% of GDP. This may worsen the fiscal balance of the accession countries to such an extent that almost all of them will fail on the fiscal test. Therefore, the countries need further fiscal consolidations.

Before a country is admitted into EMU, it must keep its exchange rate within the normal fluctuation band without initiating a devaluation of the central parity for at least two years. The current definition of 'the normal fluctuation band' is ±15% around the central parity. Table 3.4 shows that all the eight accession countries maintained their exchange rates vis-à-vis the euro within a ±15% fluctuation band during the two-year period from July 2000 to June 2002, if the central parities are defined as the average euro exchange rates for this period.

Finally, it is required that the nominal long-term interest rate in the accession countries should not exceed by more than 2 percentage points that of the three best performing member states in terms of price stability. This corresponds to a reference interest rate at 6.8% per annum for 2001. Only three countries could meet this criterion: the Czech Republic (5.3%), Estonia (6.8%) and Lithuania (6.3%). For the other five countries, country risk premia may play a role in pushing up their nominal interest rates.

Summary

If an assessment had been made in June 2002, based on data available then, to determine which accession countries could join EMU at the beginning of 2003, the above analysis of nominal convergence suggests that only Lithuania would join the euro area immediately, as it was the only country that passed all the five tests. The other two Baltic states scored four in the test, while the Czech Republic and Slovenia met three criteria. The chances would be the least for Hungary, Poland and the Slovak Republic, as they fulfilled only two of the five criteria. In general, there is no clear correspondence between exchange rate policies and convergence performance, and no particular exchange rate regime is preferred to others in terms of overall convergence performance. However, the accession to the EU and EMU may impose constraints on the conducting of exchange rate policies in the accession countries, and exchange rate regimes still need to be chosen appropriately to meet the new challenges.

3 CHALLENGES TO EXCHANGE RATE POLICIES

The CEE countries conduct their exchange rate policies with the aim of early and smooth accession to the EU and EMU. This broad objective justifies their emphasis on exchange rate stability, since it is regarded not only as a common interest of the EU member states, but a precondition for the entry into EMU as well. However, exchange rate stability is difficult to achieve if capital flows are volatile, a likely by-product of increasingly liberalized capital accounts. Moreover, exchange rate stability may be achieved at the cost of price stability if trend appreciations are inevitable. These two issues pose great challenges to exchange rate policies in the accession countries.

3.1 The Influence of Heightened Capital Mobility

Capital account liberalization in the CEE accession countries has proceeded with enormous speed since the beginning of transition. The aspiration to EU membership played a key role behind this trend, as the EU regulations envisage the free movement of persons, goods and capital within the Union. While the accession countries must fully liberalize their capital accounts upon entry into the EU, they are allowed to do so in two stages, with medium- and long-term capital flows being liberalized in the first stage and short-term capital flows in the second. After joining the EU, however, restrictions on capital movements cannot be re-imposed except in exceptional cases and with the approval of the EU. Meanwhile, four CEE countries — the Czech Republic, Hungary, Poland and the Slovak Republic — are also member states of the Organization for Economic Co-operation and Development (OECD), so they need to adopt the Code of Liberalization of Capital Movements of the OECD.[19]

Table 3.5 displays the number of categories of capital transactions that are subject to controls in the eight CEE accession countries. Among the eleven categories identified by the IMF,[20] the three Baltic states imposed controls only on two or three categories in 2001, not very different from the average level in the EU. Poland and the Slovak Republic still maintain controls on many types of capital flows, despite the obligations of OECD membership. Only Hungary and, to a lesser extent, the Czech Republic seem to be fulfilling OECD obligations in this regard. The capital account in Slovenia is semi-open.

Table 3.5 Capital controls and capital flows

Country	Number of Capital Controls[1]		Net FDI Inflows[2] (% of GDP)		Gross Capital Flows[3] (% of GDP)	
	1998	2001	1998	2001	1998	2001
Czech Republic	5	3	6.6	8.7	12.0	13.3
Estonia	1	3	11.0	9.7	16.9	24.0
Hungary	9	0	4.3	4.7	12.1	16.0
Latvia	9	2	5.8	2.3	13.0	16.4
Lithuania	2	2	8.6	3.7	15.0	8.2
Poland	10	10	4.0	3.2	9.1	11.4[6]
Slovak Republic	8	6	2.6	6.3	11.3	24.8[6]
Slovenia	7	6	1.3	1.9	6.3	9.2
CEE average[4]	*6.4*	*4.0*	*5.5*	*5.1*	*12.0*	*15.4*
EU average[5]	*2.1*	*1.9*	*–1.5*	*–1.5*	*20.6*	*20.8*

Notes:
(1) Number of capital transaction categories subject to controls. The total number of categories is 11. *Source*: Own calculations based on IMF, *AREAER* (various issues).
(2) *Source*: European Commission, *Regular Report* (2002).
(3) Gross capital flows are the sum of outflows and inflows of direct investment, portfolio investment and other investment. *Source*: IMF, *IFS*.
(4) Simple average across eight CEE accession countries.
(5) Number of capital controls is simple average across 15 EU member states; Net FDI flows and gross capital flows are GDP-weighted average for the euro area.
(6) Data for 2000.

It should be noted that capital controls are de jure measures which might be less effective de facto or circumvented in practice. As a result, the actual degree of capital mobility might well be different from what was implied by the existence of capital controls. One way to measure the actual degree of capital mobility is to look at the magnitude of capital flows, such as net foreign direct investment (FDI) inflows, or gross capital flows, which is the sum of inflows and outflows of FDI, portfolio investment and other investment. Table 3.5 reports that net FDI inflows stabilized at 5% to 6% of GDP on average around the turn of the century. Gross capital flows are gaining importance, with their average share in GDP rising from 12% in 1998 to 15% in 2001. Given the presumably stable share of gross FDI flows, this increase reflects to a large extent a rising share of portfolio investment, banking credits and other types of capital flows.

From a medium- to long-term perspective, the CEE accession countries are expected to experience even more capital mobility in the future. On the de jure side, further capital account liberalization will allow more freedom in the cross-border movement of capital. On the de facto side, higher profitability associated with faster economic growth in the accession countries will attract more capital inflows and the integration of these countries into the international financial market will lead to a substantial increase in gross capital flows.

Given high capital mobility, central banks are likely to be involved in large-scale foreign exchange interventions, if they wish to achieve exchange rate targets. Meanwhile, the probability of abandoning the exchange rate target is rising as the magnitude of capital flows surges. This is because a large, if not the largest part of all capital inflows takes the form of portfolio investment or other financial investments, a substantial part of which is short-term ('hot money'). The experience of the 1990s shows that such capital flows can easily revert in the case of political or economic instability in the host country, swings in market expectations or contagion of financial crises from abroad. When this happens, central bank interventions are limited by the availability of international reserves, which can be overwhelmed by the magnitude of capital outflows. In that case, a crash of an exchange rate regime of limited flexibility is inevitable. In the case of capital inflows, sterilization is, in principle, not limited. However, sterilized intervention can be costly and unsterilized intervention can lead to excessive inflation and, consequently, real appreciation and a deterioration of external account. This is, in essence, the 'convergence play' experienced by countries in the ERM of the late 1980s and early 1990s. Empirical studies show that the combination of large capital inflows and real exchange rate appreciations are typical leading indicators of currency crises in emerging economies.[21]

As a result, high capital mobility will make exchange rate stability an ever more difficult objective, unless monetary policies are fully devoted to this end. Large amounts of foreign capital expected to flow into the accession countries will push the national currencies towards appreciation. Exchange rate volatility tends to be increased, which can be avoided only by subordinating all monetary instruments towards the objective of exchange rate stability.

3.2 The Influence of Real Appreciations

The other major challenge to the monetary authorities in the CEE accession countries is to achieve exchange rate and price stability in the presence of real appreciations of their currencies. The real appreciation of the accession countries' currencies vis-à-vis that of their main trading partner (i.e. the euro) reflects the fact that the inflation differentials between the accession countries and the EU are larger than can be offset by the depreciation of the candidates' currencies against the euro (if any). The common causes of higher inflation in the accession countries include the monetization of fiscal deficits and the adjustment of relative prices. Given the fact that the former cause becomes less likely as fiscal discipline is strengthened in the accession countries, the latter becomes increasingly prominent. The main driving force of relative price adjustment is productivity growth.[22] Since this is inevitable during the accession process, the monetary authorities face a trade-off between exchange rate stability and price stability.

The relationship between productivity growth and relative price changes is usually summarized in terms of the Balassa-Samuelson (B-S) effect, which refers to 'a tendency for countries with higher productivity in tradables compared with non-tradables to have higher price levels' (Obstfeld and Rogoff, 1996, p. 210). The mechanism linking relative productivity growth with price level differentials is wage equalization across tradable and non-tradable sectors. The wage increase in the tradable sector caused by productivity growth pulls up the wage level of the non-tradable sector through wage equalization and inter-sectoral labour relocation. If productivity growth in the non-tradable sector is slower, the price of non-tradables will rise. Since the price of tradables is determined by the world price, assuming that the law of one price holds for tradables, the price of non-tradables relative to the tradables will rise and so it is with the overall price level. If the relative productivity growth of the tradables as compared with non-tradables is faster at home than abroad, the home price level will rise faster than the foreign, so a positive inflation differential will be observed.

The B-S effect is frequently cited as a factor underlying the inflation differentials of the CEE accession countries relative to the EU. Productivity growth in the tradable sector is faster than in the non-tradable sector in the accession countries, since the modern production technology of the tradable sector can easily be transferred into the accession countries, leading to substantial improvement in labour productivity, while the non-tradable sector is, by definition, closed to foreign competition.[23] Moreover, the productivity growth differential is more pronounced in the accession countries than in the EU due to the catching-up process. As a result, the accession countries' currencies tend to appreciate in real terms vis-à-vis the euro. If nominal exchange rates are fixed, these real appreciations lead to higher inflation in the accession countries than in the EU.

Empirical studies do find some support for the B-S effect in the CEE accession countries in the 1990s. Table 3.6 summarizes the main findings of a selection of studies by reporting the estimated elasticity of real appreciation with respect to productivity growth. Table 3.6 also shows the implied consumer price inflation differentials between the CEE accession countries and the EU if the former adopt fixed exchange rates against the euro. These studies use, in essence, the following empirical approximation:

$$\Delta q = \beta_T a_T - \beta_N a_N + \text{Control Variables},$$

where Δq measures real appreciation and a_T (a_N) is the rate of productivity growth of the tradable (non-tradable) sector. Foreign productivity growth is assumed to be zero for simplicity. Some studies use the productivity growth differentials ($a_T - a_N$) as a regressor under the restriction that $\beta_T = \beta_N$. Most studies use the relative price of non-tradables in terms of tradables as the measure of the real exchange rate so that $\Delta q = \pi_N - \pi_T$, with π_N (π_T) denoting the inflation rate of non-tradables (tradables). Let π (π^*) denote the home (foreign, here the EU) consumer price inflation rate and α the share of tradables in the consumer price index. It can be shown that $\pi - \pi^* = (1 - \alpha)(\pi_N - \pi_T)$. This is obtained under the assumption that $\pi^* = \pi_T$, which is valid if the exchange rate is fixed, the law of one price holds and $\pi^* = \pi_T^*$. Some studies use instead the real effective exchange rate so that $\Delta q = \pi - \pi^*$ in case of fixed exchange rates.[24]

Table 3.6 Real appreciation due to the Balassa-Samuelson effect: some estimates

Empirical Study[(1)]	β_T	β_N	$\pi_N - \pi_T$[(2)]	$\pi - \pi^*$[(3)]	Country Sample
Begg et al. (2001)	0.61	0.78	4.7	2.5	8 CEECs, Russia
Coricelli and Jazbec (2001)	0.54	0.54	4.2	2.3	10 CEECs, 9 TEs
De Broeck and Sløk (2001)	0.30	0.30	–	2.3[(4)]	10 CEECs
Halpern and Wyplosz (2001)	0.43	0.32	3.4	1.8	8 CEECs, Russia
Kovács and Simon (1998)	–	–	4.6[(5)]	1.6[(5)]	Hungary
Lommatzsch and Tober (2002)	0.56[(6)]	0.56[(6)]	4.4	2.4	5 CEECs
Pelkmans et al. (2000)	–	–	–	3.8[(5)]	10 CEECs
Rother (2000)	1.10	1.10	8.6	4.6	Slovenia

Notes:
CEECs: Central and Eastern European Countries. TEs: Transition Economies.

(1) The real exchange rate is the relative price of non-tradables in terms of tradables, except for De Broeck and Sløk (2001), where the CPI-based real effective exchange rate is used.
(2) $\pi_N - \pi_T \approx \beta_T a_T - \beta_N a_N$. Expressed in per cent per annum (p.a.). It is assumed that the average productivity growth of tradable sector (a_T) is 8.4% p.a. and the average productivity growth of non-tradable sector (a_N) is 0.6% p.a.
(3) $\pi - \pi^* \approx (1 - \alpha)(\pi_N - \pi_T)$. Expressed in per cent per annum. This is obtained under the assumption that $\pi^* = \pi_T$, which is valid if the exchange rate is fixed and $\pi^* = \pi_T^*$. The average share of tradable goods in consumer price index (α) is set at 0.46.
(4) $\pi - \pi^* \approx \beta_T a_T - \beta_N a_N$. Expressed in per cent per annum.
(5) Taken from original studies.
(6) Simple average of five country-specific coefficients: 0.28 (Hungary), 0.34 (Poland), 0.37 (the Czech Republic), 0.78 (Slovenia) and 1.02 (Estonia).

For our calculations we gauge the annual productivity growth of tradable sector (a_T) at 8.4%, that of non-tradable sector (a_N) at 0.6% (implying an annual relative productivity growth ($a_T - a_N$) at 7.8%),[25] and the share of tradables in CPI (α) at 0.46.[26] The results reported in Table 3.6 show that for most CEE accession countries the magnitude of inflation differentials that can be attributed to relative productivity growth differentials ranges from 2% to 4% in each year. Note that these inflation differentials are relative to the average inflation rate in the euro zone, which must be higher than the reference rate defined as the average inflation rate of three best-performing EU member states in terms of price stability. Therefore, the accession countries maintaining a fixed euro exchange rate will very likely fail to meet the inflation criterion of the Maastricht Treaty, which allows, at maximum, a 1.5% inflation differential above the reference rate. Although productivity growth in the EU, especially the relative growth of the tradable sector, can offset the above mentioned B-S effects to some extent, the magnitude is rather small due to slow relative productivity growth in the euro area. Our estimations for the euro area during 1997–1999 show that the average annual productivity growth of tradables is 2.3% and that of non-tradables is 1:6%.[27] Taking into account these developments, the implied annual inflation differentials reported in Table 3.6 will be reduced by 0.1%–0.4%, which is not sufficient to reverse the main conclusion.[28] As a result, a careful balance must be sought between the two objectives of price and exchange rate stability.

There are several caveats to the above-mentioned analysis.[29] First of all, the B-S effect is a long-run tendency, which may be less prominent over a shorter time horizon. Second, productivity growth of the service sector, which is the main constituent of the non-tradable sector, can be very fast in the accession countries, as it is developing essentially from a very low starting level. Third, the productivity growth of the tradable sector will gradually lose its momentum as it reaches a higher level. Fourth, the pressure of high unemployment rates may prevent the wage rate from equalizing at a level compatible with tradable-sector productivity growth. All these factors tend to reduce the inflation differentials caused by the B-S effect. Despite these qualifications, the B-S effect cannot be ignored as a source of inflation differentials. In the medium to long run, the productivity-driven relative price adjustment is likely the dominant factor of high inflation rates, which may constrain the exchange rate policies of the accession countries over a longer time span.

3.3 Policy Responses

Facing the challenges of high capital mobility, one response is to follow the 'bi-polar' approach in the choice of exchange rate regimes.[30] At the one extreme end, more flexible exchange rate regimes, such as free or managed float, are adopted, which allow the exchange rate to adjust more freely to absorb the shocks caused by volatile capital flows. At the other extreme end, very rigidly fixed regimes, such as currency board arrangements, are adopted, which strengthen the commitment to exchange rate stability by devoting all monetary instruments to that objective. Another response is to conduct conservative fiscal policies, especially in the presence of capital inflows, which can prevent capital inflows from fuelling domestic price pressures and the build-up of external debts that would eventually threaten the financial system and the exchange rate arrangement.[31]

To cope with the challenges caused by real appreciations, one needs to find measures that reduce the magnitude of such real appreciations in the first place. One measure is to promote non-tradable sector development, especially the improvement of its productivity, so that those real appreciations attributable to the B-S effect are attenuated. Another measure is to strengthen fiscal discipline to contain aggregate demand, especially demand for non-tradable goods, so that the relative price of non-tradable goods does not rise too fast.

These responses and measures, however, have their own shortcomings. Floating exchange rate regimes may result in volatile exchange rates, which have negative consequences for small open economies like the CEE accession countries. With hard pegs, the monetary authority loses control on domestic monetary supply and, henceforth, inflation. The measures dealing with real appreciations can only partially attenuate the magnitude of real appreciations, but are unable to solve the issue completely. The remaining real appreciation driven by relative productivity growth is an equilibrium phenomenon, which will be manifested by nominal appreciation, higher inflation rates, or both.

4 ENTRY INTO EMU VIA ERM-II

According to the official position of the EU, the procedure leading to the adoption of the euro involves three steps: (1) entry into the EU, (2) participation in the ERM-II and (3) entry into EMU after meeting the convergence criteria. While there is no separate national monetary and exchange rate policy after the entry into EMU, during the period leading to that third stage the monetary authorities of the CEE accession countries must still carefully formulate their exchange rate policies to facilitate a smooth accession to the EU and EMU. However, there are alternative ways leading to EMU.

4.1 Exchange Rate Regimes Consistent with EMU Accession

Before joining the EU, the CEE accession countries have free choices as to their exchange rate regimes. Upon accession, the new EU members will still have much freedom to choose their exchange rate arrangements, except that they must now treat their exchange rate policies (as well as other economic policies) as a matter of common concern to all the EU members. This requirement is aimed at avoiding competitive devaluations among member countries. All exchange rate regimes satisfying this requirement are consistent with the EU accession, including those with fixed central parities (currency boards, pegged rates, horizontal bands) and those under which exchange rates are determined mainly by market forces without heavy manipulations of the authorities (managed or free float). From this perspective, the eight CEE accession countries that will join the EU in 2004 now have exchange rate regimes consistent with EU accession (see Table 3.1).

After joining the EU, all the new members are expected, sooner or later, to participate in the second stage of the Exchange Rate Mechanism (ERM-II) for at least two years before the final entry into EMU. The ERM-II is in essence a horizontal band regime where the euro exchange rate of a member state currency is allowed to fluctuate within a ±15% band around the fixed central parity. Several exchange rate regimes are excluded from the option list, including independent float (the Czech Republic and Poland) and managed float (the Slovak Republic and Slovenia), which have no announced central parity vis-à-vis the euro and the fixed peg not anchored by the euro (Latvia). The other exchange arrangements — euro-based currency boards (Estonia and Lithuania) and euro pegs with horizontal bands (Hungary) — have fixed central parities vis-à-vis the euro and bands not wider than ±15%. From this perspective, they can be considered as valid regime options leading to EMU.

The five countries whose current exchange arrangements are not compatible with EMU entry may switch to a standard ERM-II regime with wide bands, or may go all the way to unilateral euroization. Under the latter option the euro parity is decided by the accession country unilaterally without agreement from the ECB. This is also the case for currency board arrangements. However, since the ERM-II is a cooperative arrangement between the ECB and the non-euro EU members, the setting of the central parity requires an agreement between the ECB and the accession country in question. From this perspective, currency boards and unilateral euroization can be viewed as non-standard approaches towards EMU.

4.2 EMU Entry via the ERM-II

The standard route towards EMU is via ERM-II. The CEE accession countries willing to take this route need to decide on the timing of their entry into ERM, which influences the timing of EMU assessment and that of the adoption of the euro. There are also technical issues that need to be solved, including the determination of the central parity and the band width. Before we discuss these issues faced by the CEE accession countries, we first take a look at the experience of the first-wave EMU members before they joined EMU on 1 January 1999. These experiences are relevant for the CEE accession countries because the first-wave EMU members all entered into EMU via the standard route of ERM-II.

Past experiences

On 1 May 1998 the European Council announced that eleven EU member states fulfilled the Maastricht Criteria on nominal convergence and would participate in the third stage of Economic and Monetary Union on 1 January 1999. The relevant assessment for EMU entry was made in March 1998. Data for 1997 was used for the evaluation of fiscal performance. The assessment of inflation and interest rates was based on data for the year ending January 1998. The two-year window for ERM participation referred to the period from March 1996 to February 1998.

Besides a relatively loose interpretation of the criteria pertaining to fiscal deficits and public debts, the assessment also treated the requirement of a two-year ERM participation in a flexible way. Finland joined, and Italy rejoined, the ERM in October and November 1996 respectively. When the assessment was conducted in March 1998, they had not been in the ERM for two years, but they did meet this requirement by the time EMU started. The European Council nevertheless concluded that both countries had displayed sufficient exchange rate stability within the past two years and fulfilled the relevant criterion, since both the Finnish markka and the Italian lira had appreciated vis-à-vis other ERM currencies between March 1996 and their ERM entry and were stable within ERM afterwards.[32] This leads to two possible interpretations. Either one may conclude that what is important is to avoid devaluations within the two-year period; whether a country is formally participating in the ERM for the whole period is of less importance. Or one may conclude that formal ERM-II does matter, but the relevant period is between the entry to the ERM-II and the entry into the euro. That is, the decision to permit that entry can be made substantially before two years have elapsed (8 months or 32% of the required period in the example). This is significant, since the announcement of a date for EMU entry and a terminal exchange rate will stabilize the exchange rate and make it easier to meet the criterion.

Setting the terminal conversion rates of the national currencies into the euro was difficult for the first EMU member states, because it had to meet two conditions set by the Maastricht Treaty. First, the conversion rates had to be equal to the market exchange rates of the national currencies on the last day of currency trading before the start of EMU. Second, the conversion was not allowed to change the value of the national currencies vis-à-vis the ECU, a currency basket of the 15 national currencies including those of the countries with a derogation from EMU. Since the exchange rates between the 'ins' and the 'outs' were not fixed, the exchange rates of the 'ins' into the ECU or the euro could not be fixed before 1 January 1999 either. Leaving the announcement of the conversion rates until the very last moment could have heightened speculative pressures and created exchange rate volatility in the run-up to EMU that might have derailed the entire process. This risk was particularly large in view of the fact that setting the conversion rates was necessarily a political decision. The outcome of bargaining in the European Council over the conversion rates right before the start of EMU would have been highly unpredictable, since each country would have had a large incentive to take the others hostage and demand a favourable conversion rate, i.e. one giving its economy a competitive advantage.[33]

In the end, the countries that first joined EMU adopted a solution that promised to minimize uncertainty and exchange rate volatility in the critical phase before the start of EMU. Specifically, the finance ministers had already announced in 1997 that the cross-rates among the participating currencies should be those implied by the central parities in the ERM. This provided clear anchors to guide market expectations and eliminated the scope for opportunistic strategic manipulation of conversion rates (Begg et al., 1997). This decision was confirmed in May 1998 by the European Council, which decided that the EMU member currencies would be converted into each other at the fixed central parities prevailing on 1 May 1998. Furthermore, the width of the exchange rate band was left unchanged allowing for maximum fluctuations of 15 per cent around the target rate in both directions. Begg et al. (1997) argued that this would minimize the risk of speculative attacks on the central parities, as speculators could not engage in one-sided bets. Nevertheless, the central banks made clear to the markets that they were ready to intervene in unlimited amounts to achieve the central parities in the last trading period before the start of EMU. As it was, the actual transition to EMU proved to be smooth and stable, giving credit to the strategy adopted.

In an interesting theoretical study, De Grauwe et al. (1999) confirm the stabilizing properties of a strategy for conversion into the euro that combines a pre-announced terminal rate with wide exchange rate bands. The key insight is provided by the forward-looking nature of the exchange rate as an asset price. Consider the basic equation of the monetary approach of exchange rate determination:

$$s_t = \alpha x_t + (1-\alpha)E_t s_{t+1}.$$

This says that the current exchange rate (in logs), s, is a weighted average of a fundamental equilibrium rate, x, and the expected exchange rate next period, $E_t s_{t+1}$. The latter results from the impact of speculative trading in the foreign currency market, which ensures that the expected rate of return on domestic and foreign assets is the same. Let x be constant for simplicity and assume that the exchange rate is announced to be fixed at rate s^* after $n+1$ periods. Then

$$s_t = \alpha \sum_{j=0}^{n} (1-\alpha)^j x + (1-\alpha)^{n+1} s^*.$$

This equation says that, as the date when the exchange rate is fixed approaches, the influence of the terminal rate, s^*, on the actual rate becomes increasingly larger. Thus, speculation leads the exchange rate to converge smoothly towards the terminal rate. However, this is true only if the announcement of the terminal conversion is credible. As De Grauwe et al. (1999) show, any change in the expected terminal rate results in changes in the current exchange rate, and the resulting fluctuations are stronger than in the absence of the conversion announcement. The authors use numerical simulations to compare the variances of the market exchange rate under three scenarios: (1) free float without any guidance on the final conversion rate or its determination, (2) the final conversion rate being the average of past exchange rates and (3) the final conversion rate being fixed and known to the market. They find that the variance of the market exchange rate is the smallest with a pre-announced fixed conversion rate. Note, finally, that the closer the terminal rate, s^*, is to the fundamental equilibrium rate, the less variable will be the actual rate as it approaches the terminal date.

Three points can be drawn from the success of the first-round EMU entry. One is that a country should fix its euro conversion rate upon the confirmation of its entry into EMU or even before that. For future EMU entrants, the rule that the conversion rate must be a market exchange rate of the last trading day will remain, but its implications are less difficult than in the case of the first members of EMU, since the problem of outside currencies no longer exists. Avoiding uncertainty and the risk of disruptive speculative pressures then suggests that they should announce their terminal euro parities as early as possible.

Another point is that, as long as the announced conversion rate is credible, the market exchange rate will converge smoothly towards this target with the smallest variance. The readiness of the ECB to intervene in support of currencies in the ERM-II is obviously critical for this. Under the rules of the ERM-II, the ECB is obliged to provide unlimited support at the edges of the band, but it can unilaterally withdraw from intervening, if the monetary stability of the euro is endangered otherwise. Since the target rate for entry into EMU is unlikely to be at the edge of the band, this may create unnecessary uncertainty. Instead, the ECB should make clear its willingness to intervene and support the target rate on the last day of trading before a country enters EMU. Such a signal would deter speculative pressures. It is a credible promise, since it would have no adverse consequences for the ECB's monetary policy: if the ECB acquires a new member's currency on the last day of trading at the rate s^*, and this is the conversion rate of that currency into the euro, the intervention does not affect the ECB's monetary base on the first day after the new member has entered EMU. Obviously, such a promise should only be made conditional on the decision that the country in question joins EMU.

Beyond that, the third point is that, after fixing the conversion rate, the market exchange rate should be allowed to move freely during the interim period leading to the EMU entry. Central banks should avoid committing themselves to exchange rate bands smaller than the 'normal' ones of ±15 per cent in the ERM-II, so that speculators cannot place one-sided bets against the exchange rate. In other words, both the central bank of the new member country and the ECB should refrain from large-scale interventions prior to the last day of trading before the new member country enters EMU. Such interventions would only signal to the markets that the central banks pursue secret exchange rate targets within the normal bands of the ERM-II and invite destabilizing speculation.

Slow versus fast track to EMU

There are four important dates for the CEE accession countries during their quest for EMU membership: the date of EU accession, the date of ERM-II entry, the date of assessment for joining EMU and the date of EMU membership. The date of EU accession is very likely in the middle of 2004 for these countries. From there on, there is a fast-track and a slow-track scenario for the entry into EMU. Under the fast-track scenario, the new EU members would strive for the earliest possible date to become full members of EMU. Because one precondition for joining EMU is at least two-year-long participation in ERM-II without devaluation of the currency against the euro, in strict terms, such assessment can only be made two years after a country enters ERM-II. Since the ERM-II is a cooperative exchange rate arrangement, the earliest date for participation in ERM-II is that of the EU entry. However, it may take time for the new EU members to discuss with the incumbent members and with the ECB the appropriate central parities for ERM entry. Allowing a few months for negotiations on that issue, the new EU members may enter ERM-II in the second half of 2004. If they prefer an early entry in May 2004, they need to start the negotiations before they join the EU.

The two-year membership requirement without a devaluation then implies that the assessment regarding the Maastricht Criteria can be carried out for these countries in the second half of 2006. However, the past experiences with Finland and Italy suggest that the earliest possible date for the assessment of the entry criteria would seem to be in the spring of 2006, when data on required macroeconomic variables (especially fiscal deficits and public debts) for the year 2005 become available. If these countries pass the examination on convergence performance in accordance with the Maastricht Treaty, they could become formal members of EMU on 1 January 2007.

Under the slow-track scenario, countries could take a more relaxed attitude and aim at full EMU membership only a few years later. This implies that there is no need to join the ERM-II immediately after joining the EU. Countries on the slow track could wait until the conditions for joining the exchange rate system and, later on, for holding the assessment regarding the Maastricht Criteria seem right.

The main advantage of the fast-track scenario is that the instabilities created by the combination of an intermediate exchange rate system, high capital mobility and the expectation of a 'convergence play' can be overcome in a relatively short time. The main disadvantage is that the new EU members will have to make extra efforts to meet the Maastricht Criteria and prepare for the adoption of the euro. To the extent that this requires solutions for inherited structural fiscal problems and further efforts at reducing inflation, the fast track eliminates the possibility of using monetary policy to ease the macroeconomic consequences of structural reforms. The main advantage of the slow-track scenario is that this possibility can be used to some extent, since the exchange rate can still adjust.

This reasoning suggests that those new EU members that have already given up the use of monetary policy for domestic policy purposes should find the fast-track option more attractive. For the others, which include Poland, the Czech Republic and Hungary, the slow-track option deserves consideration, all the more so, the more they perceive that they can use monetary policy effectively to steer their economies. Commitment to an inflation target would then be an appropriate policy framework. Importantly, these countries should not fall into the trap that led to the collapse of the 'New ERM' in the early 1990s.[34] That trap was created by the fact that realignments of the central parities became increasingly impossible for reasons of national political prestige, while at the same time monetary and fiscal policies were not fully consistent with a fixed exchange rate. Market beliefs that monetary union was imminent allowed that situation to prevail for some time. However, when the failure of the Danish voters to ratify the Maastricht Treaty shattered those beliefs, the system collapsed in a series of speculative attacks.

For countries on the slow track, the lesson to learn from the collapse of the 'New ERM' is twofold. First, these countries should stay out of the ERM-II as long as the conditions for joining EMU are not yet reachable within a period of two or three years. Second, if they decide to join the ERM-II earlier anyway, realignments should remain technical rather than political actions. This can be ensured by establishing regular (annual) and transparent reviews of the appropriateness of the central parities, conducted jointly with the ECB, and timely parity adjustments, if these reviews suggest such steps.

However, choosing the slow-track option may have a negative influence on the momentum of structural reforms and on the commitment to policy discipline. Structural reforms aiming at deeper integration into the euro area, such as dismantling barriers to foreign competitors and abandoning protections on domestic agents, can create unpleasant shocks to the domestic economy in the short run. Even worse, these negative shocks cannot be easily absorbed by appropriate fiscal and monetary policies, since the fast-track option requires fiscal discipline to ensure small budget deficits and public debt as well as monetary tightening to ensure low inflation rates. If countries are committed to the fast-track strategy, and the markets believe it, a favourable environment for policy-making may emerge, including declining country risk premia, converging interest rates to the euro area level, stable exchange rates and low inflation expectations. These developments can ease the difficulties associated with the fast-track option and help countries to achieve the nominal convergence required for EMU entry.

In contrast, if countries lack strong political will to join EMU as early as possible, a vicious circle may be the outcome. Politicians may suspend painful reform efforts and follow more lax policies appealing to the electorate. Because of weak commitment to policy discipline, the markets view these countries as unfit for EMU in the foreseeable future and attach high-risk premia when dealing with them in international financial transactions. High interest rates worsen the fiscal position and create depreciation expectations. Exchange rates will be less stable and inflation rates, due to pass-through effects, will be high. These unfavourable conditions make the efforts aiming at reducing fiscal deficits and inflation rates even more difficult, and the incentive to abandon disciplined policies even stronger. As a result, EMU entry will be further postponed as the political enthusiasm diminishes. This possibility suggests that, although countries are given the slow-track option, they should generally be encouraged to take the fast track towards EMU.

Choosing a central parity

Our discussion above and the experience of the first EMU members suggest that market forces will cause the nominal exchange rate of a prospective EMU member's currency to converge smoothly towards the pre-announced terminal conversion rate. The actual value of the terminal rate is not of great importance from that perspective. However, once the terminal rate has been reached, and given that output prices and wages are sticky, the choice of the nominal exchange rate determines the country's real exchange rate at least for a while. If the terminal rate for the euro is set too low (in terms of national currency units per euro), the country will enter EMU with an overvalued real exchange rate and experience a period of price level adjustment subsequently, in which the domestic price level falls relative to the price level in the rest of EMU. If the terminal rate is chosen too high, the country will enter EMU with an undervalued real exchange rate and will subsequently experience higher rates of price increases than the rest of EMU. Both deviations from the equilibrium real exchange rate can have significant real costs. In the first case, the industries lose competitiveness and go through an adjustment recession with low growth and rising unemployment. In the second case, overemployment will be the result. As the experiences of Ireland and the Netherlands, among others, suggest, the adjustment may also result in property price bubbles which ultimately can have adverse effects on the financial system.

In addition, the choice of the central parity can affect a country's ability to meet the nominal convergence criteria. A country choosing an undervalued central parity when entering the ERM-II may experience high consumer price inflation rates that violate the inflation criterion for EMU participation, unless the actual exchange rate is allowed to adjust within the normal ERM-II band. But if the expectation of EMU entry drives the nominal rate towards the central parity, this adjustment does not take place. Under such circumstances, the exchange rate criterion and the inflation criterion could be conflicting goals.[35] If the market perceives the entry rate as appropriate, the transition into the ERM-II will be easy. Such rates are also viewed as credible, which in turn facilitates smooth convergence of market rates towards the announced parities.

In view of this, the choice of the initial central parity in the ERM-II is of particular importance for the countries on the fast track to EMU, as this parity is likely to be their terminal rate as well. However, equilibrium (real) exchange rates are difficult to determine. The difficulties are further augmented by the fact that the real exchange rate of the new member countries cannot be expected to be a constant. Thus, choosing the central parity entails considerable uncertainty. In principle, there are two ways to resolve this uncertainty. One is to fix the nominal exchange rate for some time and let goods prices adjust to find an equilibrium real exchange rate. The other is to use monetary policy to control domestic inflation and let the nominal exchange rate adjust to find an equilibrium. Which of these is the appropriate solution depends on a country's monetary policy regime before entering the EU. Those countries that have followed a fixed-exchange rate regime for some time already should use the first option and enter EMU on the fast track, using their past parity to the euro as a guide to pick the central parity in the ERM-II. Should these countries experience rates of price level increase in excess of the inflation criterion, the assessment of nominal convergence should show that this cannot be due to too lax monetary policy, i.e. it reflects real exchange rate adjustments. Since there are then no good reasons to deny these countries entry into EMU, the assessment should make the point transparent and permit their entry.

In contrast, countries that have adopted flexible exchange rates in the recent past should focus on inflation targeting and postpone entry to the ERM-II until domestic inflation is in line with EMU inflation. To the extent that they experience trend appreciations of their currencies during this period, this trend could be accounted for in the choice of a central parity, when these countries eventually decide to initiate the process of entering EMU.

5 NON-STANDARD ROUTES TOWARDS EMU

5.1 EMU Entry via Currency Board Arrangements

While standard ERM-II regimes have wide fluctuation bands (up to ±15%) around the agreed central parities, narrower bands can also be declared as a unilateral commitment of the non-euro area national central bank. As an extreme case, the euro-based currency board arrangements (CBAs) have the band width set to zero. Another feature that makes CBAs different from standard ERM-II regimes is that their central parities were determined unilaterally by the relevant accession countries without agreement of the ECB, since the CBAs were established well before these accession countries join the EU.

Nevertheless, the existing central parities and the zero band width of the CBAs are likely to be accepted by the ECB as relevant parameters for the ERM-II entry. The regime itself is perfectly compatible with the idea of monetary union with the EU, since all the CBAs now use the euro as the backup currency. The central parities have been stable since the launch of the arrangement, reflecting their appropriateness as the exchange rates between accession countries' national currencies and the euro, as well as the ability of the monetary authorities of these countries to stabilize the exchange rates without severe pressures. Therefore, the existing euro parities should be used as the conversion rates upon entry into EMU. Any deviations from the existing parities would only result in unnecessary redistribution of wealth and damages to the established credibility of the regimes. Similarly, introducing broader bands now that the credibility of the CBAs is proven would only create unnecessary uncertainty. Since it is a unilateral commitment, there is no need for the ECB to intervene on the foreign exchange market to support the relevant currencies, hence no risk to price stability in the eurozone from these arrangements.

With a CBA, the money supply is determined solely by reserve changes, and there is no independent monetary policy instrument to control inflation. Fiscal policy may take this responsibility, but its efficacy is rather limited. Given that the currencies of the accession countries tend to appreciate in real terms against the Euro, the accession countries with CBAs will likely exhibit higher inflation rates than in the euro area. Thus, although countries with euro-based CBAs have already effectively adopted the ECB's monetary policy, there is a risk that they violate the Maastricht criterion on inflation because of the B-S effect. For these countries, any deviation from euro-area inflation should be properly interpreted as relative price adjustment rather than an indicator of weak monetary discipline. Since they have proven their willingness and ability to maintain an absolutely fixed exchange rate with the euro, the inflation criterion should be used in a flexible way when their readiness for EMU is tested.[36]

5.2 EMU Entry via Unilateral Euroization

Unilateral euroization has been proposed by some researchers as a safer stepping-stone towards EMU than the semi-fixed, crises-prone ERM-II regime.[37] With unilateral euroization, a country completely gives up its national monetary policy in favour of that of the ECB. However, it is unable to influence the monetary policy of the ECB before it formally joins EMU, which requires the fulfilment of all the Maastricht Criteria.

The main argument in favour of unilateral euroization is that it eliminates all room for speculative attacks on a currency in the run-up to joining EMU. The combination of large capital inflows and high capital mobility means that exchange rate targets are extremely vulnerable to shifts in market expectations. If market expectations depend on economic fundamentals only, this threat can be regarded as a useful disciplinary device. It forces governments and central banks to maintain safe and sound policies; as long as this is the case, they need not be afraid of being punished by the markets. But if market expectations also depend on sentiments and beliefs independent of fundamentals, the possibility of self-fulfilling and contagious speculative attacks arises. Fixed exchange rates might come under attack because there are problems in neighbouring countries, even if domestic policies are fully consistent with the exchange rate target. From this perspective, sound domestic policies are a necessary but not a sufficient condition for avoiding speculative attacks. Even if governments and central banks adopt all the right measures, a country could be thrown off the path to EMU when a currency crisis spills over from abroad. Empirical and theoretical research to date does not allow us to rule out such effects. How important the threat is, therefore, depends on the degree of risk aversion of the policy-makers.

The impact of unilateral euroization on accession countries' convergence performance is not clear-cut. For real convergence, the impact is likely positive, since a common currency will generally promote trade growth and encourage capital inflows, which are growth-enhancing.[38] For nominal convergence, by contrast, the nature of the impact differs across various aspects. With unilateral euroization, the criterion of exchange rate stability is automatically fulfilled. Unilateral euroization has positive influence on the fulfilment of the interest rate criterion, since the currency risk premium is eliminated. The country risk premium can also be reduced, if euroization eliminates currency mismatches in foreign liability and, as a result, default risks.[39] However, risk premia may also rise if the euroization is unsustainable due to policy inconsistency or lack of readiness for monetary union.[40] In that case the fulfilment of the interest rate criterion is made more difficult. The impact on fiscal policy is ambiguous too. On the one hand, fiscal discipline will be strengthened, leading to low deficits and small debt stocks, as governments realize that they can no longer rely on monetary financing any more. On the other hand, a fall in the interest rate reduces the cost of borrowing, which allows governments to pursue lax fiscal policies. As far as inflation is concerned, unilateral euroization deprives the countries of the possibility of nominal appreciation in the case of strong real appreciation, so the inflation rate at home may well exceed that prevailing in the EU. No matter how the convergence performance is affected, the point is that it is still possible to check the fulfilment of the Maastricht Criteria even if a country has euroized. There is no reason to worry that unilateral euroization would be a cheap way of sneaking into the eurozone.

A major problem with unilateral euroization is the European Commission's opposition to it as a strategy for EMU entry. Obviously the EU loses its influence on the selection of the rates at which the national currencies are converted into the euro. However, since the Commission accepts currency board arrangements with unilaterally selected central euro parities, it has no reason to object to unilateral euroization because of this. More important is the concern that unilateral euroization might be used as a substitute for serious reforms and to circumvent convergence efforts. This concern is nevertheless not well grounded, as our previous discussions show that the convergence performance of the euroized countries can still be examined based on the Maastricht Criteria. And only by fulfilling all the convergence criteria can a country be granted membership of EMU.

However, just as with a currency board arrangement, inflation rate convergence is difficult to achieve in a euroized accession country in the presence of trend equilibrium real appreciation. As a result, accession countries adopting unilateral euroization are advised to persuade the EU to adjust the inflation criterion to make it easier for the accession countries to fulfil.[41] It is not clear whether the EU will soften its position on this issue, which currently insists on applying equal treatment to the new entrants as to the previous ones. If the convergence criteria remain unchanged, the route towards EMU via unilateral euroization might be a difficult one for the accession countries.

6 CONCLUSIONS

In this chapter we analysed exchange rate policies in the CEE accession countries during the run-up to EMU. We argued that these countries are confronted with challenges associated with the EU and EMU accession. On the one hand, capital account liberalization, coupled with a brighter economic future, generates substantially larger capital flows, leading to high volatility in the foreign exchange market, unless the exchange rate is fixed under a CBA or unilateral euroization. On the other hand, the accession to EMU requires the fulfilment of various convergence criteria, including exchange rate stability and low inflation rates. Since the currencies of the accession countries tend to appreciate in real terms due to relative productivity growth, there is an apparent conflict between the Maastricht Criteria and the economic reality of the accession countries.

Given real appreciation in place, different exchange rate regimes during the run-up to EMU have different implications for nominal convergence. Currency board arrangements ensure exchange rate stability, but price stability is not guaranteed, though fiscal policy can be of some use in attenuating real appreciation. In the case of large real appreciation, the inflation target is likely to be missed. A more extreme regime choice is unilateral euroization, which completely eliminates exchange rate risk and reduces interest rates by lowering risk premia. However, as under CBAs, inflation tends to be higher under euroization than under a standard ERM-II regime. The suggested solution is to soften the inflation criterion to make it compatible with the situation of the CEE countries.

The standard choice is to enter the ERM-II with a fixed central parity and a wide fluctuation band. A wide band is necessary to accommodate exchange rate volatility associated with enhanced capital mobility. The euro central parities during the ERM-II should be, in normal cases, the final conversion rates between national currencies and the euro. These euro parities, as well as their importance as the predecessor of the final euro conversion rates, should be made clear to the markets as early as possible, as this can reduce much confusion in the prediction of the conversion rates and much fluctuation in the market rates as they converge towards the announced targets. However, if the pressure of real appreciation is strong, the central parities can be revalued to ease the fulfilment of the relevant nominal convergence criteria.

NOTES

* This is a revised version of the paper presented at the conference on Monetary Strategies for Accession Countries, February 27–28, 2003, Budapest, organized jointly by the National Bank of Hungary (NBH), the Institute for World Economics of the Hungarian Academy of Sciences (IWE), and the Center for European Integration Studies (ZEI), University of Bonn.

** Correspondence: ZEI, Walter Flex Strasse 3, D-53113 Bonn, Germany. Tel: +49(0)228-734928. Email: zhou@united.econ.uni-bonn.de.

1. European Union (2002).
2. Recent currency crises in EMS (1992), Mexico (1994), East Asia (1997), Russia (1998), Brazil (1999) and Turkey (2000) all involved some type of adjustable exchange rate peg in a financially open economy. See Eichengreen (1994), Fischer (2001) or Mussa et al. (2000)

for more discussions on the fragility of semi-fixed exchange rates under high capital mobility.

3. Halpern and Wyplosz (1997, 2001).
4. See von Hagen and Zhou (2002) for an empirical analysis of the exchange rate regime choices in transition countries in the 1990s.
5. For example, in 2001 the average inflation rate in the eight CEE accession countries was 5.7%, while the inflation rate in the euro area was 2.6%.
6. In 2001 the GDP values of Estonia and Lithuania, measured by purchasing power standard, were 13.4 billion euro and 30.3 billion euro respectively, ranking number 8 and 6 in the eight CEE countries and much below the group average of 96 billion euro.
7. See, among others, Ghosh et al. (2000). Another feature is that CBAs tend to be adopted by countries with a very poor track record in macroeconomic policy management. A case in point from the CEE countries is Bulgaria, which adopted the CBA in 1997 in the aftermath of a severe currency crisis and a hyperinflationary episode.
8. The Lithuanian currency board originally used the US dollar as the back-up currency. To make the exchange rate regime more compatible with the requirement of the EU accession, it has been replaced by the euro as the reserve currency since 2 February 2002.
9. Amato and Gerlach (2001) point out that central bank independence, especially instrument independence, is an essential precondition for the success of an inflation targeting framework. Goal independence, by contrast, is less important, as the UK experience suggests.
10. The EBRD indices are valued on a 1,2,3,4 scale, with 'x–' or 'x+' indicating a value slightly below or above x, and with '4+' denoting full convergence with the standards and norms of advanced industrial countries. To derive the index reported in the text, a '+/–' perturbation is interpreted as '0.3 more or less', i.e., '3–' is valued as 2.7 and '3+' as 3.3. The EU reference value is set at 4.3.
11. Orlowski (2000) argues that the CEE accession countries should gradually replace inflation targeting by exchange rate targeting when they are preparing for final entry into EMU.
12. IMF (2001).
13. The so-called 'Copenhagen Criteria' for the accession into the EU require that accession countries ensure (1) stability of institutions guaranteeing democracy, the rule of law, human rights and the respect and protection of minorities; (2) the existence of a functioning market economy as well as the capacity to cope with competitive pressure and market forces within the Union; and (3) ability to take on the obligations of membership, including adherence to the aims of political, economic and monetary union.
14. One obvious disadvantage of focusing on per capita data is the negligence of income distribution.
15. For example, the average PPP-adjusted per capita GNP of Greece, Ireland, Portugal and Spain was 55% of the EU average in 1986 and 69% of the EU average in 1997. See Buiter and Grafe (2001).
16. Simple average based on 2001 data.
17. The preliminary data for 2002 show that the Czech Republic (1.8%) and Poland (1.9%) successfully reduced their inflation rates down below the threshold (3.0%), together with Latvia (1.9%) and Lithuania (0.3%).
18. These numerical targets should be interpreted with flexibility. Larger deficits or public debts may be allowed as long as they are falling substantially and approaching the reference values at a satisfactory speed.
19. See Buch and Lusinyan (2002).
20. Since 1997 the IMF's Annual Report on Exchange Arrangements and Exchange Restrictions identifies eleven categories of capital transactions that may be subject to controls. They include controls on (1) capital market securities, (2) money market instruments, (3) collective investment securities, (4) derivatives and other investments, (5) commercial credits, (6) financial credits, (7) guarantees, sureties and financial backup facilities, (8) direct investment, (9) liquidation of direct investment, (10) real estate transactions and (11) personal capital movements.
21. See, for example, Kaminsky and Reinhart (1999), Ho (2003).

22. Price liberalization may also contribute to the adjustment of relative prices, but its importance fades away as the scope of price controls becomes increasingly smaller in recent years in the accession countries.
23. See, among others, Halpern and Wyplosz (2001).
24. Obstfeld and Rogoff (1996, p. 212) show that the B-S effect can be characterized by the following equation:

    $$\pi - \pi^* = (1 - \alpha)\,[\gamma\,(a_T - a_T^*) - (a_N - a_N^*)],$$

    where γ denotes relative labour intensity of the non-tradable sector compared to the tradable sector, and variables with asterisk denote foreign counterparts. Assuming zero productivity growth abroad, we have

    $$\pi - \pi^* = (1 - \alpha)\,\gamma\,(a_T - a_N) + (1 - \alpha)(\gamma - 1)\,a_N,$$

    which leads to the approximation used in the text, if we assume that a_N is small, and γ is not far above unity.
25. This is the simple average of relative productivity growth ($a_T - a_N$) in eight CEE accession countries. For each country a_T (a_N) is the average productivity growth rate of the tradable (non-tradable) sector during 1994–1999. The tradable sector is proxied by the manufacturing, while the non-tradable sector covers trade, repair, hotels etc. and financial services, and real estate. The data source is UNECE.
26. This corresponds to the average trade-to-GDP ratio in the eight accession countries over 1995–1999. The trade value is the average of export and import values.
27. For each sector labour productivity growth rate is used, which is the balance between the growth rate of value added and that of employment. For the growth rate of value added, the tradable sector refers to 'manufacturing, energy, and mining', and the non-tradable sector refers to 'trade, repairs, hotels, etc' and 'financial services, real estate, etc'. For the growth rate of employment, the tradable sector is 'industry excluding construction', and the non-tradable sector is 'services'. Data source is ECB (2002).
28. Rother (2000) reports that the relative productivity growth in the EU can offset the inflation differential by roughly 0.8%.
29. See Backé et al. (2002) and Lommatzsch and Tober (2002).
30. See Fischer (2001) and Eichengreen (1994).
31. See Begg et al. (2001).
32. ECOFIN (1998).
33. Note that the economic cost of such implied devaluation in terms of inflation could be expected to be small, since the ECB was to take over monetary policy and fight inflation immediately afterwards.
34. The 'New ERM', a term used in the monetary policy debates of the late 1980s and early 1990s, was built on the assumption that, after 1987, countries would not use the option of realignments anymore and that the ERM, therefore, was already a de facto monetary union with some remaining exchange rate flexibility. See Fratianni and von Hagen (1992).
35. This discussion implies that the strategy adopted by Greece, which devalued the drachma by 12.3% just before the entry into the ERM in March 1998 bears considerable risks. See Bank of Greece (2000).
36. See Szapáry (2000), Buiter and Grafe (2001), and Begg et al. (2001).
37. See Begg et al. (2001), Rostowski (2002), Buiter and Grafe (2002).
38. See Goldstein (2002) and Rostowski (2002).
39. See Berg and Borensztein (2000).
40. Begg et al. (2001).
41. See Rostowski (2002).

REFERENCES

Amato, Jeffrey D. and Stefan Gerlach (2001), 'Inflation targeting in emerging market and transition economies: lessons after a decade', CEPR Discussion Paper No. 3074.

Backé, Peter, Jarko Fidrmuc, Thomas Reininger and Franz Schadarx (2002), 'Price dynamics in Central and Eastern European EU accession countries', Oesterreichische Nationalbank Working Paper 61.

Bank of Greece (2000), *Monetary Policy*, Interim Report 2000.

Begg, David, Francesco Giavazzi, Jürgen von Hagen and Charles Wyplosz (1997), 'EMU: Getting the end-game right', *Monitoring European Integration*, **7**, CEPR.

Begg, David, Barry Eichengreen, László Halpern, Jürgen von Hagen and Charles Wyplosz (2001), *Sustainable Regimes of Capital Movements in Accession Countries*, CEPR.

Berg, Andrew and Eduardo Borensztein (2000), 'The pros and cons of full dollarization', IMF Working Paper 00/05.

Buch, Claudia M. and Lusine Lusinyan (2002), 'Short-term capital, economic transformation, and EU accession', Deutsche Bundesbank Discussion Paper 02/02.

Buiter, Willem H. and Clemens Grafe (2001), 'Central banking and the choice of currency regime in accession countries', SUERF Studies No. 11.

Buiter, Willem H. and Clemens Grafe (2002), 'Anchor, float or abandon ship: exchange rate regimes for accession countries', CEPR Discussion Paper No. 3184.

Coricelli, Fabrizio and Bostjan Jazbec (2001), 'Real exchange rate dynamics in transition economies', CEPR Discussion Paper No. 2869.

De Broeck, Mark and Torsten Sløk (2001), 'Interpreting real exchange rate movements in transition countries', BOFIT Discussion Paper 2001 No. 7.

De Grauwe, Paul, Hans Dewachter and Dirk Veestraeten (1999), 'Price dynamics under stochastic process switching: some extensions and an application to EMU', *Journal of International Money and Finance*, **18** (1999), pp. 195–224.

ECOFIN (1998), 'Recommendation on member states participating in EMU', Brussels.

Eichengreen, Barry (1994), *International Monetary Arrangements for the 21st Century*, Washington, DC: Brookings Institution.

European Bank for Reconstruction and Development, *Transition Report* (various issues).

European Central Bank (2002), *Monthly Bulletin*, September 2002.

European Commission (2002), *Strategy Paper*, available from http://europa.eu.int.

European Commission (1998, 2002), *Regular Report*, available from http://europa.eu.int.

European Union (2002), *Presidency Conclusions*, Copenhagen European Council, available from http://europa.eu.int.

Fischer, Stanley (2001), 'Exchange rate regimes: is the bipolar view correct?', mimeo, IMF.

Fratianni, Michele and Jürgen von Hagen (1992), *The European Monetary System and European Monetary Union*, Boulder and Oxford: Westview Press.

Ghosh, Atish R., Anne-Marie Gulde and Holger C. Wolf (2000), 'Currency boards: more than a quick fix?', *Economic Policy*, October 2000, pp. 271–335.

Goldstein, Morris (2002), *Managed Floating Plus*, Washington, DC: Institute for International Economies.

Halpern, László and Charles Wyplosz (1997), 'Equilibrium exchange rates in transition economies', IMF *Staff Papers*, **44** (4), pp. 430–61.

Halpern, László and Charles Wyplosz (2001), 'Economic transformation and real exchange rates in the 2000s: the Balassa-Samuelson connection', mimeo.

Ho, Tai-kuang (2003), Four Essays in the Economics of Banking and Currency Crises, PhD dissertation, ZEI, University of Bonn.

International Monetary Fund (2001), 'Monetary and exchange rate regimes in the Central European economies on the road to EU accession and monetary union', mimeo.

International Monetary Fund, *Annual Report on Exchange Arrangements and Exchange Restrictions* (various issues).

Kaminsky, Graciela and Carmen Reinhart (1999), 'The twin crises: the causes of banking and balance-of-payments problems', *American Economic Review*, **89** (3), pp. 473–500.

Kopits, George and István Székely (2002), 'Fiscal policy challenges of EU accession for the Baltics and Central Europe', mimeo, IMF.

Kovács, M. András and András Simon (1998), 'Components of the real exchange rate in Hungary', National Bank of Hungary Working Paper 1998/3.

Lommatzsch, Kirsten and Silke Tober (2002), 'Monetary policy aspects of the enlargement of the euro area', Deutsche Bank Research, Research Notes No. 4.

Mussa, Michael, Paul Masson, Alexander Swoboda, Esteban Jadresic, Paolo Mauro and Andrew Berg (2000), 'Exchange rate regimes in an ncreasingly integrated world economy', IMF *Occasional Paper* 193.

Obstfeld, Maurice and Kenneth Rogoff (1996), *Foundations of International Macroeconomics*, Cambridge, MA: MIT Press.

Orlowski, Lucjan T. (2000), 'A dynamic approach to inflation targeting in transition economies', ZEI Working Paper B00-11, University of Bonn.

Pelkmans, Jacques, Daniel Gros and Jorge N. Ferrer (2000), 'Long-run economic aspects of the European Union's eastern enlargement', WRR Working Documents W109.

Rostowski, Jacek (2002), 'Why unilateral euroization makes sense for (some) applicant countries', mimeo.

Rother, Philipp (2000), 'The impact of productivity differentials on inflation and the real exchange rate: an estimation of the Balassa-Samuelson effect in Slovenia', IMF, mimeo.

Szapáry, György (2000), 'Maastricht and the choice of exchange rate regime in transition countries during the run-up to EMU', National Bank of Hungary Working Paper 2000/7.

von Hagen, Jürgen and Jizhong Zhou (2002), 'The choice of exchange rate regimes: an empirical analysis for transition economies', ZEI Working Paper B02-03, University of Bonn.

COMMENTS

Vítor Gaspar* (jointly with Fiorella De Fiore)

We very much enjoyed reading the chapter by Jürgen von Hagen and Jizhong Zhou. The authors start by identifying key dates for the acceding countries in their path towards full integration into the European Union. They proceed to discuss the main (policy) challenges along this timeline, focusing particularly on monetary and exchange rate policies 'on the last stretch'. Finally, they provide conclusions and main recommendations. The chapter is well-structured and well-written. The policy challenges identified by the authors are certainly relevant. Nevertheless we have, or so we think, serious objections to the main conclusions and policy recommendations that the authors draw from their analysis. In our comments, we will start by presenting a short summary of the chapter. We will then go through the timeline and work out the implications, from a policy viewpoint, as time unfolds. As you will see, our conclusions and recommendations will differ from those reached by the authors.

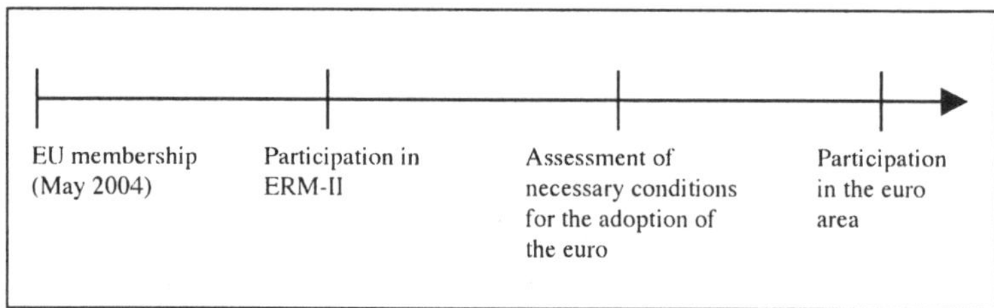

Figure 3.1 Key dates in the accession process

The authors identify four key dates in the accession process: EU membership, participation in ERM-II, assessment of the necessary conditions for the adoption of the euro and participation in the euro area (see Figure 3.1). Associated with this timeline, they derive two main policy challenges. First, with EU membership comes participation in the Single Market and full freedom of capital movements.[1] Paraphrasing von Hagen and Zhou, freedom of capital movements makes these countries fully vulnerable to the whims of international financial markets. At the same time, the authors argue, acceding countries aim at exchange rate stability as a way to ensure a smooth and early access to EMU. This is consistent with the requirement for EU members to treat exchange rate policies as a 'matter of common interest' (Article 124(1) of the European Union Treaty) and with the convergence criteria necessary for participation in the euro area. From these two elements, the authors derive the first challenge: how to ensure exchange rate stability in an environment of unrestricted capital mobility and whimsical financial markets? The second challenge, in turn, is derived from the need to fulfil the convergence criteria for membership in the euro area and from the implications of structural change and a successful catching-up process. The goal of early participation in the euro area implies that price stability and exchange rate stability have to be satisfied simultaneously. Therefore it requires *real* exchange rate stability. This is problematic, since a successful catching-up process implies relative productivity differentials between accession countries and the euro area. Such differentials are associated with relative price changes and a trend appreciation of the equilibrium real exchange rate. The second challenge then is how to solve this contradiction.

Given these challenges, the authors proceed to discuss monetary and exchange rate policy options after recognizing the wide diversity of initial exchange rate regimes and the common end point provided by the adoption of the euro. Notwithstanding the relevance of each country's own history, the authors are able to put forward three general policy conclusions. First, the criterion of price stability should be softened, reflecting the need for real exchange rate adjustment for countries with fixed exchange rates. Second, the final euro conversion rates should generally coincide with the central parities during ERM-II. They should be fixed and made clear to markets as soon as possible to reduce speculative pressures and fluctuations in the market rates, as these rates converge to the announced target. Third, unilateral euroization in accession countries should be seen as a permissible option.

Now, let us go through the timeline from the beginning and work out the policy implications, as we see them. The first stage in the accession timeline is the phase following EU membership. In this phase new EU members join a stability-oriented community. In the EU, there is a firm consensus on the importance of stability-oriented policies, which provide the best possible environment for sustainable economic growth and for convergence of economic performances among member states. As applied to acceding countries, this basic idea implies that sound and stability-oriented policies provide the best environment for sustainable economic growth, integration into the EU and successful catching-up. In general terms, this belief is reflected in Article 4 of the Treaty, which establishes that economic policies in the EU must be conducted according to the principles of an open market economy with free competition, stable prices, sound public finances and sustainable balance of payments. The Treaty also clearly states that exchange rate policies are a matter of common concern (Article 124), as the authors rightly emphasize. It is, however, key to recall that the same applies to *all* economic policies of member states (Article 99). As a matter of fact we believe it is correct to say that all economic policies in the Community are a matter of common concern. In particular, the common concern also covers member states' budgetary policies, structural policies and reforms, incomes policies and much else. A number of procedures have been established to ensure consistency of national policies with the common interest – such as the excessive deficit procedure, the stability and growth pact, the broad economic policy guidelines, the macroeconomic dialogue (Cologne Process), the employment guidelines (the Luxembourg Process) and Reports on Economic Reform, focusing on product and capital markets (the Cardiff Process). In a context where monetary and exchange rate policies are part of a broader set of stability-oriented policies, the exchange rate cannot be seen as an end in itself. It is a means to an end. And the end goal is the achievement and maintenance of price stability. It is clear that member states' monetary policies should be directed towards the achievement of this goal. The process of monetary policy coordination within the EU also aims at ensuring price stability.

The second important stage of the accession timeline is participation in ERM-II. Let us briefly recall some fundamental elements of ERM-II. First, the resolution of the European Council meeting in Amsterdam, by which the ERM-II was set up on 16 June 1997, states that 'The ERM will help to ensure that member states outside the euro area participating in the mechanism orient their policies to stability … It will provide those member states with a reference for the conduct of sound economic policies in general and monetary policy in particular.' Hence, ERM-II presupposes policy decisions directed to a stable environment and to a sustainable convergence process. Moreover, it provides enough flexibility to ensure convergence and stability through standard fluctuation bands of ±15% around central rates. A second important element of ERM-II is that the choice of the monetary and exchange rate strategy remains primarily the responsibility of the member state — subject to the obligations deriving from participation in a stability-oriented Community. These obligations include the pursuit of disciplined and responsible monetary policy aimed at achieving price stability. Additionally, the functioning of ERM-II must be compatible with the primary objective of the ECB and the member states' National Central Banks: again price stability. A further crucial aspect of the overall design of ERM-II is its multilateral dimension, where decisions concerning central rates and bands need to be taken by mutual agreement. Intervention at the margins is in principle automatic and unlimited, although it can be suspended if this were to conflict with the primary objective of price stability.

The last key date in the timeline of accession is EMU membership. This involves important issues such as the decision of final conversion rates and the announcement of these rates to the market, with the related possibility of triggering speculative pressures and excessive exchange rate volatility. To minimize this risk, previous ERM experiences suggest that adjustments in central parities within ERM-II should be conducted in a timely manner and should reflect 'technical' rather than 'political' decisions.

Let us now come to our conclusions on the set of questions raised by the authors. The first conclusion is that the criteria and procedures established in the EU Treaty — including the inflation criterion — should be maintained. This ensures sustainable economic growth for the euro area as a whole, convergence of economic performances among its members and equal treatment to all countries at the time of assessment of the conditions for the adoption of the euro. Under some circumstances, pursuing the objective of price stability in a small open economy leads to a stable path for the exchange rate. The degree of exchange rate volatility depends on the structure of the economy and on the nature of the shocks.[2] Additionally, if the economy experiences equilibrium phenomena that imply an appreciation of the real exchange rate (such as large capital inflows or relative price changes), the exchange rate should be able to accommodate the necessary adjustment. This is indeed compatible with ERM-II, given in particular the fact that the possibility of revaluating the central rate is not excluded by the criterion on participation in the exchange rate mechanism (according to the Protocol to Article 121 of the Treaty). What is important is that new members carefully and realistically assess their degree of convergence when deciding the timing of entry in ERM-II. The wide diversity of initial exchange rate regimes makes clear that no single policy choice or recommendation is appropriate for all cases. In this respect, we share the authors' views. However, arguing that the requirement of exchange rate stability implies the need to soften the requirements for price stability seems to us a clear case of putting the cart before the horse.

Our second conclusion is that no ex ante limitation on the length of participation in ERM-II or guarantee that the central parity will be the final conversion rate can be given. Such guarantees would be incompatible with the requirement of no conflict with the objective of price stability. Conversion rates that do not reflect economic fundamentals at the time of EMU entry may trigger speculative pressures and be incompatible with sustainable convergence. Such rates need to be set at a level that reflects fundamentals at the end of the convergence process to guarantee the best economic performance of new members and of the euro area as a whole. The risk of speculative pressure and exchange rate volatility needs to be minimized by conducting adjustments in central parities in a timely manner. Here, we do agree with the authors when they emphasize the need to consider the full use of the fluctuation bands foreseen in ERM-II. Moreover, in our view, ERM-II allows for enough flexibility to enable a well-structured case-by-case approach.

The third conclusion is that acceding countries are not to be allowed to enter the euro area by undertaking a process of unilateral euroization. First, the exchange rate could not be used as a convergence criterion for EMU entry, implying an unequal treatment of acceding countries in the assessment of the convergence criteria. Second, unilateral euroization is in clear contrast to the idea underlying ERM-II, where the final conversion rate should reflect the economic performance of new members and their exposure to market discipline. Finally, euroization is not compatible with the nature of ERM-II as a multilateral framework, where decisions on central parities and on final conversion rates should be mutually agreed. Indeed, currency board arrangements are only deemed compatible with ERM-II following a case-by-case assessment, where the appropriateness of the existing central parity is evaluated.

To conclude, we think the chapter asks a set of relevant questions. The answers we reach, however, are very different from those of the authors. First, the criteria established in the EU Treaty — including the inflation criterion — should be maintained. Second, no ex ante guarantee that the central parities will be close to the conversion rates for euro adoption is possible. Third, unilateral euroization is not compatible with the Treaty and with the ERM-II resolution. Hence we finish with a second disclaimer: the views presented in the chapter do not reflect the views of the discussants.

NOTES

* The views expressed by the discussants are their own and do not necessarily reflect those of the European Central Bank or the Eurosystem.

1. Freedom of capital movements already prevails in all accession countries, as testified by their 2002 Pre-Accession Economic Programmes.
2. See Detken, C. and V. Gaspar (2003), 'Managed floating: a fearless way out of the corner?', mimeo, European Central Bank, Frankfurt.

4. Disentangling the Balassa-Samuelson effect in CEC5 countries in the prospect of EMU enlargement

Mihály A. Kovács

1 INTRODUCTION[1]

Since the opportunity to join the common market has come within reach of the accession countries, there has been much economic debate regarding the costs and benefits, and especially the timing, of EMU membership. Most authors agree that, in the longer term, EMU membership is beneficial to both the accession and the current EMU countries. The traditional arguments in this respect are built on the strong trade relations and historical ties between these countries. Furthermore, as most of the accession countries are small open economies, it is also frequently argued that monetary independence and the resulting exchange rate volatility may be damaging for long-term macroeconomic development in the accession area.

Buiter (2000) and Szapáry (2000) and later Buiter and Grafe (2002) came to the conclusion quite early that the earliest possible EMU entry strategy for the accession countries would be highly beneficial, mainly by avoiding unnecessarily volatile capital flows and exchange rates. Csajbók and Csermely (2002) advocate early EMU membership on a more complex ground, by presenting a detailed cost benefit analysis in terms of GDP gains from EMU membership. They argue that the costs of complying with the Maastricht criteria and giving up monetary independence are temporary, while the gains via a decreasing risk premium and expanding international trade are permanent. While the 'when' seemed to be more obvious, the 'how' remained very questionable. Most of the authors above and others, including Halpern and Wyplosz (2001) and Hobza (2002), have raised a number of caveats related to the issue of nominal convergence, and more specifically, the real exchange rate.

According to the traditional argument it is said that due to the equilibrium real appreciation, arising mainly from the Balassa-Samuelson (B-S) effect, these countries cannot achieve an EMU-consistent inflation level and stable exchange rate at the same time. This may cause problems at least in two respects. First, the equilibrium real appreciation, together with disinflationary efforts prior to accession, may require nominal appreciation during ERM-II, which may be inconsistent with the exchange rate corridor. Second, due to the presence of nominal rigidities, the nominal appreciation required for disinflation may cause unnecessary output losses.

Several possible solutions have been proposed to tackle this problem. Buiter (2000) argues in favour of an asymmetric ERM-II band, and a reinterpretation of the inflation criterion of the Maastricht Treaty in terms of tradable price inflation. The argument is further elaborated by Buiter and Grafe (2002), who suggest a flexible treatment of the ERM-II period as was in effect done in the case of Italy, Finland and Greece. By contrast, Szapáry (2000) suggests setting the inflation criterion of the Treaty in terms of the average rate of inflation within EMU instead of the average rate of the three countries with the lowest inflation. But as our calculations show, that B-S effect might be low enough that it could be accommodated within the current Maastricht inflation criterion. Finding the possible rate of equilibrium real appreciation requires an assessment of the most important factors, including the B-S effect, in these countries. It is important to note, however, that since the B-S effect is a sectoral story, *real convergence* does not inevitably imply at all stages of the catch-up process a higher *traded/non-traded* productivity differential, i.e. real appreciation.

On the other hand, the B-S effect was not the only possible factor of real appreciation in these countries, especially in the early years of transition. As is well known in international economics, real exchange rates may reflect persistent trends if a country's underlying fundamentals are changing over time.[2] As rapidly changing economic fundamentals are one of the most important characteristics of transition economies, the assessment of actual exchange rates in relation to some equilibrium value is a really formidable task. As shown by pioneering econometric evidence provided by Halpern and Wyplosz (1997), equilibrium exchange rates are expected to appreciate as transition proceeds. However, it is very difficult to give a precise estimate of the equilibrium rate of real appreciation.

Figure 4.1 clearly shows the existence of trend appreciation in five Central and Eastern European Countries: the Czech Republic, Hungary, Poland, the Slovak Republic and Slovenia (hereinafter CEC5) since the start of the transition. Between 1991 and 2002, all five countries experienced real appreciation in the range of 2% to 6% per annum. It is also obvious that the first half of the nineties was characterized by much sharper appreciation tendencies than the latter part of the decade. While between 1991 and 1993 real appreciation ranged from 3.6% to 10.3%, after 1993 the annual rate decreased to 0.7%–4.4%.

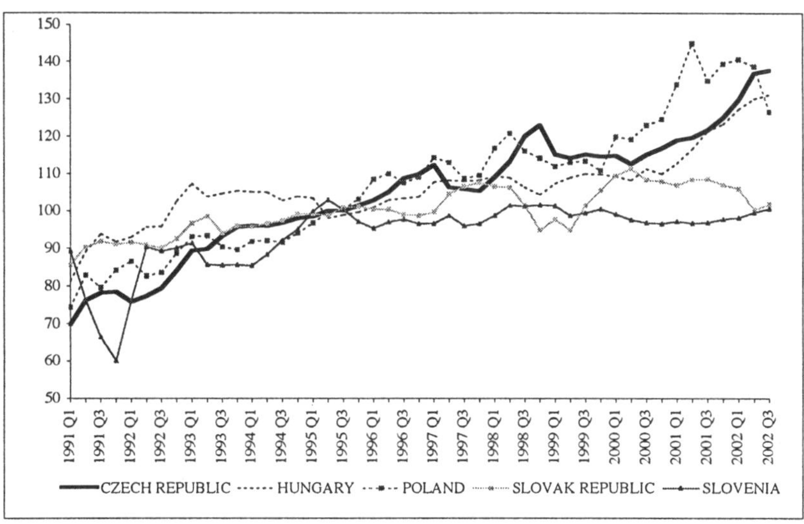

Sources: IMF, *International Financial Statistics* and Bank of Slovenia.

Figure 4.1 CPI-based real exchange rates in the CEC5 (real effective indices, 1995 = 100)

The underlying factors of the real appreciation in the two stages of transition were presumably markedly different. Several authors, like Halpern and Wyplosz (1997), Kovács (1998) and Corricelli and Jazbec (2001), argue that in the early 1990s the deregulation of goods and labour markets and financial deepening were the main explanations behind the real appreciation observed. At that time, productivity improvements had been modest, in some countries even negative, compared to those in developed countries. In the late 1990s, after a period of successful transition, the CEC5 began to resemble the former catching-up European countries, such as Spain, Portugal or Greece prior to EU accession. In a recent chapter,[3] the Magyar Nemzeti Bank (MNB) argues that by 2001 Hungary had become in several respects similar to the above-mentioned countries in terms of both nominal and real convergence. In fact, for almost all of the CEC5, a high share of trade with the EU, a high share of intra-industry trade, relatively sound legal infrastructure and sustainable financial conditions were already prevailing.[4]

These advances in their economic systems also meant that more standard channels of real exchange rate determination had started to play a dominant role in the appreciation, with the B-S effect playing the most influential role. While the productivity differential hypothesis seems to be supported by several authors,[5] relatively little focus has been given to other potential explanations. While the real appreciation may have been generally associated with productivity improvements in the CEC5 in relation to the developed economies, the productivity differential has much less explanatory power within the CEC5. Table 4.1 shows that the higher real appreciation was not necessarily associated with the higher sectoral productivity differential at all. For example, the Czech Republic, experiencing one of the highest annual real appreciations, had the smallest productivity differential, while Hungary, the country with the highest productivity improvements, experienced the second smallest real appreciation.

Table 4.1 Real appreciation vis-à-vis Germany and sectoral productivity differentials in the CEC5

Annual change (%)	Real appreciation*	Productivity**	Period covered
Czech Republic	3.8	2.4	1994–2001
Hungary	2.6	6.2	1992–2001
Poland	6.7	na	1995–2001
Slovakia	1.5	3.3	1995–2001
Slovenia	1.5	4.1	1992–2001

Notes:
* CPI based rates.
** Labour productivity rates, traded/non-traded in the domestic economy. The exact sectoral classification might be found in Kovács et al. (2002).

Source: Kovács et al. (2002).

Table 4.1 suggests that the B-S effect is only one aspect of the observable real appreciation within the CEC5, which is what prompted us in this chapter to give a simple but comprehensive accounting model for real exchange rate determination. This framework is then employed to decompose real exchange rate movements within the CEC5 countries. Several interesting results emerge from the analysis. The B-S effect for the CEC5 countries seems to be less than 2% annually, which is of similar magnitude to that estimated by Alberola and Tyrvainen (1998) for Spain, and Canzoneri et al. (1998) for a few non-core EMU countries prior to EMU membership. Though not uniformly, other important determinants of real appreciation have also emerged. First, the CPI-based real appreciation has a high correlation with the tradable-price-based real appreciation, indicating that nominal exchange rate movements play a significant role in the development of the real exchange rate. Second, the B-S hypothesis is only one of the explanations for internal real exchange rate movements. In the Czech Republic and Slovakia, non-traded/traded relative wages have increased systematically, thereby reinforcing real appreciation. In the Czech Republic and Slovenia, mark-ups in the traded and non-traded sectors have evolved differently, indicating possibly changing demand elasticity in the markets. Finally, in almost all countries, other effects like indirect tax and perhaps commodity price changes have influenced the CPI-based real appreciation.

The chapter is organized as follows. Section 2 discusses the assumptions of the textbook B-S model, indicating possible sources of contradiction to real-world observations. Section 3 summarizes empirical research on the B-S model regarding both developed and less-developed countries. Section 4 presents our simple theoretical framework for the analyses. Section 5 presents the results, and Section 6 offers conclusions.

2 THE B-S MODEL

Since the publication of the seminal papers of Balassa (1964) and Samuelson (1964), economic policy debate has never been so lively about this issue, with particular regard to the link between EMU enlargement and the Balassa-Samuelson effect.[6] This is not surprising, since EMU membership offers an excellent empirical experiment of the theory of real exchange rate determination during the catch-up process. At the same time, the Maastricht criterion on inflation gives explicit political relevance to this topic.

By the mid-1990s, the B-S effect had been modelled in a general equilibrium framework by several authors.[7] All agree that the B-S model relies on the following assumptions:

1. Perfect competition in the goods market.
2. Perfect international capital mobility.
3. Perfect intra-national labour mobility.
4. No role for regulation and intermediate goods.

Perfect competition in the goods market assures that, in the long run, *PPP* holds for traded goods, which implies that only the relative price of non-tradables matters. Perfect intra-national labour mobility assures that *nominal wages* are similar in the traded and non-traded goods sectors of the economy, while perfect international capital mobility determines traded and non-traded *real wages*, i.e. the relative price of non-tradables in the model. Condition four is necessary for the simple decomposition of costs into *wages and capital costs*, so that other costs do not complicate the issue.

Not surprisingly, none of these assumptions seems to be valid in *absolute* terms in the real world. PPP does not seem to be valid in its absolute form at the macro level, even for tradable prices. There are several possible explanations for this.[8] First, tradable price indices usually contain many products which, due to the structure of consumption and production, are not necessarily similar across countries. This causes an *aggregation bias*. This means that even when the law of one price (LOP) holds for every individual good, persistent relative price changes may run contrary to the PPP hypothesis.[9]

Second, there are several possible explanations for the deviations from the LOP for traded goods. In a real-world economy, products are differentiated and produced under monopolistic competition. This means that the same products may vary in price across the different markets, due to *price discrimination* and *adjustment costs.* Krugman (1987) derives optimal price setting under variable nominal exchange rates for a monopolistically competitive firm. *Pricing to market* means that after a nominal depreciation of the local currency, local import prices of foreign exporters increase less than the change in the nominal exchange rate, since, under optimal price setting, firms make their decisions by taking into account the price elasticity of demand. In the end, this means that exchange rate swings, in large part, are absorbed by the profit margins of companies. Furthermore, under monopolistic competition, it is not only the exchange rate-induced price adjustment that may contribute to the deviations from the LOP. Changes in consumer preferences may also cause demand elasticity to change which, via changes in the mark-up, may in turn lead to differing prices in different markets, given the same costs.

Adjustment or menu costs may also explain the deviation from the LOP, even in the case of traded goods. If prices are not fully flexible, that is they are only adjusted after certain time intervals, the result may be a temporary deviation from the LOP. In the new open economy macroeconomics literature, Gali and Monacelli (2002), and Smets and Wouters (2002) use models which can produce highly persistent deviations from the LOP. Using a Calvo (1983) type of price setting, the persistence in the deviation depends on the probability of individual price changes over a certain time period.

Perfect *capital mobility* seems to be the closest to the theoretical model, although country and exchange rate risks create a heavily segmented international capital market. In chapter 7 of Obstfeld and Rogoff (1996), a simple model is presented showing how credit market imperfections may slacken convergence of capital/labour ratios. *Labour mobility* is also far from perfect within national economies, due both to the high costs incurred in transferring skilled labour between sectors and to labour market regulations.

Intermediate goods may also have a very strong influence on the validity of the B-S hypothesis. In the real-world production process, it is not only wages and capital costs that determine total production costs, since imported or intermediate products may also play a major role. Shocks to the price of highly volatile commodities, especially oil, may induce a trend change in relative prices without any relationship with traded and non-traded productivity. Although in a market economy *administrative prices* cannot substantially deviate from the market level in the long run, government regulation may have a very persistent effect on administered prices. As the latter constitute a substantial share in the CPI,[10] this might also distort the analysis of the B-S effect.

3 EMPIRICAL RESULTS REGARDING THE B-S EFFECT

In a formal examination of the empirical relevance of the B-S effect, Balassa (1964) first regressed the real exchange rate on productivity in a cross-section of twelve industrial countries, and found strong evidence in support of the hypothesis. His conclusion was confirmed in a similar regression in Balassa (1973). By contrast, Officer (1976) obtained much less favourable results. Officer argues that Balassa's results are extremely sensitive to the year chosen and the countries included.

More recent evidence on comparable national price levels is more conclusive about Officer's view. Using the Summers and Heston ICP database,[11] Rogoff (1996) concludes that a scatter plot of GDP per capita and real exchange rates shows developed and less developed countries as separated into two groups. While investigating the whole sample, there seems to be a positive relationship between the two variables. However, that correlation disappears when looked at separately within developed and within less developed economies. However, this is not the only shortcoming of the regression analyses in the early literature. As is readily apparent from the theoretical models of the B-S effect, the models cannot necessarily predict the link between *aggregate* productivity and the real exchange rate. They simply require that productivity should grow more in the traded sectors of the catch-up countries than in the non-traded sectors, compared to the corresponding sectors of developed countries. Consequently, the B-S effect may be associated in principle with both rising and declining *aggregate* productivity compared to a developed country. This also means that the 'correct' test of the B-S hypothesis would require sectoral data for productivity. Nevertheless, this is still not the end of the story. A correct scientific testing of the B-S hypothesis would require simultaneous testing of the four assumptions listed above. Although there has been an increasing number of attempts, especially since the 1990s, to test the B-S effect in the sectoral context, relatively few papers have endeavoured to assess all the assumptions of the model simultaneously. In the following review of the literature, we will divide our discussion into developed and less developed economy regressions for two main reasons. First, as already mentioned, the empirical validity of the B-S model seems to be strikingly dependent on the country group considered. Second, in view of the high persistence of real exchange rate movements, the considerably longer data series available for the developed economies may generate different results from those relevant to the less developed economies.

3.1 Empirical Results in Developed Economies

Among the first papers to test the B-S hypothesis as a sectoral story was Hsieh's (1982). The author ran sectoral time series regressions on German and Japanese real exchange rates vis-à-vis the US dollar. The explanatory variables employed were sectoral productivity and aggregate wages. The significance of productivity terms was established, though, as pointed out by Froot and Rogoff (1995), the inclusion of the ULC-based real exchange rate on the right-hand side of the regression may have induced instability problems. Marston (1987) used OECD sectoral output and employment data to construct non-traded and traded productivity series, arguing that the sectoral productivity might provide a good explanation of the real appreciation of the yen against the US dollar during the 1970s.

Asea and Mendoza (1994) formalized a two-country neo-classical growth model so as to derive two key propositions of the B-S model, i.e. non-tradable relative prices may be explained by productivity differentials, whereas deviations from PPP can also explained by trend movements in non-tradable relative prices. Using the long-term trend of OECD sectoral data, the authors found that while productivity differentials provided a good explanation of trend changes in the relative price of non-tradables, deviations from PPP cannot be linked to the former. Similarly, using sectoral OECD data for the period between 1970 and 1985, De Gregorio et al. (1994) provided evidence on trend changes in non-traded/traded relative prices. However, compared to Asea and Mendoza (1994), they also controlled some possible demand side factors at various time horizons. Their results indicated that in the short run demand side factors seemed to be much more important in explaining relative prices, while long-term regressions leave room in the explanation only for Total Factor Productivity (TFP) factors.

Canzoneri et al. (1998) sought to assess the possible relevance of dual inflation in EU countries from the early 1970s to the early 1990s. The paper intended to assess the feasibility of the Maastricht criterion in high-inflation EU countries. Several important conclusions have emerged from their analyses. First, they argued that the ratio of relative labour productivity to prices exhibited mean reversion. This means that the sectors studied might have been aptly described by a certain class of production functions and relative wages and that mark-ups did not play a long-term role in changing relative prices of non-tradables. Second, in contrast to Asea and Mendoza (1994), they concluded that PPP seemed to be valid in the traded sector for all of the European countries studied. The two results combined fully substantiated the B-S hypothesis for EU countries.

A similar investigation was presented in a study by Alberola and Tyrvainen (1998), though with slightly different conclusions. Using various lengths of data periods leading up to 1995 in eight of the EMU countries, the productivity hypothesis was tested for non-tradable relative prices. The results revealed that though there seemed to exist a long-term relationship between relative prices and productivity, the coefficients estimated were nowhere near what this theory would have required. However, when controlling for the changes in sectoral wages, estimates were closer to the expected theoretical relationship. Thus, in contrast to the Canzoneri paper, Alberola and Tyrvainen argued that European data contradicted the labour mobility assumption of the B-S hypothesis.

In their most recent paper, MacDonald and Ricci (2001) further expanded the original B-S model by endowing the distribution sector with an explicit role. Having used annual data pertaining to the period between 1970 and 1992 in ten developed economies, the authors established the significance of the productivity of the distribution sectors on the real exchange rate. Surprisingly, however, the estimated relationship suggested that any increase in productivity induced real exchange rate appreciation, similarly to what was the case in the traded sector. MacDonald and Ricci (2001) argue that this phenomenon may be explained by important services and retail sector supplies to the traded sector.

3.2 Empirical Results in Less Developed Economies

Of the less developed economies, the wave of empirical research of the B-S model first reached the *Southeast Asian* economies. This was hardly surprising, since following the publication of Marston's paper on Japan, it was safe to assume that the real exchange rate could be explained satisfactorily by productivity growth differentials in fast-growing Asian countries. Using sectoral data in the APEC region, Isard and Symansky (1996) decomposed the real exchange rate movements into the external and internal components of real exchange rates. The conclusions of the paper were similar to those of Asea and Mendoza's (1994), in the sense that productivity growth differentials provided a good explanation of trend changes in non-tradable prices; however, PPP for traded goods seemed to be strongly rejected by the data. Actually, a considerable part of real appreciation detectable in these countries at the aggregate level was attributable to the real appreciation of the traded real exchange rate rather than to fast sectoral productivity growth.

Using a co-integration approach, Wu (1996) sought to explain the trend appreciation of the Taiwanese dollar against the US dollar in the 1980s. Relying on impulse response analyses, Wu argued that both changes in the nominal exchange rate and relative productivity exerted permanent effects on the real exchange rate. It was also found that the role of unit labour cost was significant. Finally, Wu arrived at the conclusion that while the productivity differential would have depreciated the Taiwanese currency, this was more than offset by nominal appreciation and an increase in unit labour costs, which in turn caused real appreciation. This result clearly rejected the predictions of the B-S model as far as traded PPP and labour mobility were concerned.

Using sectoral data for nine Asian countries, Chinn (1998) arrived at a similar conclusion. The explanatory power of productivity concerning non-tradable relative prices was firmly established. Likewise, the high persistence of traded real exchange rate movements was also identified. Interestingly, Chinn also found that the real price of oil had significant explanatory power in several countries.

Due to the high real appreciation observed and the prospective EU and EMU membership, the B-S literature has also reached *transition economies* more recently. This again was a safe bet, as substantial real appreciation has been experienced in most of these countries since the early 1990s. However, here the issue is even more complex than in the case of the South Asian countries mentioned above. As the process of transition generated significant changes in relative prices in almost all sectors of the economy, the productivity hypothesis seemed to be only one side of the coin. As far as these countries are concerned, the literature can be divided into two groups, where the grouping reflects mainly the historical evolution of research. The first one approaches the issue at an aggregate level while the other one uses a sectoral approach. Using a selection of usually aggregate explanatory variables including aggregate productivity, Halpern and Wyplosz (1997, 1999) produced estimates of manufacturing dollar wage equations in 80 countries. The significance of increasing aggregate productivity pertaining to dollar wages was established, and the results also indicated that real appreciation could be associated with several transitional factors, such as financial deepening and goods and labour market deregulation. The authors also argued that the real appreciation detected was also the result of the initial undervaluation of the currencies in the countries concerned relative to their long-term equilibrium value.

Krajnyák and Zettelmeyer (1997) used panel techniques to estimate the regression equation of a similar form. When the results were decomposed with respect to the various regions in these countries, it was found that the equilibrium real exchange rate appreciated in the most advanced Central and Eastern European (CEE) countries while it remained relatively flat for most of the CIS countries. The study also concluded that real exchange rates had been substantially below the estimated equilibrium rate in most of the countries studied even in 1996. Nevertheless, as the time series horizon of the data is very short, and the standard errors of the equations are large in both studies, it would be hard to find any statistically significant under- or overvaluation of real exchange rates.

Also dealing with the aggregate level, De Broeck and Slok (2001) estimated whole-economy real exchange rate equations for several CEE and Baltic countries for the period between 1993 and 1998. Their results suggested that a substantial portion of real appreciation might be explained on the basis of productivity gains in the CEE accession countries. By contrast, productivity gains were not obvious in the case of former CIS countries. The paper also presented the cross-sectional regression of the aggregate real exchange rate and productivity in 1999 for a large number of non-transition countries. The elasticities thus obtained implied that a 1 per cent catch-up results in a 0.4 per cent real appreciation. This regression was also used to illustrate real exchange rate movements in these countries between 1993 and 1999. A general pattern was outlined in the analysis, namely more developed accession countries had eliminated initial undervaluation by an increase in per capita GDP, i.e. the actual real appreciation was larger than the equilibrium one. On the other hand, in the case of the rest of the countries (mainly members of the CIS), declining undervaluation was associated with declining per capita GDP. This might have happened as the actual real exchange rate depreciation was smaller than the productivity-based equilibrium one in some cases; in certain cases declining GDP per capita was associated with real appreciation.

Darvas (2001) employed state space models to estimate equilibrium exchange rate models, as well as the exchange rate pass-through simultaneously and separately for four accession countries. Explanatory variables included aggregate productivity in some cases and sectoral productivity in others. In addition to productivity, several other variables like net assets, terms of trade and the real interest rate were also included in the regressions. The results indicated that sectoral productivity movements had relatively modest transmission into equilibrium real exchange rates in Hungary and Slovenia. However, more significant coefficients were found in the case of the Czech Republic and Poland at the aggregate level. At the same time, the significance of other explanatory variables remained weak. Dubravko (2002) explained relative inflation equations with sectoral productivity differentials in six CEE accession countries. The significance of the productivity differential was again supported, though the author argued that productivity gains alone were unable to fully explain the inflation differential vis-à-vis that in Euroland.

Given that longer sectoral time series have become available, the more recent literature pursued sectoral investigations on non-traded/traded relative prices. A higher level of disaggregation provided an excellent opportunity to tackle the hypotheses of the B-S model separately, though not fully comprehensively. Using simple statistical methods, Kovács and Simon (1998) assessed the importance of internal and external movements in the real exchange rate in Hungary based on the sectoral decomposition of SNA data. Their results indicated that sectoral productivity differentials had excellent explanatory power in the real appreciation of the Hungarian currency, the forint, which was partially offset by the real depreciation of the traded real exchange rate. Jakab and Kovács (1999) used a simple two-sector, small open economy model to derive identification restrictions in a SVAR model of the Hungarian real exchange rate. Using these restrictions, they isolated various shocks from real exchange rate fluctuations in Hungary during the period between 1991 and 1998. The primary importance of productivity shocks for non-tradable relative prices was established; as far as the traded real exchange rate was concerned, it was tradable supply shocks that played the most prominent role.

Rother (2000) ran dynamic time series regressions for Slovenia in the period between 1993 and 1998. Besides sectoral productivity variables, the effect of monetary and fiscal policies was also examined. The results indicated that in the short run government policies might have had significant impact on the relative price of non-tradables to tradables. In the long run, however, these effects phased out and productivity-related explanations were able to fully underpin relative price changes.

Halpern and Wyplosz (2001) estimated a simple system of equations pertaining to nine accession countries in order to test the relationship between FDI, productivity, wages and relative prices. The results indicated that FDI had significant impact on productivity, which brought about an increase in real product wages. According to their argument, this might cause the services to industrial goods ratio to increase. Though it seems clear that FDI increases productivity in general, looking at the estimated elasticities and the sectoral composition of FDI, it was much less clear whether it was the inflow of FDI that had caused the traded/non-traded productivity gap. Nevertheless, the estimated service to industrial goods price regression supports the view that increased industrial productivity increases service prices compared to industrial goods prices.

Corricelli and Jazbec (2001) decomposed non-traded/traded relative price differentials applicable to several accession countries into different structural components. The decomposition revealed that, while in the first phase of transition the process had been dominated by special factors such as the deregulation of goods and labour markets, in the second, more recent period the productivity channel started to gain importance. Jazbec (2002) employed the former framework so as to give an estimate of the B-S effect in Slovenia.

In a series of papers, Égert (2001, 2002a, 2002b, 2003) , Égert et al. (2002) tested both the role of non-tradable prices in real exchange rate movements and that of productivity in explaining non-traded versus traded inflation. Using time series and panel co-integration methods, the authors, similarly to others (Kovács and Simon (1998), Jakab and Kovács (1999), Darvas (2001), Dubravko (2002)), found that sectoral productivity growth had good explanatory power for the relative price of non-tradables. The link between relative non-traded prices and the real exchange rate was, however, much less unambiguous. Égert et al. (2002) explained this result with persistent traded price-based real exchange rate movements, the low share of non-tradables in accession country CPIs and the role of regulated and food prices in the index.

Summarizing the empirical studies mentioned above, several observations can be made. First, sectoral productivity gains have explained non-traded/traded relative prices relatively successfully. Second, a few studies have confirmed the significance of relative wages in explaining real appreciation. Third, persistent deviations in the traded real exchange rate have also been observed. And, last but not least, intermediate goods prices, e.g. the real price of oil, and government regulations have also influenced the real exchange rate significantly.

4 OUR ACCOUNTING FRAMEWORK

The foregoing observations question the simultaneous validity of the four key assumptions of the B-S model mentioned earlier. Given these differences between theory and empirical results, it is tempting to use a relatively comprehensive framework for assessing the deviations from the various assumptions of the B-S model simultaneously. To the best of our knowledge, such a test has not been performed so far, either for developed economies or for accession countries. In this section, we present our simple, but comprehensive framework used for evaluating these problems.

The real exchange rate between two countries can be decomposed into two main components:[12] the relative prices of tradables between the countries involved and the relative non-tradables to tradables price ratio between the two countries. For the purposes of simplicity, in what follows, we refer to them as external and internal real exchange rates:[13]

$$RER = \frac{P}{EP^*} = \frac{1}{E}\left(\frac{P_T}{P_T^*}\right)^{\alpha}\left(\frac{P_N}{P_N^*}\right)^{1-\alpha} = \left(\frac{P_T}{EP_T^*}\right)\cdot\left(\frac{P_N/P_T}{P_N^*/P_T^*}\right)^{1-\alpha} \tag{1}$$

where[14]
RER is the CPI-based real exchange rate,
E is the nominal exchange rate (home/foreign),
P^*_T, P_T are CPI tradable prices abroad and at home,
P^*_N, P_N are CPI non-tradable prices abroad and at home and
α is the share of tradables in the CPI.

As already discussed, the B-S effect is closely related to the internal real exchange rate — differences in productivity developments in the two sectors are translated into a trend increase in non-tradable/tradable relative prices. In terms of price setting, the usual assumption is applied, namely that prices are set as a mark-up over unit labour costs.[15] However, this formula assumes that the role of intermediate goods is negligible in the period examined. This is clearly not the case in transition economies, where the entire structure of production changes continuously, and the ratio of intermediate products to value-added prices may contain significant trends. For this reason, we cannot neglect the role of intermediate goods. Rather than explicitly modelling price setting with such goods, we simply assume that there is a term called 'the other factor' that can capture the difference between value-added deflators and final (CPI) prices. Consequently, this term also reflects the effect of indirect tax changes. We can formalize our previous statements in the following equations.

The ratio of non-tradable to tradable value-added deflators is determined by the usual pricing formula:

$$\frac{P_N^{VA}}{P_T^{VA}} = \frac{m_N}{m_T}\frac{W_N/PROD_N}{W_T/PROD_T} \tag{2}$$

where
P_N^{VA}, P_T^{VA} are value-added deflators in non-tradables and tradables
m_N, m_T are mark-ups in non-tradables and tradables
W_N, W_T are wage rates in non-tradables and tradables
$PROD_N$, $PROD_T$ are labour productivity rates in non-tradables and tradables.

The difference between CPI prices and value-added deflators can be straightforwardly captured by what is called the 'other' multiplicative factors:

$$\frac{P_N}{P_T} = \frac{o_N}{o_T} \frac{P_N^{VA}}{P_T^{VA}} \tag{3}$$

where

o_N, o_T are other effects in non-tradables and tradables.

Combining (2) with (3), the following formula for CPI prices can be obtained:

$$\frac{P_N}{P_T} = \frac{o_N}{o_T} \frac{m_N}{m_T} \frac{W_N / PROD_N}{W_T / PROD_T} \tag{4}$$

We assume that similar equations are valid both at home and abroad. From (4) it is clear that changes in the internal exchange rate are driven by four main factors of non-tradables to tradables:

- changes in the difference between relative *value-added prices and CPI prices*,
- changes in relative *mark-ups*,
- changes in relative *wages* and
- changes in relative *productivity.*

Of these four factors, only the fourth is the B-S effect in a strict sense.[16]

5 EVIDENCE

Experts from the respective five national central banks in a joint research project computed the simple accounting framework presented above for the CEC5 countries.[17] While basically the same methodological framework was used for each country, some room was left to national experts in respect of the calculations. The manner in which data periods were selected was at the discretion of country experts, so that both data availability and economic relevance could be achieved. The period analysed was also divided into early and late transition phases, so that structural stability in the study patterns could be detected. We opted for Germany as a benchmark, in order to assess real appreciation due to the B-S effect in the five countries. Either the EU or Euroland could have also been used; however, no detailed productivity and price series were readily available for such aggregates. Our choice of Germany meant that we did not lose too much information, Germany being the largest economy in the EU and also the most important trading partner of CEC5.

We adopted a methodology similar to the one applied by Kovács and Simon (1998). Manufacturing was classified as a tradable sector, whereas non-tradables were defined as the sum of the following categories: market services, construction, retail trade, transport and telecommunications. The state sector was excluded from the analyses for two main reasons. First, prices in this sector are largely distorted by the discretionary policies of the individual governments. Second, the measurement of output in the state sector was based on assumptions about productivity, rather than on observing real output. Energy and agriculture were also excluded, as the role of government in determining prices was non-negligible in both cases.

Table 4.2 shows the results of the decomposition for equation (1). Two subgroups can be observed in the CEC5 countries. While Hungary and Slovenia experienced very modest real appreciation, annual real appreciation in the Czech Republic and Poland was around 4%–5%. With respect to the importance of external and internal real exchange rates, dispersion was even more accentuated in these countries. In the Czech Republic and Slovakia, the bulk of real appreciation occurred through an external component, while in Poland and Slovenia it was internal real appreciation which proved to be the most significant. The situation seems to have been the most balanced in Hungary, where internal real appreciation was slightly higher than external appreciation.

Table 4.2 Decomposition of the CPI-based real exchange rate

Annual change (%)	Total	External	Internal	Period covered
The Czech Republic*	4.4	2.8	1.6	1994–2001
Hungary**	2.3	1.0	1.5	1992–2001
Poland	5.3	1.6	3.7	1995–2001
Slovakia***	4.3	2.7	1.8	1995–2001
Slovenia*	1.9	0.4	0.9	1992–2001

Notes:
* CPI excluding regulated prices.
** CPI excluding food + regulated prices.
*** Value-added deflator.

Source: Kovács et al. (2002).

It is tempting to argue that internal real appreciation in these countries accounted for the size of the B-S effect, which stood at 1%–2% in most cases, except in Poland where it was close to an annual rate of 4%. However, equation (4) makes it clear that some further refinement is required: the role of relative mark-ups, wages and intermediate goods should also be considered, in addition to productivity. Table 4.3 contains a more detailed description of the non-traded-traded relative price ratio.[18] In the next few paragraphs, we briefly summarize the results for the individual countries.

Table 4.3 Components of the non-traded/traded relative price ratio in CPI

Annual change (%)	Prices (CPI)	Productivity	Wages	Mark-ups	Other	Period covered
Czech Republic*	5.8	2.4	2.3	−3.0	4.1	1994–2001
Hungary**	5.2	6.2	−0.2	−0.3	−0.4	1992–2001
Slovakia***	3.3	3.3	1.9	na	na	1995–2000
Slovenia*	6.8	4.1	−0.7	0.1	3.2	1992–2001

Notes:
* CPI excluding regulated prices.
** CPI excluding food + regulated prices.
*** Value added deflator.

Source: Kovács et al. (2002).

Compared with variations in productivity, the other factors seem to have had more explanatory power in the *Czech Republic*. The most dominant change in other factors was indirect tax changes in 1997. While productivity accounted for less than half of the relative price changes, relative wages also changed substantially, and mark-ups in the non-traded sectors declined compared with the traded sectors. The decline in relative non-tradable mark-ups may in part represent cyclical behaviour, but the effect of the micro level restructuring in 1997 also needs consideration. A simultaneous increase in relative wages can offer some evidence of the adverse B-S effect.[19]

A glance at the results reveals that *Hungary* seems to approximate the best to the theory predicted by the B-S model. Relative productivity movements explain relative price movements quite well, while the effect of wage mark-ups and other factors seems to be of very modest importance. In our view, the presence of the B-S effect in such a textbook form in Hungary can be explained by the crawling peg exchange rate regime maintained for a six-year period between 1995 and 2001. Predictable currency depreciation within the system enabled producers to set prices with more certainty than in regimes with nominal exchange rate volatility. At the same time, the crawling peg regime also gave wage-setting policies some sort of nominal anchor.[20] These provided a possibility of smooth variations in both the price-setting behaviour and productivity of companies, although at the cost of higher inflation.

Improved productivity was instrumental in relative price changes in *Slovakia*, where productivity and relative prices actually increased one for one. Relative wages rose by approximately 1.9% annually, which must have been offset by mark-ups and other effects. The increase in relative wages, as in the case of the Czech Republic, might indicate some adverse B-S effect. Relative price changes were the most marked in Slovenia, where the bulk of the increase can be explained by improved productivity. Other factors also played a dominant role, while the importance of wages and mark-ups was negligible.

Table 4.4 Components of the non-traded/traded price ratio in two subperiods

	Prices (CPI)	Productivity	Wages	Mark-ups	Other	Period covered
Czech Republic*	5.8	6.8	4.7	−5.0	−0.3	1994–1997
Hungary**	5.3	6.6	−0.1	−0.1	−1.0	1992–1995
Slovenia*	12.6	1.2	0.2	3.2	7.7	1992–1995
Czech Republic*	5.8	−2.5	2.1	−0.2	6.5	1998–2001
Hungary**	5.1	5.8	0.1	−0.2	0.1	1996–2001
Slovenia*	2.4	6.5	−1.4	−2.2	−0.3	1996–2001

Notes:
* CPI excluding regulated prices.
** CPI excluding food + regulated prices.

Source: Kovášçs et al. (2002).

Splitting the *Czech* sample reveals that, while the growth rate of non-traded/traded relative prices was nearly the same in the early and late transition periods, the underlying determinants were dramatically different. After a period of rapid improvement, relative tradable productivity turned negative, which calls into question the relevance of the B-S effect. However, caution is advised when drawing conclusions on the basis of three years' data. The dramatic change in the productivity pattern was offset by an opposite change in the pattern of other factors which, as mentioned earlier, represented the effect of indirect tax modification since 1997. The growth rate of relative wages declined in the late transition period, which again supports our former view, namely, that some kind of adverse B-S story may be behind the figures. While relative mark-ups changed dramatically in the early transition period, their effect practically disappeared after 1997. This may be attributable to the fact that market structure changed more dramatically in the first part of the period.

In *Hungary*, both relative prices and the underlying fundamentals behaved very similarly during the two periods: improved productivity accounted for the majority of the relative price changes, while relative wages and mark-ups practically remained stable. It was only the other effects that differed slightly between the two periods. A decrease in the other effects in the early transition period can be explained by changes to the tax regime. Relative prices and their underlying determinants were the least stable in *Slovenia*. A two-digit change in non-tradable/tradable relative prices in the early period decreased to 2.4% in the late period. While in the early transition period the change in the other effects and mark-ups was the primary cause of the relative price changes, the pace of change in relative prices decreased dramatically once these effects had faded away. It is, however, important to note that at the same time the productivity differential increased markedly which, if it proves to be permanent, may indicate future potential acceleration of the B-S effect.

5.1 Calculation of the B-S Effect on CPI

Once the various underlying determinants of relative price changes are identified, the B-S effect on CPI can be calculated on the following assumptions. First, we assume that the external real appreciation is zero, ignoring deviations from relative PPP for traded prices. Second, we assume that the change in relative wages, mark-ups and other effects is zero. Third, we assume that improved productivity affects relative prices by a unit coefficient in the long run. This assumption is consistent with a relatively large class of production functions.[21] Finally, we use the non-traded share in CPI (market and administered prices), which is approximately 40% in the majority of the countries considered. Table 4.5 summarizes the results of the project.[22] As can be seen in each country presenting the calculation, the B-S effect seems to have been under an annual rate of 2% over the past years.

Table 4.5 The Balassa-Samuelson effect for the CPI in CEC5 countries

Annual change (%)	Actual	B-S	Period covered
Czech Republic*	4.4	1.6	1994–2001
Hungary**	2.3	1.9	1992–2001
Poland	5.3	na	1995–2001
Slovakia***	4.3	1.0–2.0	1995–2001
Slovenia*	1.9	0.7	1992–2001

Notes:
* CPI excluding regulated prices.
** CPI excluding food + regulated prices.
*** Value added deflator.

Source: Kovács et al. (2002).

It is interesting to observe that there is not an obvious correlation within the five countries among the actual and the productivity-based real appreciation. This means that the B-S effect is only part of the story and other potential explanations of internal real appreciation were present, although they seemed to be much less systematic than the productivity explanation. In the Czech Republic, it was only relative wages and other effects that contributed positively to the increase in non-tradable/tradable prices in the late transition period. Even in this case, the contribution of relative wages declined markedly, and that of other effects was connected with a discretionary increase in indirect taxes. In Slovenia, on the contrary, both relative wages and mark-ups contributed negatively to the observed increase in non-tradable relative prices in the second period. In Hungary, there is no clear trend of other relative price determinants, so that productivity is the main determining factor.

5.2 Some Policy Consequences

After EMU accession, once the nominal exchange rate becomes irrevocably fixed, traded prices are expected to converge to the aggregate European level. This result has already been supported by recent research conducted in the current EMU member states[23] and by several earlier papers for cities in the US.[24] Nevertheless, even in this case marginal excess inflation in the tradable sectors is imaginable, mainly on account of the increasing demand for the products of catching-up countries, although it is much harder to quantify. Within EMU, most of the traded component of the real exchange rate will be eliminated, hence only non-tradable relative prices will matter in the B-S framework from the point of view of long-term inflation differentials. Among the possible factors effecting non-tradable/tradable prices, we were interested in the B-S effect in this chapter. Are our findings in line with other estimates of the B-S effect?

Some of the papers mentioned in Section 3 gave numerical estimates of the B-S effect using the estimated sectoral regressions. Table 4.6 summarizes a few results. We found two papers presenting comparable estimates of the B-S effect in EU periphery countries prior to EMU accession. These are the papers by Canzoneri et al. (1998) and Alberola and Tyrvainen (1998) which may be considered as benchmarks. It is interesting to compare our results with the estimates of other authors for accession countries, as well as with the numbers in the benchmark papers mentioned above. The comparison might give a picture of the difference between the current enlargement of the EMU and the first wave in 1999, at least from the point of view of inflation differentials.

Table 4.6 Estimated B-S inflation differentials in different studies

	Country	%	Period	Weighting
Alberola and Tyrvainen (1998)	Spain vs Germany	1.9	1970–1995	CPI
Canzoneri et al. (1998)	EU periphery vs Germany	2–2.5	1973–1991	GDP deflator
Cipriani (2000)	Hungary	0.8	1995–1999	CPI
Corricelli and Jazbec (2001)	Hungary vs Germany	1.6	1990–1998	CPI
Dubravko (2002)	Hungary vs EMU	0.6	1996–2002	Estimated
Égert (2001)	Hungary vs Germany	2.5–2.9	1991–2000	Estimated
Égert (2002a)	Hungary vs Germany	1.3–1.7	1993–2000	CPI
Halpern and Wyplosz (2000)	Six Country Average vs Germany	0.0	1992–1998	CPI
Kovács and Simon (1998)	Hungary vs effective	1.6	1992–1996	CPI
Sinn and Reutter (2001)	Hungary vs Germany	6.9	1994–1997	GDP deflator

Source: Papers mentioned above and author's calculations.

For the sake of comparability, we have examined a few of those studies that provided elasticities for sectoral productivity in accession countries.[25] In most cases, the studies are not readily comparable, as the countries considered are different, and one needs assumptions to derive comparable results. Where it was possible, we used Hungary for the calculations, not only because of the best availability of data, but also because Hungary is usually considered as having the highest B-S effect among the accession countries.[26] In the case of the Corricelli and Jazbec (2001) and Halpern and Wyplosz (2001) papers, we applied the non-traded weights in the Hungarian consumer price index and used available German data on the non-tradable/tradable inflation results to achieve comparability. In the case of the other studies, it was not possible to perform this calculation, so we present the authors' results.

Looking at Table 4.6, the following conclusions can be drawn. First, in most of the studies it was found that B-S inflation was *less than 2%*. These numbers are of the same magnitude as that found by Alberola and Tyrvainen (1998) for Spain before EMU entry, and slightly smaller than in the paper by Canzoneri et al. (1998). Second, there are *two outlier* results. Égert (2002a) estimated the effect to be slightly higher, between 2%–3%, while Sinn and Reutter gave an extreme value of 6.9% for Hungary. Third, *weighting* is very important for the comparability of the calculations. The Canzoneri paper may give slightly higher estimates than the Alberola and Tyrvainen one, as the former is based on GDP weights, which have higher shares of non-tradables than in the CPI. This problem is even more severe in the case of accession countries, where the non-traded share in CPI is even smaller than in more developed economies.[27] This fact also partially explains the sizeable figures obtained by Sinn and Reutter (2001). Also, the higher figures of Égert (2002a) may be partially explained by the estimated weights used in the calculation. Fourth, not only the weights, but also *other data concepts* are important. The Sinn and Reutter (2001) paper used gross output for the traded sector, which was growing at a substantially higher pace than value-added figures. This again caused an upward bias in their B-S estimate.

Examining the studies using the 'more correct' weights and data (i.e. CPI and value-added figures), all the numbers presented in the table are similar in magnitude. This magnitude of 1%–2% on annual CPI inflation also indicates that the CEC5 countries are no more exposed to excess B-S inflation than were non-core EU countries prior to their EMU entry. However care must be taken when interpreting our results as a consequence for possible future EMU membership. First, the results were obtained on the basis of a relatively small sample with large structural changes. As the B-S effect is a long-run phenomenon, it is very hard to disentangle the real long-run effect from the sample.[28] Second, the fact that the B-S effect seemed to be modest in the past might give some indication, albeit limited, of its future size. As EMU membership might cause sectoral structural changes, it is very hard to be precise on the exact future magnitude. Third, although other sources of the internal exchange rate appreciation were less systematic, they were present in our sample, indicating even more uncertainties for the possible inflation differential in the CEC5 within EMU. Finally, fiscal policy as a possible source of excess inflation is not explicitly presented in our framework. The effect of fiscal policy might have an impact via almost all of the variables of our accounting framework. In our set-up, it is impossible to disentangle causality, i.e. to what extent the observed relative factor movements represent technology shocks (as is to be expected in the B-S framework), or are the result of possible excessive fiscal policies. In the case of the latter, fiscal policy might play a prominent role in reducing inflation differentials to EMU-consistent levels.

6 CONCLUSION

In this chapter, we have presented a simple accounting framework that can be used to assess the empirical validity of the assumptions of the B-S model. The framework was applied to CEC5 data so as to obtain a more correct measure of the B-S effect in these countries. Other empirical studies were also reviewed in order to ensure the broad comparability of our results with other papers on this topic. The analysis provided clear evidence that the B-S effect on CPI inflation in these countries has not exceeded 2% per annum vis-à-vis Germany over the past few years. The numbers obtained are somewhat different from the actual change in the real exchange rate for two reasons. First, the traded real exchange rate had appreciated substantially, violating PPP for this price category. Second, other factors, such as changes in sectoral wage rates, pricing behaviour and intermediate product prices, have also contributed to the development in the non-tradable/tradable price ratio in the past. The estimated size of the B-S effect for the CEC5 is comparable in magnitude to the figures obtained for former EMU periphery countries prior to EMU membership. This would suggest that the CEC5 are no more exposed to the B-S effect than were Spain, Portugal or Ireland prior to 1999. Nevertheless, the results should be interpreted with caution, since the B-S effect is not the only source of the possible inflation differential, although these other sources seem to be much less systematic in our sample.

NOTES

1. The author would like to thank Jean-Philippe Cotis for discussing the chapter, and participants of the seminar 'Monetary Strategies for Accession Countries' in Budapest, February 2003, for useful comments and suggestions.
2. See Williamson (1994).
3. Csajbók and Csermely (2002).
4. See for example the more recent EBRD transition reports.
5. See Égert (2003) for an extensive overview of the models and test applied in the B-S analyses of accession countries.
6. A simple proof of the popularity of the Balassa-Samuelson model in accession countries is that entering 'Balassa Samuelson effect' in the Google search engine finds 2230 occurrences, while for 'Balassa Samuelson effect + accession' there are 742 occurrences.
7. See Asea and Mendoza (1994), Obstfeld and Rogoff (1996), and Balvers and Bergstrand (1997).
8. See Froot and Rogoff (1995) for an excellent review.
9. Simply the B-S hypothesis in itself would cause such persistent relative price changes for a broader price index, but for traded prices one can imagine several other factors, like change in the relative price of agricultural products or other commodities like oil.
10. It is around 20% of the CPI in Hungary.
11. See Summers and Heston (1991).
12. See Isard and Symansky (1996) and Kovács and Simon (1998).
13. Kovács and Simon (1998).
14. As can be seen, in (1) we assume that the composition of the CPI basket is similar both abroad and at home. Although empirically CPI weights vary from country to country, the magnitude of differences is not large; thus, we can use this simplification without losing too much information.
15. This formula can be derived under simple theoretical assumptions. See Varian (1992).
16. In a strict sense, the B-S effect is related to total factor productivity, which may deviate from labour productivity owing to changes in capital intensity. Due to lack of capital stock data, we use labour productivity measures.
17. See Kovács et al. (2002) and Zumer (2002).
18. The Polish expert did not complete this decomposition in the project, while the Slovakian expert carried out only a certain part of the analysis.
19. Compared with the original B-S model, the productivity-price relationship in the adverse B-S effect works in the opposite direction. Thus, increased demand for services pushes up non-tradable wages which, through labour mobility, forces the traded sector to increase productivity. See Grafe and Wyplosz (1997).
20. See Kovács (1998).
21. See Canzoneri et al. (1998)
22. Unfortunately, we do not have numerical results from the project for Poland.
23. See Goldberg and Verboven (2001).
24. See Engel and Rogers (1996), and Parsley and Wei (1996).
25. As we already mentioned, the B-S effect has implications for a sectoral story, which does not necessarily mean an aggregate story. Therefore, we neglected studies from the analyses that estimated aggregate productivity elasticities.
26. Looking at Table 4.1 it becomes clear that the productivity differential was the highest in Hungary among the CEC5.
27. The small share of services in consumption might explain the small share of non-tradables in the CPI of accession countries. As the income elasticity of services is larger than that of industrial goods, catching-up will also mean closing the gap in the structure of consumption.
28. There are quite a few estimations (Rother (2000), Halpern and Wyplosz (2001), Begg et al. (2002)) indicating that the B-S effect might be larger in the longer than in the short term.

REFERENCES

Alberola, I. and T. Tyrvainen (1998), 'Is there a scope for inflation differentials in EMU', Bank of Spain Working Papers No. 9823.

Asea, P. K. and E. G. Mendoza (1994), 'The Balassa-Samuelson model: a general-equilibrium appraisal', *Review of International Economics*, **2** (3), pp. 244–67.

Begg, D., B. Eichengreen, L. Halpern, J. von Hagen and C. Wyplosz (2002), 'Sustainable regimes of capital movements in accession countries', CEPR Policy Paper No. 10.

Balassa, B. (1964), 'The Purchasing Power Parity doctrine: a reappraisal', *Journal of Political Economy*, **72**, pp. 584–96.

Balassa, B. (1973), 'Just how misleading are official exchange rate conversions: a comment', *Economic Journal*, **83**, pp. 1258–67.

Balvers, R. J. and J. H. Bergstrand (1997), 'Equilibrium real exchange rates: closed form theoretical solutions and some empirical evidence', *Journal of International Money and Finance*, **16** (3) pp. 345–66.

Buiter, W. H. (2000), ' Exchange rate regimes for accession countries', Lecture given at a luncheon hosted by Deutsche Bank and the EBRD Annual General Meeting in Riga, Latvia on 21 May 2000.

Buiter, W. H. and C. Grafe (2002), 'Anchor, float or abandon ship: exchange rate regimes for accession countries', paper presented at the conference 'Alternative exchange rate regimes in the globalized world' in Tallin, 11 June 2002.

Calvo, G. (1983), 'Staggered prices in a utility maximising framework', *Journal of Monetary Economics*, **12**, September, pp. 383–98.

Canzoneri, M., R. Cumby, B. Diba and G. Eudey (1998), 'Trends in European productivity: implications for real exchange rates, real interest rates and inflation differentials', OENB Working Paper Series 27.

Chinn, D. M (1998), 'The usual suspects? Productivity and demand shocks and Asia-Pacific real exchange rates', OENB Working Paper Series 31.

Cipriani, Marco (2000), 'The Balassa-Samuelson effect in transition economies', September, mimeo, New York University.

Corricelli, F. and B. Jazbec (2001), 'Real exchange rate dynamics in transition economies', CEPR Discussion Paper Series No. 2869.

Csajbók, A. and Á. Csermely (2002), 'Adopting the euro in Hungary: expected costs, benefits and timing', MNB Occasional Papers 24.

Darvas, Z. (2001), 'Exchange rate pass through and real exchange rate in the EU candidate countries', Discussion Paper 10/01 of the Economic Research Centre of the Deutsche Bundesbank.

De Broeck, M. and T. Slok (2001), 'Interpreting real exchange rate movements in transition economies', IMF Working Paper 01/56.

De Gregorio, J., A. Giovannini and H. C. Wolf (1994), 'International evidence on tradables and nontradables inflation', *European Economic Review*, **38** (6), pp. 1225–44.

Dobrinsky, R. (2001), 'Convergence in per capita income levels, productivity dynamics and real exchange rates in the candidate countries on the way to EU accession', International Institute for Applied Systems Analysis, Interim Report no. 038 2001.

Dubravko, M. (2002), 'The Balassa-Samuelson effect in Central Europe: a disaggregated analysis', paper prepared for the 8th Dubrovnik Economic Conference, Dubrovnik, Croatia, 27–29 June 2002.

Égert, B. (2001), 'Estimating the impact of the Balassa-Samuelson effect on inflation during the transition: does it matter in the run-up to EMU?', paper presented at the conference on East European Transition and EU Enlargement: A Quantitative Approach, Gdansk, 15–21 June 2001, http://seminar2001.bg.univ.gda.pl/papers/Egert.pdf.

Égert, B. (2002a), 'Estimating the impact of the Balassa-Samuelson effect on inflation and the real exchange rate during the transition', *Economic Systems*, **36**, pp. 1–16.

Égert, B. (2002b), 'Investigating the Balassa-Samuelson hypothesis in transition: do we understand what we see?', BOFIT Discussion Papers No. 6.

Égert, B. (2003), 'Nominal and real convergence in Estonia: the Balassa-Samuelson (dis)connection: tradable goods, regulated prices and other culprits', Bank of Estonia Working Papers 2003/4.

Égert, B., I. Drine, K. Lommatzsch and C. Rault (2002), 'The Balassa-Samuelson effect in Central and Eastern Europe: myth or reality', William Davidson Institute Working Paper No. 483.

Engel, C. and J. H. Rogers (1995), 'Regional patterns in the law of one price: the roles of geography and currencies', NBER Working Paper 5395.

Froot, A. K and K. Rogoff (1995), 'Perspectives on PPP and long-run real exchange rates', in G. Grossmann and K. Rogoff, *Handbook of International Economics*, Ch. 32, Volume 3, North Holland Press, Amsterdam.

Gali and Monacelli (2002), 'Monetary policy and exchange rate volatility in a small open economy', CEPR Discussion Paper Series, No. 3346.

Goldberg, P. and F. Verboven (2001), 'Market integration and convergence to the law of one price: evidence from the European car market', CEPR Discussion Paper Series No. 2926.

Grafe, C. and C. Wyplosz (1997), 'The real exchange rate in transition economies', CEPR Discussion Paper Series No. 1773.

Halpern, L. and C. Wyplosz (1997), 'Equilibrium exchange rates in transition economies', IMF Staff Papers 44/4, pp. 430–61.

Halpern, L. and C. Wyplosz (1999), 'Equilibrium exchange rates', in L. Ambrus-Lakatos and M. E. Schaffer (eds), 'Monetary and exchange rate policies, EMU and Central and Eastern Europe', Forum Report of the Economic Policy Initiative No. 5.

Halpern, L. and C. Wyplosz (2001), 'Economic transformation and real exchange rates in the 2000s: the Balassa-Samuelson connection', Chapter 6 in *Economic Survey of Europe 2001*, No. 1, Economic Commission of Europe, Geneva, United Nations, 2001.

Hobza, A (2002), 'CEE countries on the way to euro zone', CEPS Working Paper, June.

Hsieh, D. (1982), 'The determination of real exchange rates: the productivity approach', *Journal of International Economics*, **12**, pp. 355–62.

Isard, P. and S. Symansky (1996), 'Long-run movements in real exchange rates', in Takatoshi Ito, Peter Isard, Steven Symansky and Tamim Bayoumi, 'Exchange rate movements and their impact on trade and investment in the APEC region', IMF Occasional Paper 145.

Jakab, M. Z. and M. A. Kovács (1999), 'Determinants of real exchange fluctuations in Hungary', MNB Working Papers Series 1999/6.

Jazbec, B. (2002), 'Balassa-Samuelson effect in transition economies: the case of Slovenia', William Davidson Institute Working Paper No. 507.

Kovács, M. A. (1998), 'Mit mutatnak? A különféle reálárfolyam-mutatók áttekintése és a magyar gazdaság ár és költség-versenyképességének értékelése (The information content of various real exchange rate indicators)', MNB Working Papers 1998/8 in Hungarian.

Kovács, M. A. (2001), 'The equilibrium real exchange rate in Hungary', MNB Background Studies 2001/3.

Kovács, M. A. and A. Simon (1998), 'Components of the real exchange rate in Hungary', MNB Working Paper Series 1998/3.

Kovács, M. A., J. Benes, M. Klima, J. Borowski, M. Dudek, P. Sotomska-Krzysztotik, F. Hajnovic and T. Zumer (2002), 'On the estimated size of the Balassa-Samuelson effect in CEC5 countries', prepared by experts from the CEC5 Central Banks, edited by M. A. Kovács, MNB Working Paper Series 2002/5.

Krajnyák, K. and J. Zettelmeyer (1997), 'Competitiveness in transition economies: what scope for real appreciation?', IMF Working Paper 97/1.

Krugman, P. (1987), 'Pricing to market when the nominal exchange rate changes', NBER Working Paper No. 1926.

MacDonald, R. and L. Ricci (2001), 'PPP and the Balassa-Samuelson effect: the role of the distribution sector', IMF Working Paper 01/38.

Marston, R (1987), 'Real exchange rates and the productivity growth in the United States and Japan', in S. Arndt and J. D. Richardson (eds), *Real-Financial Linkages among Open Economies*, The MIT Press, Cambridge, Massachusetts.

Obstfeld, M. and K. Rogoff (1996), *Foundations of International Macroeconomics*, The MIT Press, Cambridge, Massachusetts.

Officer, L. (1976), 'The productivity bias in purchasing power parity: an econometric investigation', IMF Staff Papers 23, pp. 545–79.

Parsley, D. C. and S. J. Wei (1996), 'Convergence to the law of one price without trade barriers or currency fluctuations', *Quarterly Journal of Economics*, **111**, November, pp. 1211–36.

Rogoff, K. (1996), 'The Purchasing Power Parity puzzle', *Journal of Economic Literature*, **XXXIV**, June, pp. 647–68.

Rother, P. (2000), 'The impact of productivity differentials on inflation and real exchange rates: an estimation of the Balassa-Samuelson effect in Slovenia', IMF Country Report, Republic of Slovenia, Selected Issues 00/56, April, pp. 26–39.

Samuelson, P. (1964), 'Theoretical notes on trade problems', *Review of Economics and Statistics*, **46**, March, pp. 145–54.

Sinn, H. W. and M. Reutter (2001), 'The minimum inflation rate for the euroland', NBER Working Paper No. 8085.

Smets, F. and R. Wouters (2002), 'Openness, imperfect exchange rate pass-through and monetary policy', *Journal of Monetary Economics*, **49**, pp. 947–81.

Summers, R. and A. Heston (1991), 'PENN world table (MARK 5): an expanded set of international comparisons 1950–1988', *Quarterly Journal of Economics*, **106**, May, pp. 327–68.

Szapáry, Gy. (2000), 'Maastricht and the choice of exchange rate regime in transition during the run-up to EMU', MNB Working Paper 2000/7.

Varian, H. (1992), *Microeconomic Analysis*, Third Edition, New York and London: W. W. Norton and Company.

Williamson, J. (1994), 'Estimating equilibrium exchange rates', Institute for International Economies, Washington DC.

Wu, H. L. (1996), 'Testing for fundamental determinants of the long run real exchange rate: the case of Taiwan', NBER Working Paper Series No. 5787.

Zumer, T. (2002), 'The Balassa-Samuelson effect in Slovenia', *Prikazi in analize*, **X/1**, September, Ljubljana.

COMMENTS

Jean-Philippe Cotis

I liked this chapter a lot and so did my colleagues at the OECD. Since I have the obligation to offer some criticisms, let me say that the only thing I really miss in the chapter is a clearer exposition of the policy implications. As it stands, it seems too complacent about the challenges central European countries will face in the run-up to EMU membership and afterwards. More specifically, we should not lend credence to the notion that central European countries are already in a way protected from 'excess inflation' risks. By 'excess inflation' I mean over and above a level consistent with a catch-up process and the EMU-wide inflation target. And the risks apply both in the 'pre-entry' and the 'post-entry' phase. I shall start my comments with a short presentation of the chapter and its motivations, followed by some methodological comments and a policy discussion.

The chapter endeavours to shed light on a difficult question: do accession countries have a good chance of entering the EMU in the near future? More specifically, can they comply in terms of inflation convergence? This is a question worth asking: Poland and the Czech Republic have recently achieved very low rates of inflation in line with the euro area average. Hungarian inflation is down to 4–5 per cent, i.e. not too far off eurozone target. However, these good results might have been achieved at the price of disequilibria in the rest of the economy such as, for instance, exceedingly weak activity. Achieving and maintaining low inflation is indeed a difficult process.

In this context, a main issue is how difficult it will be to cope with autonomous, structural inflationary pressures[1] in the run-up to EMU membership, knowing that exchange rate policies will be more constrained and less able to allow for the sort of disinflationary appreciation of the currency so widely used in the past. It would be good altogether to avoid or at least to minimize these potential tensions. It would indeed be a relief if, for instance, the sources of autonomous inflation were to abate spontaneously in the future, easing in the process the task of accession countries. Whether autonomous inflationary pressures will abate depends in turn on their inner nature. They may reflect successive one-off shocks, such as price liberalizations and tax increases or, on the contrary, more continuous phenomena, such as the so-called 'Balassa-Samuelson effects' (B-S). In this respect, the best of worlds would be for current inflation to reflect strong one-off effects, while pressures of the continuous type are weak. If that were true, we could expect 'one-off effects' to vanish, leading to a spontaneous deceleration of inflation.

To disentangle the B-S effect from one-off and other effects, the chapter provides us with a very interesting and careful accounting exercise. It finds that the B-S effects might have contributed from 1 to 2 per cent to overall inflation over the past decade in central Europe, and it expects this contribution to decline in a context where the productivity catch-up will moderate progressively. In parallel, the chapter gives a very thorough survey of empirical literature devoted to assessing the qualitative importance of B-S effects, both in accession and other countries. The survey finds that the most reliable papers tend to conclude that 'non-core' EU countries were experiencing B-S effects of a similar — 1 to 2 per cent — magnitude before entering EMU. If it worked for Spain, Portugal and Greece, why would it not work for central European countries?

I find the 'inflation' accounting exercise very useful and well-inspired. It is good to have a systematic comparison between central European economies and it is useful to look at the sectoral level in a very precise way. Furthermore, it is indeed very important to break down the appreciation of the aggregate real exchange rate into the real exchange rate of traded goods, which is unrelated to the B-S effect, and the relative price of non-traded goods, which precisely captures the B-S effect. The results look robust, but they are of necessity drawn from a small sample.

However, it might be dangerous to extrapolate this sort of '*ex post*' accounting into the future. EU membership will be a new experience. It might speed up the productivity catch-up and therefore increase the B-S effects rather than the opposite. We do not know how robust the chapter's assumption of a progressive decline in the productivity catch-up is. Structural changes can indeed be non-linear. Furthermore, the framework is not in a true sense an inflation accounting exercise. It is dealing with changes in relative prices, such as real exchange rates (internal and external), while inflation is, in the end, a nominal phenomenon. It is here that the chapter is overreaching when it gets to policy conclusions. An obvious source of trend inflation left out by the chapter is the impact of strong capital inflows when nominal exchange rates are not fully flexible. These capital inflow pressures may show up in both rising consumer and asset prices (housing and financial assets). We should therefore not jump from moderate B-S effects in the past to strong conclusions about the likely absence of 'excess inflation' in the future.

The contributions in this volume are very focused on EMU accession. This is natural, but we should not forget that there is life, and a tough one, once in EMU. 'Balassa countries' should already incorporate this challenging perspective in their policy thinking. What past EMU experience shows is that it is not easy to control inflation when you enter EMU with inflation above average. The main difficulty lies in the fact that a country may 'benefit' from very low short-run real interest rates. Spain, for instance, has experienced very modest or even negative real short-run rates over the past few years. There is a kind of 'inflation multiplier' here. High inflation, nurtured for instance by Balassa effects, brings accommodating real interest rates and more inflation. The correcting mechanism comes later when real exchange rate appreciation starts depressing exports and overall activity. In the process, there is a risk that the traded sector will be crowded out with potentially adverse consequences on long-term growth. To avoid these various difficulties, there is a need in 'Balassa countries' for running tight fiscal policies to contain domestic demand and carrying out vigorous economic reforms to increase downward pressure on domestic prices.

In this perspective, it might be interesting to note that the euro area has so far not performed as well as expected. After 1999, there was a resurgence of EMU-wide inflation in a context where there was not enough downward price flexibility in low growth/low inflation countries to offset upward inflationary pressures in the overheating economies. As a result, and despite some divergences in inflation rates across countries, aggregate inflation remained stubbornly above 2 per cent well into the economic slowdown. The outcome would have been much better had fiscal tightening (in overheating economies) and disinflationary economic reforms really materialized over these past few years. What applies today to EMU members will apply tomorrow to catching-up countries from central Europe. Fiscal discipline and vigorous economic reform are key to successful monetary integration.

NOTE

1. Autonomous inflationary pressures can be defined as pressures that do not originate from excess demand situations.

5. Float in order to fix? Lessons from emerging markets for new EU member countries*

Jorge Braga de Macedo and Helmut Reisen

> Argentina, Chile and Mexico, Spain and Portugal: même combat! Having established macroeconomic discipline, structural reform and democracy at home, their governments would like to set these achievements in stone by joining a rich-country club. ... With an inflationary history at their back, the authorities will then be tempted to reach out for a most visible stabilization commitment: they will fix, peg or at least shadow their currency to an anchor currency ... Just married, a honeymoon will inevitably begin. (Helmut Reisen (1993), 'Integration with disinflation: which way?', in Richard O'Brien (ed.), *Finance and the International Economy*, **7**, The Amex Bank Review Prize Essays in memory of Robert Marjolin, Oxford University Press.)

1 INTRODUCTION

The European Union has recently opted for its biggest enlargement ever in terms of scope and diversity, including ten countries in Central and Eastern Europe, namely the Czech Republic, Estonia, Hungary, Latvia, Lithuania, Malta, Poland, the Slovak Republic and Slovenia. It is envisaged that this first group of new members will join the EMU contingent upon spending two years in the new Exchange Rate Mechanism (ERM-II) without realignment of their currencies. Not surprisingly, many countries in Central and Eastern Europe are currently global investors' most favoured *convergence plays*. Positive interest spreads and expectations of currency appreciation have been directing money to Budapest and other financial markets in the region, often in the form of highly leveraged carry trades. While the discovery of the region as a target for private capital inflows amounts to a *de facto* financial opening, full *de jure* capital mobility both with the EU and with third countries is expected to prevail at the time of accession. The new EU members are thus confronted with the problem of the *impossible trinity*: they must give up one of three policy goals — monetary independence, exchange rate stability or free capital markets — as they cannot have all three at once.

Central European policy-makers have been fighting currency appreciation through repeated verbal and direct foreign exchange (FX) intervention and interest cuts.

Alas, such episodes of heavy capital inflows are well known to emerging markets and have often ended in tears. The 1990s have witnessed three distinct regional currency crises: the European crisis of 1992–93, the Latin American crisis 1994–95, and the Asian crisis 1997–98 which in turn was followed by crises in Russia and Brazil, and recently by Turkey and Argentina. Obviously, a major currency crisis every 24 months is too much for policy-makers' comfort. The virulence, speed and contagion of financial crises that have hit prospective entrants to rich-country clubs repeatedly over the past two decades have redefined policy choices and trade-offs in a world of intense capital mobility. Reviewing some of these dismal experiences, this chapter recommends earning rather than importing credibility and not foreclosing options too quickly: no sensible sailor drops the anchor until the boat stops moving.

This chapter draws on our previous work (Braga de Macedo et al., 2001a) and is organized as follows. The next two sections review some very basic theory, focusing on the choice of the exchange rate regime. Section 4 argues that multilateral surveillance has helped former EU peripheries earn credibility through the operation of what we call the ERM code of conduct. Further, Section 5 claims that the ERM code of conduct as an effective multilateral surveillance framework has implications for the new members, insofar as they are involved in the convention on the future of Europe. Specifically, flexible integration schemes are explained and their potential benefits for European institutional architecture pointed out. Section 6 describes the strategy of balancing disinflation and competitiveness demanded of the new EU members and draws lessons from emerging markets. Section 7 focuses on limiting crisis vulnerability by contrasting first- and second-generation indicators and showing the financial vulnerability of some of the new EU members, especially Hungary. The conclusion restates the basic contention that the way out of the impossible trinity is a code of conduct and an institutional architecture where currencies *float in order to fix*. To the extent that both elements can be found in the eurozone, new EU members should join the ERM-II as soon as their fundamentals allow.

2 SOME VERY BASIC THEORY

It is an almost common view now that intermediate or BBC regimes (bands, basket or crawling pegs) are not sustainable in a world of intense capital mobility. Currently, there are few efforts to revive the intermediate option (but see Williamson, 2000, and Braga de Macedo et al., 2001b). Countries are being pushed to the corners of either firm-fixing or free-floating. This clearly reflects the desire to keep capital markets open, as can be easily seen from Figure 5.1.

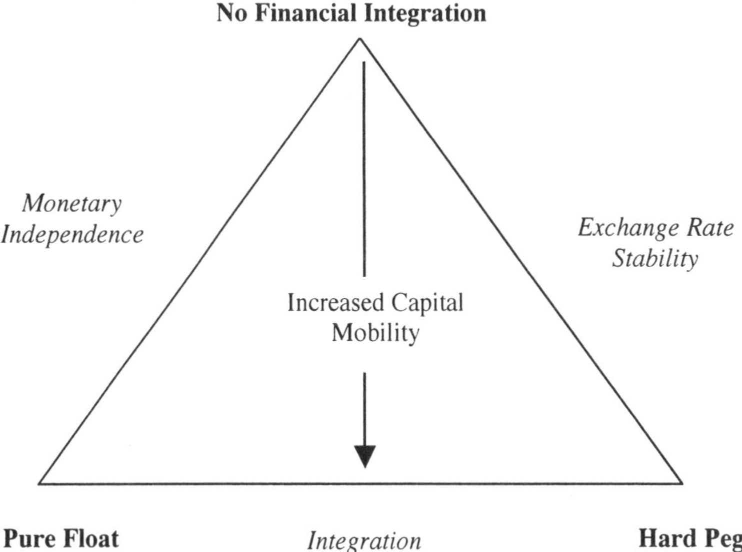

Figure 5.1 The impossible trinity

The logic behind the proposition in favour of corner solutions is the *impossible trinity* (a term coined by Tomaso Padoa Schioppa in the 1980s; see Frankel, 1999). Impossible trinity, because a country must give up one of three goals: exchange rate stability, monetary independence (useful to cope with slumps), or financial-market integration. It cannot have all at the same time. Countries can attain only two of the three goals simultaneously:

- lack of financial integration allows exchange rate stability and monetary independence;
- hard pegs (dollarization, monetary union) allow integration and exchange rate stability;
- a full float allows integration and monetary independence.

This trilemma is, in a certain way, an *embarras de richesse* at times of growing global risk aversion. Apart from many poor developing countries, entire emerging-market regions (such as Latin America) risk dropping from portfolio investors' radar screen (Reisen, 2002). Not so the new EU member countries. A tide of convergence interest has caused a surge of capital inflows in a number of central European currencies, most recently post-Irish referendum. The result has been a strong rally in local bond yields and, in many cases, a significant strengthening of the currencies.

Whatever the exchange rate regime, with free capital flows *fiscal control* is the basic requirement for avoiding macroeconomic complications. Unless the government commands fiscal control for stabilization purposes, it has to violate the *Mundell assignment* and use monetary policy for internal balance. According to Mundell (1962), however, once the capital account is open, even imperfectly, *monetary policy* acquires a comparative advantage in dealing with *external* imbalances, while *fiscal policy* is assigned to maintaining *internal* balance. Branson and Braga de Macedo (1995; also Branson et al., 2001) show for new EU member countries that fiscal rigidity in view of an investment boom forces an *unstable assignment* upon the authorities. If fiscal policy does not tighten sufficiently to cope with the investment boom, monetary policy is left to hold down aggregate demand. This in turn would *widen* the interest differential and thus reinforce the balance of payments surplus. Extending the assignment model to three targets and three instruments, Branson and de Macedo assign fiscal policy to internal balance (non-inflationary aggregate demand), the real exchange rate to the current account, and the interest rate to the external balance in terms of FX reserves.

Circumspection is required when trying to distil policy lessons from currency crises (Reisen, 1998). All too often, the isolated focus on characteristics found in countries which have fallen victim to a currency crisis yields 'causes' that are merely *endogenous effects of massive net capital inflows*. Current account deficits, overvalued exchange rates (in real terms), overinvestment in real estate and declining capital productivity all figure prominently in the list of 'culprits'. However, net flows from capital-rich to capital-poor countries can only be effected with corresponding current account deficits in the recipent countries, which are produced by a real appreciation of their exchange rate. The appreciation in turn reduces the relative incentive to invest in exportable production and tilts incentives towards non-tradables, including real estate, whose relative price has to rise. Higher capital equipment of local labour, a result of domestic investment financed (partly) by foreign savings, reduces the marginal return to capital.

3 THE CHOICE OF THE EXCHANGE RATE REGIME

The currency crashes of the 1990s underscore the evidence that the combination of pegged exchange rates and open capital accounts are prone to costly accidents. Soft pegs and narrow bands (2.25%) created a one-way bet for speculators under ERM-I in the early 1990s, as convergence plays in connection with the EU southern enlargement were encouraged by pegs that assumedly minimized currency risk and thereby created investor moral hazard. Mexico's 1994–95 highlighted the same crisis mechanism as slow disinflation in the presence of heavy intramarginal intervention to defend the crawling peg for the peso had created cumulative competitiveness problems and a large current account deficit financed by short-term bonds. The Asian crisis of 1997–98 was preceded by considerable appreciation of real effective exchange rates, in particular during the 1995–96 period, which resulted largely from the rise in the US dollar to which the Asian currencies were effectively pegged and from the depreciation of the yen, a key competitor currency. The inappropriateness of a dollar peg for the APEC currencies had long been recognized (Reisen and van Trotsenburg, 1988), although it had prevented beggar-thy-neighbour policies through competitive devaluations in the region.

The disastrous failure of the currency board system and its negative impact on growth in Argentina can be traced to insufficient fiscal discipline, which in turn produced an overvalued real effective exchange rate, and to the disincentives for savings promotion due to heavy liquidity requirements in the banking system (Braga de Macedo et al., 2001a). Argentina's dismal experience shows that no exchange rate regime will confer sufficient stability in the prolonged absence of growth. Flexible exchange rate systems have tended to favour those macro variables that have been identified in the theoretical and empirical literature as important channels for sustained economic performance, namely investment, trade openness, capital flows and fiscal or institutional rigidities. In a study that evaluates Latin American growth performance, Grandes and Reisen (2003) confirm the channels emphasized in the sparse literature that links the choice of the currency regime to growth performance. They highlight four criteria that will help guide the choice of the appropriate currency regime in emerging-market countries:

1. How does the regime impact on the mix of capital inflows? Does it encourage flows that carry positive growth externalities or does it encourage flows that raise a country's vulnerability to financial crisis?

2. How does the regime impact on the incentive to invest and save rather than to consume? Does it foster productivity growth by keeping output volatility in check?
3. How does the regime impact on the tradables sector and add to its integration into world trade, namely by providing sustainable and competitive exchange rate levels and by avoiding misalignments from the fundamental equilibrium rate?
4. How does the regime cope with a country's given rigidities, namely in the fiscal area, and to what extent can such rigidities safely be assumed to display a sufficient degree of endogeneity to the regime choice?

The hard peg advocates have argued that independent monetary policy is no longer an effective policy instrument for emerging countries for a variety of reasons: (a) the lack of credibility, (b) liabilities dollarization (Calvo, 2001), (c) the 'original sin' problem of non-existent long-term local currency finance causes currency or maturity mismatches (Hausmann, 2000), (d) excessive de facto interest rate and reserves volatility resulting in 'fear of floating' (Calvo and Reinhart, 2000) or (e) the substitution with capital market financing of relative price adjustment (Dornbusch, 2001). We would add to this list that a pure nominal float tends to encourage prolonged periods of misalignment (such as in New Zealand and the United States in the 1980s, and later in Great Britain) which threaten growth strategies based on diversifying exports away from traditional crops towards non-traditional industries (see, for example, Joumard and Reisen, 1992).

In Latin America, the hard peg view has been increasingly discredited: during the last two decades, failed attempts with hard pegs have been discontinued in favour of more flexible exchange-rate arrangements, witness Chile in the early 1980s, Mexico in the mid-1990s, Brazil in the late 1990s and now Argentina. Those who support exchange rate flexibility (e.g. Larraín and Velasco, 2001; Schmidt-Hebbel, 2000), point to nominal wage and price rigidities, to the prevalence of real shocks in emerging markets and to the moral hazards implicit in pegs to make the case for exchange rate flexibility. They attempt to prove their case by citing the main shortcomings of the hard pegs experiences: wider and more volatile sovereign spreads driven by comparatively growing default risk; heightened output volatility; wage and price stickiness; insufficient fiscal discipline and the non-compliance with optimum currency areas criteria to irrevocably peg the exchange rate.

The situation in transition countries is varied (Granville, 2001). Some of the new EU members — the Czech Republic, Poland and Slovakia — have moved to managed floats, while Hungary has already committed to an ERM-II-type exchange rate mechanism (a ±15% band around a fixed parity to the euro). However, a peg to the euro may be premature and subject to the

Walters' Critique. The one-time adviser to former UK Prime Minister Margaret Thatcher had famously pointed out the boom-bust risk of shadowing an anchor currency when local inflation remained somewhat higher than in the anchor country. With converging interest rates, real interest rates may become inappropriately low in countries with higher inflation and stimulate a twin spending and debt boom while local asset prices are pushed up. In particular the history of emerging-market crises suggests that booms are easily followed by busts and that today's financial market darlings, including former EU and OECD entrants, have become financial crisis victims within months.

Whether hard pegs such as currency boards as practised in Estonia are a better alternative for open economies depends very much on their institutional and regulatory prerequisites and their degree of endogeneity with respect to the exchange rate regime. These can be summarized as follows:

- The banking system must be strengthened, so that the central banks' more limited capacity to provide lender-of-last-resort services does not expose the country to financial instability.
- The fiscal position needs to be strong so that the absence of the central banks' ability to absorb new public debt does not end in a funding crisis.
- Commercial and intergovernmental credit lines must have been negotiated to secure liquidity in an investor sentiment crisis.
- The labour market must be made flexible in order to accommodate asymmetric shocks without higher levels of un(der)development.
- And the real economy structures should be aligned to ensure that cyclical and monetary conditions coincide with the pegging partner.

This is a long list which is not easily met; neither can its parameters be assumed to be largely endogenous to the exchange rate regime. Authorities in Central Europe are certainly better informed than us as to whether or when their country would meet that demanding list. It should be noted, however, that there is evidence that new EU member countries currently encounter shocks that are largely uncorrelated with those in the EMU core (Fidrmuc, 2002); that the EU is likely to impose transitional barriers to international migration following EU enlargement so that migration will not be an effective adjustment channel; and that there is essentially no fiscal risk sharing among the EU or EMU countries.

While hard pegs often confer initial gains in credibility and hence lower capital cost, these gains can be ephemeral when they are not supported by a sufficient degree of institutional development and economic flexibility. Braga de Macedo et al. (2001a) have shown that both francophone Africa and

Argentina became trapped by an inappropiate anchor currency – inappropriate as the anchor neither reflected their trade directions nor their cyclical needs. As there are few currencies available to borrow credibility from, this lesson will not be unique: it suggests either a basket peg or, if a realistic option, building rather than borrowing credibility.

Agnes Benassy-Quéré and Benoît Coeuré (2000) have recently stressed the *regional dimension* of the debate on corner solutions (see also Branson (2001) who computes optimal pegs for groups of developing countries). They argue that both pure floating and hard pegs make future regional cooperation more difficult. This is important in a world of regional trade blocs which look for ways to intensify cooperation. A float is an inherently unstable regime for countries competing on world markets for a similar range of products and hence sets incentives for beggar-thy-neighbour competitive devaluation. Floating induces non-cooperative strategies, especially when the competing neighbours face a common shock. Hard pegs are hard because it is so difficult to reverse them and because they lack an exit strategy. They are thus only suited for countries which aim to join a monetary union with the anchor currency in not too distant a future (such as some new EU member countries). On the other hand, the perspective of joining or creating a monetary union can make intermediate regimes more robust in the meantime. With increasing financial integration, emerging markets may thus opt to give up on *some* exchange rate stability and on *some* monetary autonomy. There is ample choice on currency regimes inside the corners, although most of the regimes will amount to some sort of inflation targeting.[1]

Fiscally disciplined Southeast Asia succeeded for quite a while (1978–96) in reconciling stable exchange rates, low inflation and massive capital inflows without resort to capital controls. In the absence of developed money markets, the Southeast Asian central banks extended the open-market sterilization instruments common in industrial countries through the use of public institutions such as social security funds, state banks and public enterprises as monetary instruments (Reisen, 1993b). But, from the mid-1990s, the regime ceased keeping the real effective exchange rate stable, and gradually turned into a dollar peg, as demonstrated by Benassy-Quéré and Coeuré (2000).

Further, exchange rate target zones with little intramarginal intervention and moderate width have been pursued quite successfully in Chile, Colombia and Israel in the early 1990s (Williamson, 1996), despite a large degree of financial openness in these countries: their crawling band helped to achieve the trade-off between the conflicting objectives of reducing inflation and maintaining export growth. That they were given up in all cases needs some explanation. A possible theoretical rationale is the complexity of basket pegs with bands, which hampers their verifiability, but is nevertheless needed for credibility (Frankel et al., 2001). In the next section we argue that, once the effectiveness of the Multilateral Surveillance Framework (MSF) is verifiable, there will be greater tolerance for intermediate regimes, so that the argument that they are 'too complicated for locals and for Wall Street' need not apply.

4 EARNING CREDIBILITY THROUGH MULTILATERAL SURVEILLANCE

This section argues that multilateral surveillance has helped former EU peripheries earn credibility through the operation of what Braga de Macedo et al. (2001a) call the ERM code of conduct. This code of conduct built up over the years and transformed the ERM from an exchange rate arrangement into a convergence instrument. The ERM code of conduct favoured a medium-term orientation of macroeconomic policy, coupled with measures designed to improve the functioning of factor markets and of the public sector. The principle of a stability-oriented policy based on the respect of property rights and open markets goes back to the gold standard, and reflects 'rules of good housekeeping' valid at the core and at the periphery. Actually, 'sustained regime change' was identified in EC (1990, chapter 9) as a condition for benefits to accrue to peripheral nations or regions. This argument was especially strong under the limited labour mobility and flexibility, coupled with low fiscal redistribution among states which prevails in the European economy. In these circumstances, exchange rate adjustments may become necessary to eliminate declines in competitiveness but they may not succeed in changing relative prices. The greater the underlying capital mobility and the more likely the repetition of exchange rate adjustments, the less effective a devaluation will be.

EC (1990) also used survey data to suggest that firms did not expect devaluation to solve their problems but rather thought that credit constraints were a more severe hindrance to expansion at the peripheries than at the centre. The fear that restrictions on fiscal policy called for by the excessive deficit procedure (EDP) contained in the treaty and later by the Stability and Growth Pact (SGP) would hurt growth and prosperity was addressed in Buti et al. (1997) who showed that the retroactive application of the SGP would not have exacerbated recessions over the 1961–97 period. With the current downturn the debate has resurfaced and led to suggestions that the SGP should be scrapped (Blanchard and Giavazzi, 2002; Wyplosz, 2002). Evidence from the markets suggests otherwise: the SGP has helped euro credibility by alleviating concerns about 'the free rider problem that potentially arises with the adoption of a common currency across a group of states with national budgets' (Persaud and Metcalfe, 2002; also Alphandéry, 2002 and Thygesen, 2002).

If correcting excessive deficits is difficult for EU member countries, buttressing the soundness of public finances is a formidable task in countries with histories of high inflation, where neither the social partners nor public employees automatically appreciate the benefits of the regime change that the policy-makers are attempting to engineer. Errors in policy appraisal can unduly raise the costs of reform, when information about the change in regime is not readily available to international financial markets. Repeated market tests of the authorities' commitment to exchange rate stability may result from this imperfect information. If these tests of the authorities' resolve greatly increase the cost of defending the exchange rate, they can lead to policy reversals. Conversely, if the volatility of the exchange rate is a direct consequence of system turbulence, market tests will be short-lived and the threat of a reversal will become less and less credible, both abroad and at home.

Since its meeting in Brussels in late 1993, the European Council has been issuing 'broad guidelines' against which policy and performance in the member states are to be gauged in what has become a regular test of the MSF for all EU member states. The progress of policy reform stands on how effective this MSF might be among union officials whose interaction with national officials should be accountable in their respective parliaments and in the European parliament.

As stated, the debate on corner solutions has a regional dimension. Regional integration reinforces peer alignment, contributing to the atmosphere in which peer review and surveillance take place. The EU and euro area policy review processes are very intensive, with peer pressure based on elements that cannot be replicated in any looser form of international institution. There are elaborate, frequent procedures sometimes based on rules, but mostly on national commitments which it is the task of the monitoring agencies such as the Commission and at the next level, committees, to keep countries to. The involvement of high-level officials is much greater than that at the IMF or the OECD. In sum, the arrangements in place within the EU give by far the greatest scope for the exercise of peer pressure and supervision.

By contrast with the Asian and Latin American experiences mentioned at the outset, candidates for membership have not been willing to set up an MSF among themselves, even when there exists an institutional vehicle like CEFTA, the Central European Free Trade Agreement (Braga de Macedo, 2000). Yet this is the way in which geographical peripheries can acquire global reputation. In a sense, they overcome the cost of physical distance through financial proximity. Of course initial and terminal conditions matter as much as the capacity to transform. Doctrinal controversies often reflect different assumptions about each one of these three factors.

In transition and developing economies, though, the institutional framework for such an orientation is lacking, so that the rules for monetary stability are not credible. The expectation of EU membership, under conditions of convergence and cohesion, provides this credibility but credible surveillance is needed for geographical peripheries to acquire global reputation. The time it takes for a nation to acquire a reputation for financial probity varies but it typically involves several general elections where alternative views of society may confront each other.

To construct a social consensus domestically, credible signals that the authorities are committed to reform may be needed. If stable democratic governments succeed in implementing reforms which help to achieve convergence between poorer and richer nations and regions, they can set off a self-reinforcing virtuous cycle of stability and growth. On the other hand, there will be a vicious cycle if short-lived governments, fearing the social conflicts associated with reforms, delay implementation and impair convergence.

With high capital mobility, exchange rate stability requires a speedy real and nominal convergence process. The indicators of budgetary discipline have become signals of regime change sustained by the structural reform of the public sector. Given that financial markets tend to exaggerate rather than to dampen such signals, apparent reversions during a relatively rapid convergence are also more liable to misinterpretation. The cohesion objective involves a degree of social awareness that may not be required with respect to the convergence of fiscal variables. In any event, whatever the credibility of national policies, it has been apparent that fast convergence is more difficult with slower growth and that the main macroeconomic costs arise before the main microeconomic benefits are felt.

If, in the final analysis, the exchange rate reflects the credibility of national policies over the medium term, it may do so with considerable noise if the entire parity grid is under attack. This is why little indication about the credibility of national policy could be gathered from the realignments which occurred during the turbulent 1992–93 period. Speculative attacks on more vulnerable currency parities will have more negative effects on the system if parities are already locked than if they continue to be flexible. Flexibility within a sufficiently wide band allows speculation not to be a one-way bet. That lesson was learned in the twelve months preceding August 2, 1993 when very wide bands of 15% replaced the normal fluctuation margins. The external discipline provided by the grid no longer obtained and each central bank decided whether or not to intervene within the old fluctuation bands. Most decided to do just that, so that the convergence process was not harmed by the decision to widen the band. The lesson from the currency crises is that the largely unwritten ERM code of conduct implied more effective coordination mechanisms among monetary and fiscal authorities than expected. Non-compliance with the code of conduct played a major role in the development of the currency turmoil, but the system regained stability after August 2, 1993, thanks to the widening of the fluctuation bands, which limited speculative pressure by eliminating one-way bets and reintroducing two-way risks.

The option to float in order to fix, a kind of financial 'cruel to be kind' (Braga de Macedo, 2001a, using a line from Hamlet, which made its way into a pop song) shows that the set of principles, rules and code of conduct which underlie the ERM have proved correct for the euro as well. That the widening of the bands was a positive step towards the euro may be easily accepted nowadays. That you may float in order to fix introduces the earning credibility process explicitly in what is the major lesson from the ERM code of conduct. When the decision to widen the bands was taken, however, many observers and prominent economists (for example Branson, 1994) stated that the euro was dead. The question of credibility is different for members of the Eurosystem because, with a single monetary policy, they are more used to following a multilateral surveillance framework. Since the best indicator of policy credibility is that multilateral surveillance is effective, it is the framework that determines the choice of an exchange rate regime.

5 FLEXIBLE EUROPEAN INTEGRATION

This section claims that the ERM code of conduct as an effective multilateral surveillance framework has implications for the new members, insofar as they are involved in the convention on the future of Europe. Specifically, flexible integration schemes are explained and their potential benefits for European institutional architecture pointed out. The creation of the euro system was followed by a difficult institutional period, which has also delayed the accession calendar. The delay reflects the propensity to procrastinate on structural reforms, rather than the recurrent European debate about whether multiple-speed convergence towards union objectives is possible and desirable. This debate does help illustrate the complementarities between global and regional common good. One extreme position in the European debate draws on the view of a unified constitutional state, for which variable geometry is impossible. The other extreme position calls for a set of contractual arrangements, where common institutions are undesirable.

From the beginning, the European Community attempted to overcome the rigid intergovernmental nature of the OECD or of the G-7 (which does not even have a permanent secretariat) by supranational institutions like the European Commission. But the convergence stopped far short of establishing Community-wide democratic legitimacy. As a consequence, the institutional framework became more and more complex, especially after a Union with three pillars, the Community and two intergovernmental pillars, was created in the 1992 Maastricht Treaty. In the process, flexibility was lost and this is why the institutional debate has resurfaced in the *Convention for the future of Europe*. The Convention deals with ongoing 'back to basics' issues such as proximity, legitimacy and accountability and takes into account the views of the accession countries.

The case for flexible integration can be made with the help of a diagram. For any given number of member states, there is a trade-off between the freedom to enter into contractual agreements which include some members and exclude others and the ultimate requirement of 'one man, one vote' which would be associated with a new state emerging from the integration of all members. In Figure 5.2, adapted from Dewatripont et al. (1996, p. 47), the vertical axis measures flexibility and the horizontal axis measures depth of integration. The origin represents purely intergovernmental cooperation among the same member states. The vertical axis represents economic efficiency and executive performance, or the forces of competition, while the horizontal axis represents legal status and legislative activity, or the forces of cooperation. Each point in the quadrant can therefore be seen as a combination between competition and cooperation.

The highest point on the vertical axis, labelled 'A la Carte', would be equivalent to a purely contractual institutional design where any combination of subgroups of member states is acceptable, so that the basic intergovernmental principle of equality of member states applies and unanimity in decision-making is preserved. During the revisions of the Union treaty in 1996 and 2000, intergovernmental schemes of 'reinforced cooperation' have been called for among some member states, as their creation still requires unanimity of all member states and their membership is open to all of the member states who qualify. The Nice Treaty made 'reinforced cooperation' possible in Community, JHA (justice and home affairs) and even some CFSP (common foreign and security policy) areas (Baldwin et al., 2001). This should alleviate cohesion countries' concerns about the proposals for flexible integration made during the preparation for Amsterdam. To the extent that flexible integration also stresses the portability of the European experience to countries in different stages of economic and financial development, it may not only facilitate enlargement but also a clearer European identity in development cooperation.

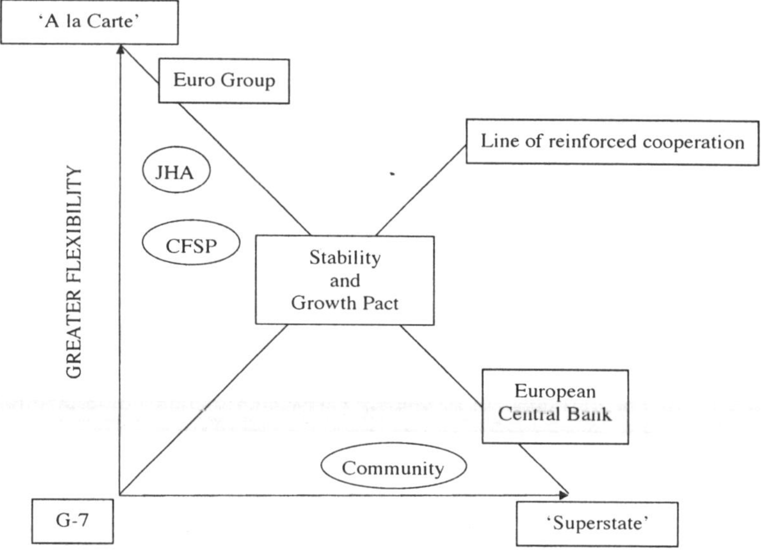

Figure 5.2 Flexibility and depth of integration

Proximity suggests governance responses at the appropriate level, through the combined action of elected officials and civil society (including business). The common good may thus be provided by regional institutions, as long as the various levels of government are appropriately combined. For these reasons schemas of flexible integration have been proposed, where the principle of proximity (or subsidiarity) is generalized from geography to issue areas. Along the same lines Kölliker (2001) shows that this generalization depends on the characteristics of the public good being provided. When there are network externalities with exclusion benefits, as is the case with the Eurosystem (also the Schengen agreement on the free movement of persons), then such flexible integration has a 'snowballing effect' which may lead initially reluctant states to join in. When there are no exclusion benefits but rather free-rider problems, flexible integration does not lead initially reluctant states to join in. This has been observed with respect to common resources (tax or otherwise).

For certain public goods, then, flexible integration recognizes national legitimacy and democratic accountability at national level. It also stresses the role of external pressure in bringing about structural reforms resisted by the operation of domestic vested-interest groups through yardstick competition. The euro delivered convergence and cohesion because the 'new politics of credibility' overcame financial hierarchy among sovereign risks. Trade unions recognized the perverse interaction between price and wage increases (which hurts the poor and unemployed disproportionately) and public opinion accepted the medium-term stance of policy. Yet it took longer to convince voters than markets, and some countries used the euro to procrastinate on their unpopular reforms, threatening the benefits of the stability culture with the 'euro hold up' (Akerlof, 1991; Buiter and Sibert, 1997, for the general point; Braga de Macedo et al., 2001a, for the application to the euro).

6 BALANCING DISINFLATION AND COMPETITIVENESS

The history of Latin American crises (e.g. Chile 1982, Mexico 1994, Brazil 1998, Argentina 2001) warns that many boom episodes have ended in tears because it proved hard to bring inflation from moderate to low levels without endangering external competitiveness and a solid FDI-based structure of capital inflows. All these countries followed exchange rate-based disinflation strategies until their currency crashed. Whether such strategy can succeed depends on (a) how quickly inflation can be brought down to the rich-country level and (b) the cost implied by the loss of international competitiveness. Inflation will persist unless wage inflation becomes forward-looking (by breaking backward indexation or by introducing incomes policy) or unless exchange rate depreciation falls below the past rate of inflation (Dornbusch and Fischer, 1991). Table 5.1 takes a closer look at the disinflation process in selected new EU member candidates.

The table demonstrates the amount of disinflation achieved in the Central European OECD member countries during the last three years. During this period, the consumer price index in the euro area rose at a stable 2.4% per annum. The Czech Republic and Poland, therefore, have brought their inflation down to target levels already; these two countries are thus released from the pressure to keep interest rates high, implying fewer incentives for hot money inflows and unwarranted currency appreciation. By contrast, disinflation remains incomplete in Hungary where incomes policy and fiscal policy have been unhelpful. Competitive positions as measured by relative unit labour cost and relative export prices have deteriorated except in Poland. The table suggests that the hardening of the euro peg in Hungary has intensified the trade-off between disinflation and competitiveness. The divergence between the sharp rise in unit labour cost and the moderate rise in relative export prices must be due to corporate profit squeezes that are unlikely to be sustained for long.

Table 5.1 Disinflation and competitiveness (annual percentage points)

	CPI	Wages	Unit Labour Cost (Export Prices)	IMF FX Reg
Czech Rep.				
2000	3.9	7.2	–0.7 (1.7)	7
2001	4.8	8.1	2.7 (2.5)	8
2002(e)	2.1	6.7	10.2 (2.7)	
Hungary				
2000	9.8	21.6	–8.8 (0.8)	6
2001	9.2	14.8	10.2 (1.2)	4
2002(e)	5.4	13.7	13.6 (2.4)	
Poland				
2000	10.1	9.7	–0.6 (–0.4)	8
2001	5.5	8.5	4.2 (–0.9)	8
2002(e)	2.1	3.5	–7.2 (–7.3)	
Slovak Rep.				
2000	12.0		10.9 (7.6)	7
2001	7.4		4.6 (2.7)	7
2002(e)	3.5		1.2 (3.7)	

Notes:
CPI = consumer price indices, percentage change from previous year.
Wages = compensation per employee in the business sector, percentage change from previous year.
Unit Labour Cost (Export Prices) = competiveness-weighted relative unit labour cost (export prices) in the manufacturing sector in dollar terms, percentage change from previous year.
IMF FX Reg = IMF exchange rate regime classification from 1 (euroization or dollarization) to 8 (independent float): 4 = horizontal bands; 6 = crawling bands; 7 = managed float with no pre-announced exchange rate path.

Source: OECD, *OECD Economic Outlook*, **72**, December 2002; IMF, *International Financial Statistics*, **55**, May 2002; authors' calculations.

Much has been made of the *Balassa-Samuelson effect to justify real currency and wage appreciation* in the so-called transition countries (Halpern and Wyplosz, 1995). From 2000/2001 on, however, productivity gains relative to the major trading partners seem to have been insufficient to compensate for real currency and wage appreciation. Moreover, while the *speed of the catch-up effect* may slow down as Central Europe approaches Western Europe's income levels, the new EU members will face the abolition of remaining barriers to trade, except in a few areas subject to temporary derogations. This means that many firms will face stronger competitive pressures from imported EU goods, that smaller firms will suffer from the new burden of legal regulations required by the EU, and that certain companies will lose certain tax advantages which are not compatible with EU regulations. Reducing the protection of sectors exposed to international competition requires a *real depreciation* of the local currency for internal and external balance, which has to be weighed against the amount of real appreciation required by the Balassa-Samuelson effect. Finally, as long as massive net inflows to the private sector were accompanied by large repayments of foreign public debt, financed by significant privatization revenues, real currency appreciation could be held in check (for Hungary, see Oblath, 1998). Family silver, alas, is not endless. Further privatization will thus be a limited option as a policy instrument to influence the real exchange rate.

Such considerations — and the numbers in Table 5.1 — point to the potential risk that the EU hopefuls will *enter the the currency union at an overvalued exchange rate*, as post-unification Germany arguably did.[2] With a low inflation target set by the ECB, real overvaluation will only be corrected over time through even lower inflation, if not deflation. This is a painful process in the presence of price and wage rigidities; the French used to call it 'competitive disinflation': suffering for an extended period until competitiveness had been restored (Blanchard and Muet, 1993).

7 LIMITING CRISIS VULNERABILITY

In order to gauge whether new EU member candidates have penetrated the crisis danger zone, economists can consult three generations of models of currency crises. The earliest models of currency crises, in particular the influential paper by former IMF chief economist Jacques Polak (1957), were based on the incompatibility of expansionary fiscal and monetary policies with fixed exchange rates. Excessive money creation would then 'leak out' through overall balance of payments deficits, until the shortage of foreign exchange reserves forced devaluation or imposed controls on capital outflows. The attempts of investors to anticipate the inevitable collapse would generate a speculative attack on the currency when reserves fell to some critical level.

The 'first-generation' crisis models (Krugman, 1979; Flood and Garber, 1984) accounted well for the many currency crises in the 1970s and also for the 1982 developing-country debt crisis, but the models failed to explain Chile's 1982 crisis, the 1992 European crisis, the Mexican peso crisis 1994–95 and the 1997–98 Asian financial crisis. The logic of the 'second-generation' crisis model (Obstfeld, 1994) developed in the aftermath of the European currency crises, stressed the trade-offs between the benefits of a credible exchange rate peg and the costs in terms of higher interest rates, higher unemployment or lower growth of defending the peg.

Table 5.2 reveals several weak spots in new EU member countries, both in view of the first- and of the second-generation models. We observe twin budget and current account deficits, which not only indicate a policy mix of loose fiscal stance and tight money, but also are at levels high enough to drive public and foreign debt up in terms of GDP. In fact, the latest OECD Economic Outlook calls for fiscal tightening in all four member countries. Foreign exchange reserves have started to dwindle in Hungary. On the other hand, moderate real GDP growth and very high levels of unemployment seriously limit the governments' capacity to defend pegs with intensified macroeconomic restraint, imposing a severe second-generation trade-off on ERM-II-type currency arrangements for now.

Table 5.2 First- and second-generation indicators, latest

	Czech Rep.	Hungary	Poland	Slovak Rep.
General gov't financial balance	–5.7	–6.7	–6.0	–5.5
Current account balance	–4.2	–5.3	–3.3	–7.0
Money growth	6.2	13.0	2.5	9.4
Foreign FX reserves growth	53.3	–16.9	3.1	103.4
GDP growth	2.5	3.1	1.2	4.3
Unemployment rate	7.4	10.1	19.7	19.0

Note: Flow data refer to avg. 2002, stock data to end 2002. If not stated otherwise, data are in % of GDP; money growth is growth of M2 and FX reserves in 2002 compared to 2001; unemployment is in % of labour force.

Sources: OECD, *OECD Economic Outlook*, No. 72, December 2002; IMF, *International Financial Statistics*; Datastream.

Both the first- and the second-generation crisis models failed to explain several of the recent emerging-market crises, in particular the Asian crisis. A third-generation model explains some of the recent events better: McKinnon and Pill (1998) show how reform countries get into the vulnerability zone through euphoric expectations about the permanent income level. Inefficient financial systems stimulate excessive optimism through credit growth and asset-price inflation. The distortions are magnified further through net capital inflows as they stimulate bank credit growth. Once short-term foreign debt exceeds official reserves, a run on a country's liquid assets is intensified by the investor knowledge that there are not enough liquid reserves to restore confidence. Short-term debt poses special problems for the maintenance of financial stability, as its rapid withdrawal can trigger sovereign default, a systemic banking and payments crisis and large-scale corporate defaults (Eichengreen et al., 1998).

Exchange rate pegs, in combination with high interest rates, typical in developing countries for structural reasons, tend to reinforce bank lending and spending booms (Reisen, 1998). They constitute an incentive for leveraged investors to exploit interest differentials as well as for offshore borrowing by creditworthy banks and non-banks to tap seemingly cheap sources of finance. Central bank intervention on the foreign exchange market to peg the currency in the face of net inflows, unless sterilized fully, is intermediated into the domestic banking system. The exchange rate peg provides the incentive to allocate those funds disregarding currency and maturity risks, as these are being implicitly transferred to the central bank (Calvo and Mendoza, 1996). Short-term foreign debt (liabilities to non-resident banks, debt securities, suppliers' credit, domestic debt held by non-residents, deposits of non-residents in domestic institutions) in relation to official foreign exchange reserves has been identified as the single most important precursor of financial crises triggered by capital-flow reversals.[3] As the level of international trade does not seem to bear any relationship to the level of short-term debt, short-term trade credit seems to play an insignificant role in driving short-term flows (Rodrik and Velasco, 1999). FDI flows, in contrast to debt-creating flows, have been found to stimulate domestic investment, rather than crowding it out by competing in domestic product markets or financial markets. The complementarity of FDI and domestic investment is explained by the complementarity in production and by positive technology spillovers (Borensztein et al., 1998).

Abundant foreign supply of capital (offered at rapidly falling sovereign yield spreads) and the greater ability of non-bank and bank borrowers to tap the international financial markets have interacted to fuel a rise in non-bank and bank foreign liabilities (towards BIS reporting banks). In terms of foreign assets, non-bank foreign liabilities exploded especially in Hungary (see Table 5.3). When short-term foreign debt starts to exceed official reserves (indicated by a ratio higher than one), each creditor knows that there are not enough liquid foreign exchange reserves, so there is a race to the exit. The table gives no warning on that front, and especially not to Hungary.

Table 5.3 Indicators of financial vulnerability, latest

	Czech Rep.	Hungary	Poland	Slovak Rep.
Short-term foreign debt/reserves	0.7	0.4	0.3	0.7
M2/reserves	2.9	2.3	3.1	3.2
Foreign liabilities/ foreign assets (towards BIS reporting banks)	0.8	3.9	0.8	1.9
FDI/current account deficit	1.8	0.4	0.8	2.5
(current account deficit as % of GDP)	(4.2)	(5.3)	(3.3)	(7.0)

Note: Data refer to 2002, but not necessarily to end of year.

Sources: BIS, www.bis.org/statistics/bankstats.htm; IMF, *International Financial Statistics*, **55**, December 2002; OECD, *OECD Economic Outlook*, **72**, December 2002.

While all four new EU members display a short-term debt/reserves ratio lower than one, they are financially open. Openness implies that the M2/reserves ratio becomes the relevant indicator for financial vulnerability, as residents may try to obtain foreign currency for their domestic currency holdings. The M2/reserves ratio exceeds one by far in all four countries. As for the reversibility of the capital flows financing the current account deficits in new EU member countries, Hungary stands out for combining a high deficit level (relative to GDP) with a low FDI cover. The country's combination of twin budget and current account deficits plus vulnerable finances risks igniting unpleasant fireworks in financial markets, if emerging-market lessons hold.

8 CONCLUSION

On the way to becoming a full member of the euro area, new EU member countries will face an intensified policy trilemma between open capital accounts, monetary sovereignty and exchange rate stability; the trilemma is most visible already in Hungary. In particular, where fiscal institutions do not yet allow full fiscal control, where the banking sector is weak and where inflation levels remain above those at the centre, loss of external competitiveness through exchange-rate misalignment and balance-sheet mismatches might lead the accession countries rapidly into the crisis danger zone. For those unaware of the history of EU enlargement and of failed hard-peg experiments in emerging markets, corner solutions – a pure float or a hard peg – are the preferred choice for the exchange rate regime to resolve such a policy trilemma and limit crisis vulnerability.

The prospect of regional integration invalidates corner solutions as non-cooperative (float) and costly to exit (hard pegs), but it revives the intermediate exchange rate regime. The EMS experience shows that target zones plus effective codes of conduct, wide enough to allow for sufficient flexibility, can indeed confer sustained credibility so as to avoid large misalignments and to reduce crisis vulnerability. What they need to achieve these objectives goes beyond the public perception that the central parity is consistent with long-term fundamentals. Expectations need to be guided by mutually agreed governance codes towards intensifying integration, based on visible progress in macroeconomic stability and regulatory reform. In the event, the transition in the mid-1990s between the ERM code of conduct and the run-up to the euro implied that a currency should float in order to fix. If this ERM-I experience is any guide, schemas of flexible integration may be the best way to generate such governance codes and to improve the multilateral surveillance thereof.

The multilateral surveillance framework has to be 'owned' by, rather than imposed on, the countries concerned. It must therefore be supported by peer pressure and yardstick competition, both of which are built gradually. The 'Eurocentric' approach to earning credibility on the way to monetary integration has had impressive successes in the former (Southern) periphery. This is why the practical operation of the ERM provides important lessons for authorities struggling to implement sustainable exchange rate regimes to support economic convergence. These lessons are beginning to spread beyond the European continent, reaching Asia and Latin America. While an EU-style multilateral surveillance framework is no panacea either, the fact that it does not seem to avoid difficult choices will certainly be welcomed by reformist governments worldwide.

NOTES

* Earlier versions of this chapter were presented at the National Bank of Hungary seminar 'Monetary Strategies for Accession Countries', at a conference in Budapest on 'The Expected Effects of the EU Accession on the Visegrad Countries' and at a seminar at the

Bank of Estonia. We are grateful to participants for comments but remain responsible for the views expressed, which do not involve the Development Centre, the OECD or their member states.

1. Sebastian Edwards (2000) lists the range of regimes from (1) free float (with the exchange rate determined in the market alone) to (2) floating with a 'feedback rule' (indirect intervention which does not result in changes in reserves), (3) managed float (with intervention resulting in changes in international reserves), (4) target zone (floating within a band, with the central parity fixed), (5) sliding band (with adjustable central parity), (6) crawling band (backward- or forward-looking change of central parity), (7) crawling peg (passive or active adjustable peg), (8) fixed, but adjustable peg, (9) currency board and (10) full adoption of another country's currency. Fischer (2001) excludes fixed, but adjustable pegs and narrow band exchange rate systems as not viable in countries open to international capital flows.
2. Financial market observers do worry about real currency overvaluation even now. Standard & Poor's MMS estimated late January 2003 that the Czech and Hungarian currencies were overvalued by up to 40%, while the estimate for the Polish zloty was 13% overvaluation (Luxton, 2003).
3. It is often maintained that distinguishing between types of flows generates little policy insight, essentially for two reasons. First, capital flows are said to be fungible. That would imply, for example, that we cannot discern a differentiated impact of foreign direct investment or short-term debt flows on private or government consumption. Second, it has been argued that capital-flow labels have become meaningless in the presence of derivatives or efforts to circumvent capital controls. These claims, however, ignore a large body of empirical, if not analytical, evidence. Sarno and Taylor (1999) measure the relative size and statistical significance of permanent and temporary components of various categories of capital flows to a large group of Latin American and Asian countries during the period 1988–97. They find relatively low permanent components in bond flows, equity flows and official finance, while commercial bank credit flows appear to contain quite large permanent components and FDI flows are almost entirely permanent. If a large portion of the variation in the time series is explained by movements in the temporary components, then the flows under consideration indicate a higher degree of potential reversibility.

REFERENCES

Akerlof, G. (1991), 'Procrastination and obedience', *The American Economic Review*, **81** (2), pp. 1–19.

Alphandéry, E. (2002), 'Need we amend the stability and growth pact?', paper presented at the Euro 50 Group meeting held in Paris on 27 November 2002.

Bailliu, J., R. Lafrance and J. F. Perrault (2001), 'Exchange rate regimes and economic growth in emerging markets', in Bank of Canada, *Revisiting the Case for Flexible Exchange Rates*.

Baldwin, R. E., E. Berglöf, F. Giavazzi and M. Widgrén (2001), 'Nice try: should the Treaty of Nice be ratified?', *Monitoring European Integration*, **11**, London: CEPR.

Bénassy-Quéré, A. and B. Coeure (2000), 'Big and small currencies: the regional connection', CEPII Working Paper No. 2000-10, June.

Blanchard, O. and F. Giavazzi (2002), 'A reform that can be done now. Improving the SGP through a proper accounting of public investment', paper presented at the Euro 50 Group meeting held in Paris on 27 November 2002.

Blanchard, O. and P. A. Muet (1993), 'Competition through disinflation: an assessment of the French macroeconomic strategy', *Economic Policy*, **16**, pp. 12–56.

Borensztein, E., J. De Gregorio and J.-W. Lee (1998), 'How does foreign direct investment affect economic growth?', *Journal of International Economics*, **45**, pp. 115–35.

Braga de Macedo, J. (2000), 'Converging European transitions', *The World Economy*, **23** (10), November 2000, pp.1335–65.

Braga de Macedo, J. (2001a), 'Statement to the preparatory committee of the UN conference Financing for Development', New York, 20 February, available at www.fe.unl.pt/~jbmacedo/oecd/un.htm.

Braga de Macedo, J. (2001b) 'The euro in the international financial architecture', *Acta Oeconomica*, **51** (3), pp. 287–314.

Braga de Macedo, J., D. Cohen and H. Reisen (2001a), *Don't Fix, Don't Float*, OECD Development Centre Studies.

Braga de Macedo, J., D. Cohen and H. Reisen (2001b), 'Monetary integration for sustained transition: earning rather than importing credibility' in J. Braga de Macedo, D. Cohen and H. Reisen (2001a), pp. 11–53.

Branson, W. (1994), 'German reunification, the breakdown of the EMS, and the path to stage three', in David Cobham (ed.), *European Monetary Upheavals*, Manchester and New York: Manchester University Press, pp. 16–28.

Branson, W. (2001), 'Intermediate exchange rate regimes for groups of developing countries', in J. Braga de Macedo, D. Cohen and H. Reisen (2001a), pp. 55–76.

Branson, W. and J. Braga de Macedo (1995), 'Macroeconomic policy in Central Europe', CEPR Discussion Paper No. 1195, August.

Branson, W., J. Braga de Macedo and J. von Hagen (2001), 'Macroeconomic policies and institutions during the transition to European Union membership', in Ronald MacDonald and Rod Cross (eds) *Central Europe towards Monetary Union: Macroeconomic Underpinnings and Financial Reputation*, Boston: Kluwer Academic Publishers, pp. 5–30 .

Buiter, W. and A. C. Sibert (1997), 'Transition issues for the European Monetary Union', in *De EMU in Breed Perspectief; Preadviezen 1997, Koninklijke Vereniging voor de Staathuishoudkunde*, pp. 1–17. Uitgeverij LEMMA BV, Utrecht, 1997.

Buti, M., D. Franco and H. Ongena (1997), 'Budgetary policies during recessions: retrospective application of the "Stability and Growth Pact" to the post-war period', European Commission, DGII mimeo, Brussels.

Calvo, G. (2001), 'The case for hard pegs in the brave new world of global finance'. in J. Braga de Macedo, D. Cohen and H. Reisen (2001a).

Calvo, G. and E. Mendoza (1996), 'Petty crime and cruel punishment: lessons from the Mexican debacle', *The American Review*, papers and proceedings, May 1996, pp. 170–85.

Calvo, G. and C. Reinhart (2000), 'Fear of floating', *Quarterly Journal of Economics*, **117** (2), pp. 379–408.

Carré, H. (2002), 'Economic governance in EMU', paper presented at the Euro 50 Group meeting held in Paris on 27 November 2002.

Dewatripont, M., F. Giavazzi, J. von Hagen, I. Harden, T. Persson, G. Roland, A. Sapir and G. Tabellini (1996), 'Flexible integration, towards a more effective and democratic Europe', *Monitoring European Integration*, **6**, London: CEPR.

Dornbusch, R. (2001), 'Fewer monies, better monies', NBER Working Paper No. 8324, available at: http://www.nber.org/papers.

Dornbusch, R. (2002), 'A primer on emerging-market crises', in E. Edwards and J. Frankel (eds), *Preventing Currency Crises in Emerging Markets*, Chicago University Press for NBER, pp. 743–54.

Dornbusch, R. and S. Fischer (1991), 'Moderate inflation', NBER Working Paper No. 3896, November.

Edwards, S. (2000), 'Exchange rate systems in emerging economies', mimeo. UCLA.

Eichengreen, B., M. Mussa et al. (1998), 'Capital account liberalization: theoretical and practical aspects', IMF Occasional Paper No. 172.

EC (1990), 'One market, one money: an evaluation of the benefits and costs of forming an economic and monetary union', *European Economy*, **44**, October.

Fidrmuc, J. (2002), 'Strategic aspects of exchange rate regime choice for the accession countries', unpublished, ECARES, Université Libre de Bruxelles.

Fischer, S. (2001), 'Exchange rate regimes: is the bipolar view correct?', www.imf.org.

Flood, R. and P. Garber (1984), 'Collapsing exchange-rate regimes: some linear examples', *Journal of International Economics*, **17**, pp. 1–13.

Frankel, J. A. (1999), 'No single currency regime is right for all countries or at all times', NBER Working Paper No. 7338, September.

Frankel, J., S. Schmukler and L. Serven (2001), 'Verifying exchange rate regimes', *Journal of Development Economics*, **66** (2), pp. 351–86.

Grandes, M. and H. Reisen (2003), 'Exchange rate regimes and macroeconomic performance: revisiting three major Latin-American experiences', mimeo (Ford Foundation/ECLAC).

Granville, Brigitte (2001), 'Exchange rates in transition', in J. Braga de Macedo, D. Cohen and H. Reisen (2001a), pp. 85–93.

Halpern, L. and C. Wyplosz (1995), 'Equilibrium exchange rates in transition', CEPR Working Paper No. 1145.

Hausmann, Ricardo (2000), 'Exchange rate arrangements for the new architecture'. in R. Hausmann and U. Hiemenz (eds), *Global Finance from a Latin American Viewpoint*, Paris: OECD Development Centre.

Joumard, I. and H. Reisen (1992), 'Real exchange rate overshooting and persistent trade effects: the case of New Zealand', *The World Economy*, **15** (3), pp. 375–88.

Kölliker, Alkuin (2001), 'Bringing together or driving apart the union? Towards a theory of differentiated integration', *West European Politics*, **24** (4) (October), pp.125–51.

Krugman, P. (1979), 'A model of balance-of-payments crises', *Journal of Money, Credit and Banking*, **11**, pp. 311–25.

Larraín, F. and A. Velasco (2001), 'Exchange rate policy in emerging markets: the case for floating', unpublished.

Luxton, P. (2003), 'Wechselkurse der Beitrittskandidaten bereiten Sorge', www.faznet.de, 30.1.2003.

McKinnon, R. and H. Pill (1996), 'Credible liberalizations and international capital flows: the overborrowing syndrome', in T. Ito and A. Krueger (eds), *Financial Regulation and Integration in East Asia*, Chicago: University of Chicago Press.

Mundell, R. A. (1962), 'The appropriate use of monetary and fiscal policy under fixed exchange rates', *IMF Staff Papers*, **9**, pp. 70–77.

Oblath, G. (1998), 'Capital inflows to Hungary and the accompanying policy responses', *Empirica*, **25** (2), pp. 183–216.

Obstfeld, M. (1994), 'The logic of currency crises', *Cahiers Economiques et Monétaires*, Banque de France, **43**, pp. 189–213.

OECD (2002), *OECD Economic Outlook*, Vol. 72, December.

Persaud, A. and M. Metcalfe (2002), 'Is it really stupid? The markets perspective on the Stability & Growth Pact and prospects for its reform', paper presented at the Euro 50 Group meeting held in Paris on 27 November 2002.

Polak, J. (1957), 'Monetary analysis of income formation and payments problems', *IMF Staff Papers*, **6** (4), pp. 1–50.
Reisen, Helmut (1993a), 'Integration with disinflation: which way?', in Richard O'Brien (ed.), *Finance and the International Economy*, **7**, The Amex Bank Review Prize Essays in memory of Robert Marjolin, Oxford University Press.
Reisen, Helmut (1993b), 'South-East Asia and the impossible trinity', *International Economic Insights*, Institute for International Economics, Washington, D.C., May/June.
Reisen, H. (1998), 'Sustainable and excessive current account deficits', *Empirica*, **25** (2), pp. 111–31.
Reisen, H. (2002), 'Prospects for emerging market flows amid investor concerns about corporate governance', OECD Development Centre Technical Paper No. 201, November.
Reisen, H. and A. van Trotsenburg (1988), 'Should the Asian NICs peg to the yen?', *Intereconomics*, July/August, pp. 172–7.
Rodrik, Dani and Andres Velasco (1999), 'Short-term capital flows', NBER Working Paper No. 7364, September.
Sarno, L. and M. Taylor (1999), 'Hot money, accounting labels and the permanence of capital flows to developing countries: an empirical investigation', *Journal of Development Economics*, **59** (2).
Schmidt-Hebbel, K. (2000), 'Chile's peso: better than (just) living with the dollar?', *Cuadernos de Economia*, **37** (110), pp. 177–226.
Thygesen, N. (2002), 'The stability and growth pact: any need for revision?', paper presented at the Euro 50 Group meeting held in Paris on 27 November 2002.
Williamson, John (1996), *The Crawling Band as an Exchange Rate Regime: Lessons from Chile, Colombia and Israel*, Institute for International Economics, Washington, D.C.
Williamson, John (2000), *Exchange-Rate Regimes for Emerging Markets: Reviving the Intermediate Option*, Institute for International Economics, Washington, D.C.
Wyplosz, C. (2002), 'The Stability Pact meets its fate', paper presented at the Euro 50 Group meeting held in Paris on 27 November 2002.

COMMENTS

Jürgen Stark

We should congratulate the authors on an extremely helpful and useful contribution to this discussion. They have done an impressive job of showing what problems the so-called impossible trinity, or the trilemma as it is also called in the chapter, could create for EU accession countries. These countries are increasingly coming under the focus of global investors' convergence plays. This is just one reason why a balance must be struck between monetary independence and exchange rate stability. Every country must itself weigh up the trade-off between greater sovereignty in economic policy under more flexible exchange rates and 'tying one's hand' owing to fixed rates. In this connection it is worth looking back to the currency crises in the 1990s. The authors claim that massive net capital inflows were the main culprit. They also state that the combination of exchange rate pegs and open capital accounts has proved to be particularly crisis-prone.

My comment on this is that intermediate regimes have justly earned their bad reputation owing to regional currency crises. Greater capital market integration makes the requirements for sustaining such regimes very demanding. I have personally never agreed with the oft-cited conventional wisdom that in a world of intense capital mobility only the corner regimes as referred to by Jürgen von Hagen — firm fixing or free floating — can survive. I have two arguments against it. First, firm fixing is a very demanding option as has been demonstrated by the Argentine example and demonstrated here by Helmut Reisen. Second, free floating is the opposite extreme. All accession countries are small and open economies, and for small countries which are closely integrated in world trade and international capital movements, this regime is often simply not a realistic option. This leaves us again with regimes inside the corners. However, it must not be forgotten that, in a vicious circle, any perception of an exchange rate guarantee encourages unhedged external borrowing. Therefore, intermediate regimes would have to be designed in such a way that they minimize the risk of excessive capital inflows and ensuing boom and bust cycles. Many countries have already figured this out. The trend towards greater exchange rate flexibility in economies with largely liberalized capital movements is desirable in my view. What I have just said applies as much to unilateral pegs as it does to multilateral arrangements. In the European integration process, the full liberalization of capital movements within the European Union in the early 1990s made it more difficult to achieve exchange rate stability. Monetary and, to a large extent, fiscal policy had to be subordinated to the objective of fixed exchange rate. The ERM crisis of the early 1990s opened the eyes of all participants to the fact that, in a world of highly mobile capital, exchange rate stability presupposes real and nominal convergence.

Let me now turn my attention to two aspects of the European integration process. First, the authors are of the view that the so-called 'flexible integration' tool created by the Treaty of Nice can, by means of 'reinforced cooperation', facilitate convergence and cohesiveness in an enlarged EU. Let me say that this may be the case in theory. In practice, however, such considerations are currently irrelevant to acceding countries, which must first meet certain minimum requirements. Second, the introduction of the euro has led to more convergence and cohesiveness thanks to what is called in the chapter the 'new politics of credibility'. However, what we see today is that the economic disparity or economic divergence between the euro-area countries seems to be increasing once more. The introduction of the euro in my view contains no automatic integration process, although I must admit it may be premature to make such an assessment already, because we started stage three of monetary union only four years ago. Participants must be willing to change their behaviour. I have to say that particularly in wage negotiations and also in fiscal policy, I do not see a real change in behaviour. There was a commitment to the Stability and Growth Pact, which is now undermined in its credibility by the behaviour in particular of the larger economies in the euro area. I think some lessons have to be drawn from this experience. There exists a danger that the will of the acceding countries to reform will soon slacken, as we see already in the euro area where there seems to be an adjustment fatigue after the introduction of the euro. My personal conclusion is that key adjustments be made prior to entry into the Eurosystem.

However, indications are that nine of the ten upcoming EU entrants intend to adopt the euro as soon as possible. All of these countries see participation in the ERM merely as a chore to be performed as quickly as possible. In my view they are overlooking an important point. The ERM gives each country an opportunity to test its ability to deal with the realities of monetary union. The mechanism still offers opportunities to make the necessary exchange rate adjustments. The accession countries should not underestimate the advantages of flexible exchange rates. Let me mention here three points. The first point is that only flexible rates offer a certain protection from speculative capital inflows from the outset. This is one of the key lessons to be learned from the emerging markets' experience. By 2002, the net capital inflows to the twelve accession countries had increased to 7% of GDP. As of late, foreign direct investment accounted for 70% of these inflows on average. However, for some time already, more volatile flows have been apparent. If not corrected in time, high current account imbalances and less reliable capital flows might create an enormous risk potential. Second, without the exchange rate as a tool in the catching-up process and as a correction mechanism for external imbalances and shocks, the donkey work has to be done by flexible labour and goods markets and domestic prices. If an exchange rate target is given priority in the absence of such support, the nominal and real convergence process, and thus the basis for fixed exchange rates, will be jeopardized sooner or later. Third, the protracted nature of the catching-up process and, in some of the accession countries, sizeable internal and external deficits will render it especially difficult to set the right conversion rates for the euro. These points also argue in favour of having such countries join ERM-II at a later date and/or for longer than two years. We must be aware of the fact that once the euro has been introduced the conversion rates can no longer be corrected. This will be the final step.

It is especially the larger accession countries that do not appear economically ready to surrender the exchange rate instrument. I am not going to involve myself in the domestic affairs of Hungary, but in the chapter of Braga de Macedo and Helmut Reisen, the Hungarian example is mentioned and in my view this example shows what problems a country can manoeuvre itself into by pegging its exchange rate without the necessary support. The dilemma becomes clearly apparent wherever monetary policy is not underpinned by fiscal discipline and wage moderation, which is precisely the case in this country. Interest rate cuts jeopardize the progress made in stability. However, high interest rates would attract even greater inflows of capital from abroad and increase upward pressure on the currency.

My conclusion is that every accession country should integrate into Europe in a manner in keeping with its circumstances, something also mentioned by Issing in Chapter 2. It is up to each new EU member state to decide when it wants to join ERM. The ERM-II Resolution has no provisions prohibiting a country from joining the mechanism immediately after obtaining EU membership. A common accord is needed only on the central rate (and on the width of the fluctuation band). As things now stand, the future EU member states will seek to keep their exchange rates close to the central rates. But, as mentioned earlier, a de facto exchange rate guarantee or an extremely early fixing of the central rate increases the risk of speculative capital movements even in multilateral pegs such as the ERM. This was one of the lessons of the 1992–93 ERM-I crisis. It is therefore in the accession countries' own best interest for market participants to construe this system as a very flexible fixed-rate regime. This argues in favour of choosing the standard band rate of ±15%. In addition, the central rate should be quickly adjusted and not be politicized as was discussed this morning. All ERM-II members or participants including the ECB could initiate such adjustments in ERM-II.

6. Portugal and the EMU: 1996–2001, the crucial years

Luís Campos e Cunha and Patrícia Silva*

1 INTRODUCTION

Portugal is often seen as a successful case of integration in the European Union (EU). The Portuguese themselves tend to be more reluctant to take that view, and have a more critical perspective of the overall process. This chapter examines that process with a critical eye and with a special emphasis on the six-year period from 1996 to 2001, the crucial years of participation in the Economic and Monetary Union.

The chapter is organized as follows. In Section 2, the road to EU integration is put into perspective. In Section 3, we look at the policy and political options that led up to the single currency. Most of these facts are well known to some, but could be of some relevance to many others less acquainted with the integration process. In Section 4, we describe the period of the preparation for the country's participation in the launch of the euro. Not only are the economic criteria under review, but the domestic political backing is also stressed. In the following sections the new economic regime created with the monetary union is analysed (Section 5), as well as its immediate consequences for the behaviour of the Portuguese economy. Special emphasis is placed on the behaviour of traditional critical variables: current account, inflation and the role of fiscal policy (Section 6). In Section 7, some final remarks are made concerning what remains to be looked at and the major challenges that will come in an enlarged European Union.

2 RECENT PAST

In 1978, Portugal initiated the formal negotiations concerning the accession to the European Community and, together with Spain, in 1986 it joined the European Community as a member state. From the start of this integration process, Portugal undertook major structural reforms aimed at increasing the role of the private sector in the economy, ensuring a growth rate above the

European Union average and giving consistency to its macroeconomic policies.

In the late 1970s, the economic activity in Portugal was subject to administrative regulations. Several sectors operated under price controls and the major firms were under direct State control. In the financial sector, entry of firms in the banking and insurance market was highly restricted, the amount of credit offered was subject to legal ceilings, and interest rates on deposits and credits were controlled by the government, with limited independence afforded by the Central Bank. In addition, international capital movements were restricted.

Structural reforms aimed at reducing the weight of the State in the economy and promoting competition first started in the financial sector in the mid-1980s. After 1984, legal barriers to entry in the banking and insurance sectors were relaxed and some private companies were allowed to enter the market. However, freedom of entry, provision of services and expansion of the number of branches in the banking sector were established only by the end of 1992, with the adoption of the Second Banking Directive. The total number of banks in Portugal has increased significantly over the last 15 years, having passed from around 20 institutions in the mid-1980s to slightly above 60 in 2000. However, it should be noted that since the early 1990s the financial sector has experienced a period of restructuring with mergers and acquisitions, which mitigated somewhat the effects of entry of new banks.

The privatization of public financial institutions started in 1989 and, by 1996, most public banks and insurance companies had been privatized, significantly changing the market share of public banks, which declined from close to 100 per cent in 1984 to below 30 per cent in 1997 (see Figure 6.1). However, despite the liberalization process, the market share of the five largest financial groups remained largely unchanged and the share of non-domestic banks remained relatively low.

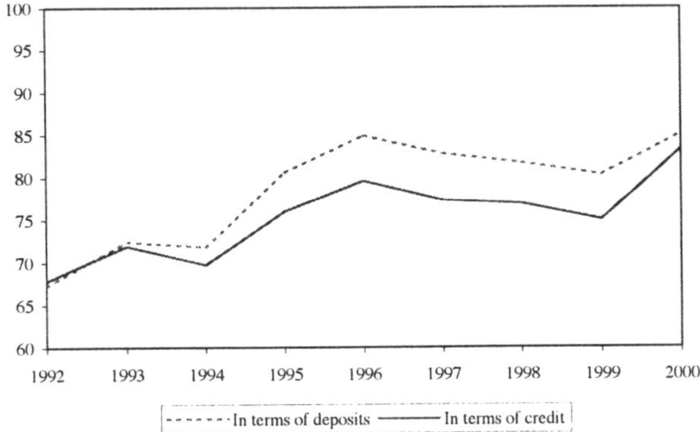

Source: Banco de Portugal.

Figure 6.1 Market share of the five largest banking groups

Within the context of preparation for the Single Market, credit ceilings were eliminated and, in mid-1992, floor limits on interest rates on deposits were removed. Interest rates on lending had already been liberalized in 1988 and 1989. Controls on capital movements were entirely removed before the end of 1992. The privatization process, the increase of the number of banks and the removal of barriers to entry and other regulations led to an increased contestability in financial markets, resulting in a sharp decline of the differential between the average interest rate on lending and borrowing (see Figure 6.2).

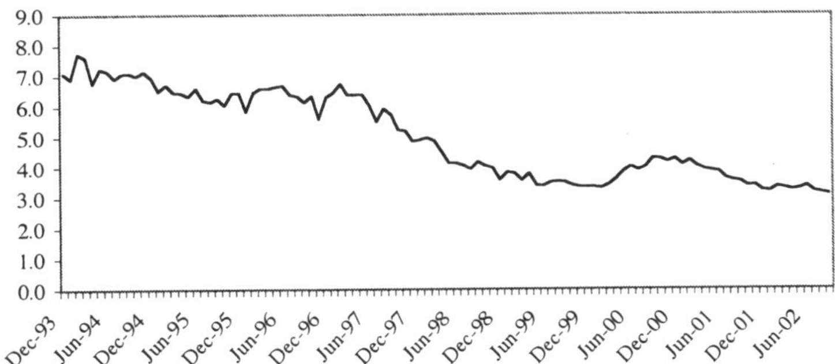

Source: Banco de Portugal.

Figure 6.2 Average lending and borrowing interest rate differential

Privatization of state-owned companies in sectors other than banking and insurance took place for the most part after 1994, along with a process of liberalization. The telecommunications and postal services were reorganized, a regulating institute was created to monitor competitiveness, and new companies were allowed into the market of mobile and fixed-line communications. Competition was also enhanced in the sectors of energy and air transportation.

International capital mobility and the privatization programme stimulated the development of capital markets. According to Carvalho (1999), there is evidence that the privatization process gave some impetus to the Portuguese stock exchange, but at the same time the capacity and innovation of the stock exchange were important factors in the success of the privatization process in Portugal. In fact, some of the State-owned companies that were privatized have been among the ten companies making the highest contribution to the stock market capitalization, accounting for more than 50 per cent of the turnover. The retail sector also went through a major increase in competition and restructuring. Starting as one of the most fragmented in the EU, it went through a sharp increase in concentration. Legislation concerning the creation of new firms was simplified, bankruptcy requirements became less stringent and monitoring of anti-competitive behaviour was strengthened.

To sum up, by the end of 1995, the Portuguese economy had changed substantially when compared to the early 1980s: it had undergone a process of liberalization and reform that rendered it more competitive and efficient and increased the role of the private sector in the economy, preparing the country for the challenge of adopting a single European currency.

3 POLICY OPTIONS BEFORE MAASTRICHT

By the time Portugal became a member of the European Community, the Current Account (CA) of the balance of payments recorded a positive balance, following the IMF programme of 1983. However, since the inflation rate remained high, reducing inflation became the main policy objective in the mid-1980s. During the second half of the decade, the programmed rate of devaluation under the crawling-peg policy[1] was lowered, which helped to reduce the inflation rate. By mid-1988, the inflation rate had decreased by more than 20 percentage points in less than four years. However, at the end of 1988, inflation accelerated again, and this, together with the lower crawling rate, led to a sizeable real appreciation (see Figure 6.3), which peaked during 1992. This took the authorities by surprise and there was no clear strategy in terms of economic policy to cope with the situation.

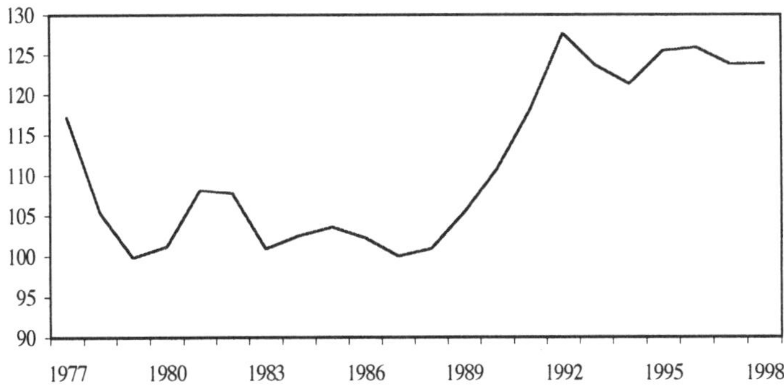

Source: Banco de Portugal.

Figure 6.3 Real effective exchange rate

At the same time, there was some erosion regarding fiscal consolidation. After posting excellent results in 1989, when the general government deficit reached 2.3 per cent of GDP, the deficit increased to more than 5 per cent of GDP in 1990 and 1991 due to expenditure overruns (see Figure 6.4). From both the inflation and fiscal points of view this was a puzzling situation.

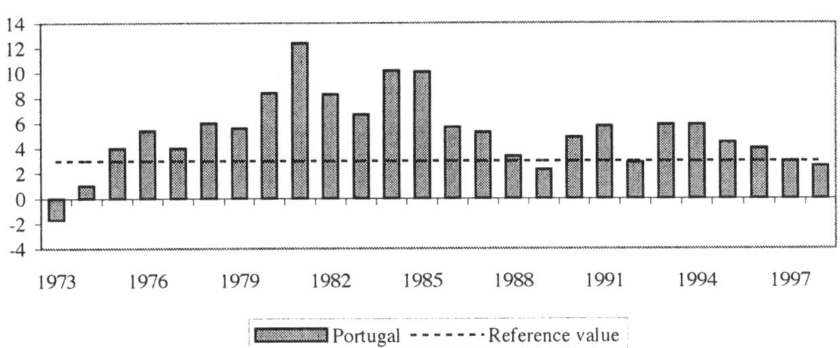

Note: (1) ESA 95 as from 1995.

Source: European Commission.

Figure 6.4 General government deficit[(1)] (percentage of GDP)

In fact, by the end of the 1980s, Portugal was facing the so-called *impossible trinity*: the impossibility of simultaneously having free capital movements, an exchange rate objective and an autonomous monetary policy.

Faced with this dilemma, the Portuguese authorities, reversing the trend and against all odds, temporarily reintroduced (until the end of 1992) some of the capital controls that had previously been removed.

Regarding the exchange rate policy, the crawling-peg regime was officially abandoned in 1990 and was replaced by an exchange rate rule of ill-defined limited fluctuation bands relative to the major five currencies of the Exchange Rate Mechanism of the European Monetary System (ERM/EMS).[2] It was a period of great uncertainty about the policy strategy of the *Banco de Portugal* and about the fiscal policy to be pursued. Policy options were clarified only after the elections at the end of 1991, when a tight fiscal policy was announced for 1992 and the Portuguese currency — the escudo — became part of the ERM/EMS in April 1992.[3] Joining the ERM/EMS greatly helped in lowering the inflation rate, since it represented a firm commitment from the Portuguese authorities to keep a stable exchange rate against the German currency, which traditionally enjoyed lower inflation rates. However, as mentioned before, the real exchange rate was too high at the time, but the realignments in December 1992 and May 1993 were able to cope with that situation.[4] Thereafter, exchange rate stability was pursued as the intermediate objective of monetary policy, the final objective of which was to reduce the inflation rate. This was the first time since the mid-1980s that a coherent exchange rate policy had been set up. This policy strategy was followed until the adoption of the euro. The exchange rate and fiscal policies became entirely focused on fulfilling the Maastricht criteria, which would allow Portugal to join the group of countries that adopted the single European currency right from the start of the monetary union in 1999.

4 POLICY OPTIONS TOWARDS THE EURO

4.1 Some Political Conditions

Joining a monetary union has enormous economic consequences but in the end it is a political decision deeply rooted in the sovereignty of a State. Therefore, a strong political commitment is necessary in order to embrace the euro as a supra-national currency. In the Portuguese case, the political support was solid and the European integration process was never seriously questioned. This political support was de facto a crucial precondition for success.[5]

The Portuguese party system is comprised of four principal parties. However, two of these — the *Partido Socialista* (PS) and the *Partido Social Democrata* (PSD)[6] — both of which have strong ties to other European political families — have dominated the political arena for the past three decades, trading the reins of government back and forth between themselves.[7] Together, in the last four parliamentary elections, the PS and PSD have won more than 75 per cent of the vote[8] and both were very supportive of the single currency project. This solid support has been crucial for the progress achieved in the European context, first in the preparations for the Single Market, and later in the efforts to meet the Maastricht criteria, which people outside Portugal considered to be an impossible task for the country to achieve, at least until very late in 1997.[9]

4.2 Fulfilling the Criteria: 1996–98

After the escudo joined the ERM/EMS in April 1992, the central parity of the Portuguese currency was realigned, first, in the context of the strong turbulence that hit the system at the end of 1992 and 1993, and then for maintaining competitiveness following the devaluation of the peseta in the wake of the Mexican crisis in 1995 (see Figure 6.5). After this realignment, the escudo remained very stable.

As the start of the monetary union was nearing, the market's belief that Portugal would be in the first group of countries to adopt the euro increased, which can be judged from the continued fall in the daily volatility of the exchange rate (see Figure 6.6). By the time of the assessment by the European Commission of Portugal's performance in relation to the convergence criteria, the escudo had remained for more than two years in the ERM with a largely stable exchange rate and without any devaluation in its central parity, thus fulfilling the Maastricht criteria for the exchange rate.

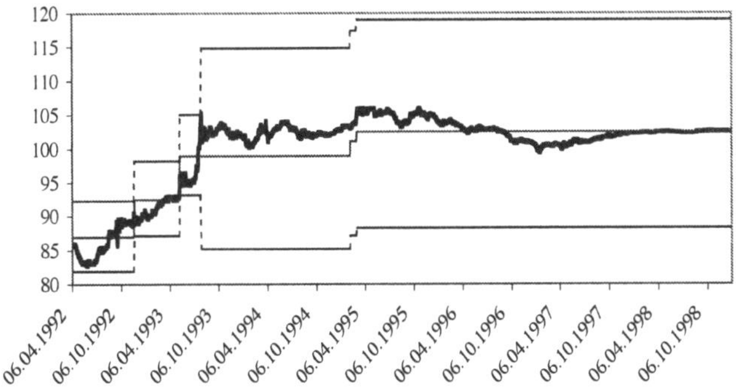

Source: Banco de Portugal.

Figure 6.5 PTE/DEM exchange rate

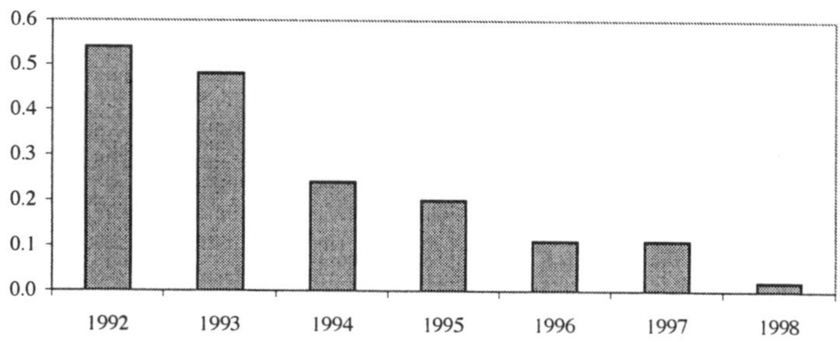

Source: Banco de Portugal.

Figure 6.6 Exchange rate volatility (standard deviation of daily changes)

The successful participation in the ERM/EMS not only contributed to lowering the inflation rate, but also increased the market's belief that Portugal would soon participate in the Monetary Union. This gave rise to the so-called 'convergence plays'. Against the background of the upcoming creation of a Monetary Union, the countries with the highest interest rates recorded a decline in the interest rate differential relative to other member states (see Figure 6.7). At the same time, progress in nominal convergence strengthened the market's belief that Portugal would participate in the Monetary Union in the first wave of entry. The expectation of entry and nominal convergence mutually reinforced each other, speeding up the pace of convergence itself. It should be stressed that market expectations are led by and start in the domestic market. In other words, convergence plays are always rooted in firm commitments and consistent actions taken by domestic authorities at all levels of government.

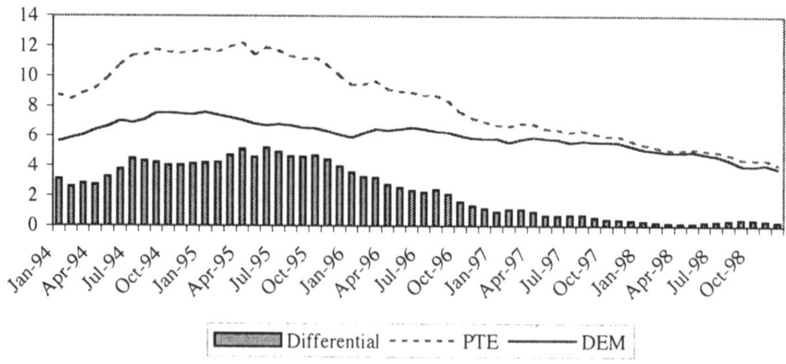

Source: Reuters.

Figure 6.7 Ten-year interest rate differential relative to Germany

Price stability was formally introduced into the statutes of the Portuguese central bank as its primary objective in 1995. In the 12-month period that ended in January 1998 — the reference date for the March 1998 assessment of the convergence process — the average inflation rate in Portugal was 1.8 per cent, below the average inflation rate of the three best-performing countries plus 1.5 percentage points, which was the reference value established in the Maastricht criteria (see Figure 6.8).[10] In addition, the long-run (ten-year) interest rate amounted to 6.2 per cent in January 1998, below the reference value of 7.8 per cent computed as the average of the interest rates of the three best-performing countries in terms of inflation plus 2 percentage points.

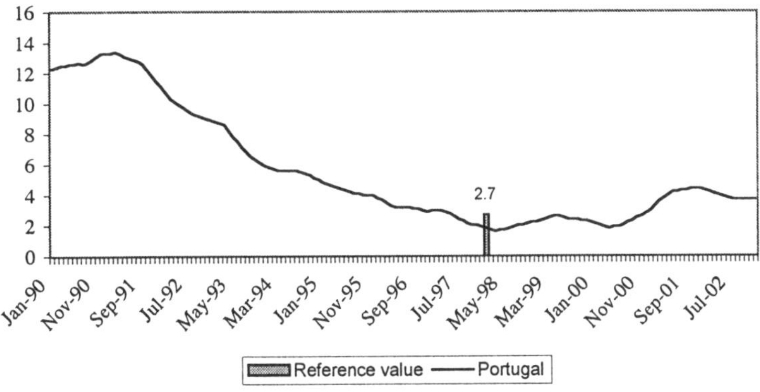

Source: European Commission.

Figure 6.8 Inflation rate (HCPI)

Fulfilling the Maastricht criteria for the general government deficit and gross consolidated debt called for important changes in policy. The public deficit widened after 1990, but it resumed a downward path in 1995. The improvement of the general government balance was achieved through lower interest payments as a result of the fall in the interest rates, and higher revenues (see Figure 6.9). As a percentage of GDP, the public deficit ratio fell by 1.9 percentage points between 1995 and 1998, aided by a fall in interest payments of 2.8 percentage points of GDP and an increase in revenue of 1.0 percentage point of GDP.

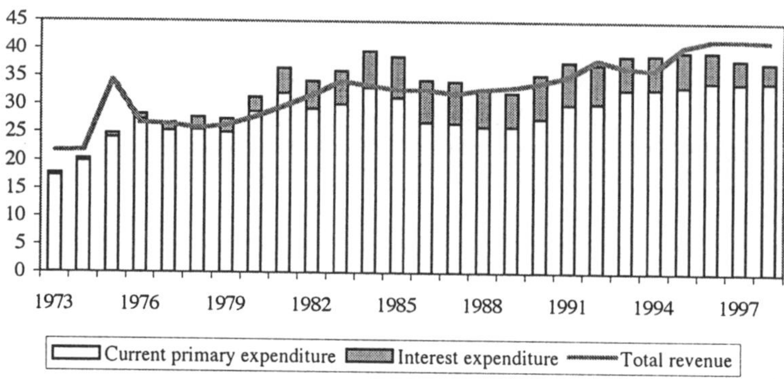

Note: (1) ESA 95 as from 1995.

Source: European Commission.

Figure 6.9 Current primary expenditure, interest expenditure and total revenue[1] *(percentage of GDP)*

By the time Portugal joined the European Community in 1986, the ratio of gross consolidated debt to GDP had risen significantly compared to the early 1970s, reaching 66.8 per cent. In 1995, it still amounted to 64.3 per cent. Thereafter, the debt ratio continued on a downward trend, as a result of the reduction of fiscal deficit and the use of part of the privatization receipts to make debt repayments. In 1997, the general government deficit stood below the reference value of 3 per cent of GDP and the public debt ratio was lower than the reference value of 60 per cent of GDP.

5 A STRUCTURAL CHANGE OF REGIME: 1999 ONWARDS

The creation of a Monetary Union brought on a change in the economic regime of the member states that participated in the eurozone. This new economic regime (NER) initiated in 1999 contrasts with the old one in three main respects: a change of rules for economic governance; a loosening up of liquidity constraints at the agent level; and a fundamental change in the nature of the external constraint of the country. These three elements are interrelated, but for ease of exposition we treat them separately. One should note that these three aspects might not be present in all countries. For instance, the change in liquidity constraints was certainly different for a resident of Germany when compared to a Portuguese or an Irish resident, since Germany was a large country and the Deutsche Mark was the anchor currency. Whatever the case may be, most of these changes were seen either as irreversible, as in the case of the adoption of the euro, or as long-lasting due to its *constitutional* nature, as is the case with the Stability and Growth Pact (SGP). Since this can be regarded as an extreme example of a Lucas change of regime, it could be better labelled as a *structural* change of regime.

Let us look at the above-mentioned three aspects of regime change. First, the NER is characterized by a new set of rules that guide economic policies. Monetary and exchange rate policies are defined by the European Central Bank (ECB), which is committed to ensure price stability in the eurozone. Not only is the ECB independent of governments, it is also the first truly supra-national institution in the EU. In contrast, the fiscal policy is pursued by each member state, but according to the SGP, it should aim at achieving a general government position close to balance or in surplus in the medium run. In this way, the automatic stabilizers built into the budget can fully operate without breaching, in an economic downturn, the reference value of 3 per cent of GDP for the general government deficit and hence without compromising fiscal sustainability.[11] These rules are subject to specified procedures and international monitoring and countries breaching the limit may be subject to pecuniary sanctions. Together, price stability and fiscal sustainability are seen as creating a stable macroeconomic environment that is considered as a necessary condition for sustainable growth and development. This institutional framework of the NER is seen as irrevocable or long-lasting.

Second, consumers and firms saw the regime change as loosening their liquidity constraints. Due to the increasing credibility of the Portuguese participation in the EMU from day one, both nominal and real interest rates fell rapidly to the EU average (as seen in Figure 6.7). The spreads were substantially reduced and have stayed that way ever since. The strong impact in terms of the liquidity constraints was amplified by the financial innovation that took place at the same time. As banks were privatized, the sector was open to international competition and new financial instruments became widely available.

Third, the NER changed the nature of the external constraint for Portugal. Prior to the single currency, any external imbalance was assessed by markets against the existing level of external debt of the country and the level of foreign exchange reserves at the central bank. After the entry into the monetary union, consumers earn their income in euros, firms' cash flows are in euros and the State's fiscal operations are carried out in euros, the very same currency that those agents are borrowing or lending in the domestic and foreign markets.[12] Before the monetary union, an international lender would be concerned not only with the credit risk of the debtor agent, but also with the solvency of the country in terms of international reserves. Under the

NER, the investor's assessment is reduced to the credit risk of the debtor agent.[13] In other words, the external constraint is nothing but the aggregation of the intertemporal budget constraint of each individual agent — families, firms and State — without an overall external liquidity constraint to be faced by the country.

6 CONSEQUENCES: 1999 ONWARDS

6.1 Market Driven Indebtness and Investment

The new characteristics of the NER led the economy to work differently with the new set of rules. However, the economic results for the period from 1999 to 2001 stemmed not only from the new medium-term steady-state path implied by the NER, but also from the transition path *towards* that steady state. Furthermore, since several of the consequences of the NER started to become noticeable before 1999, agents anticipated the change in the macroeconomic framework.

The macroeconomic effects of the regime change and the adoption of the single currency are mainly due to the reduction of the interest rates and may be divided into supply-side and demand-side effects. The supply-side effects are related to the reduction of the real interest rates. Despite the fall of the inflation rate in the euro area, the convergence process resulted in lower real interest rates (see Figure 6.10) that led to a reduction in the rental cost of capital and, therefore, to a higher accumulation of capital that in turn increased both labour productivity and the real GDP per capita. Pereira (1999) estimates that the reduction of the long-run interest rate associated with the adoption of the euro will increase the long-run Portuguese GDP per capita between 2.9 per cent and 13.6 per cent, when compared to what would have been the evolution of the Portuguese economy if neither the NER nor the euro had been adopted. Pereira (1999) also finds that the estimated past impact on GDP of the structural transfers from the EU budget is close to the lower bound for the future effects associated with the participation of Portugal in the euro area, thus stressing the high relative importance of the Monetary Union for Portugal.[14]

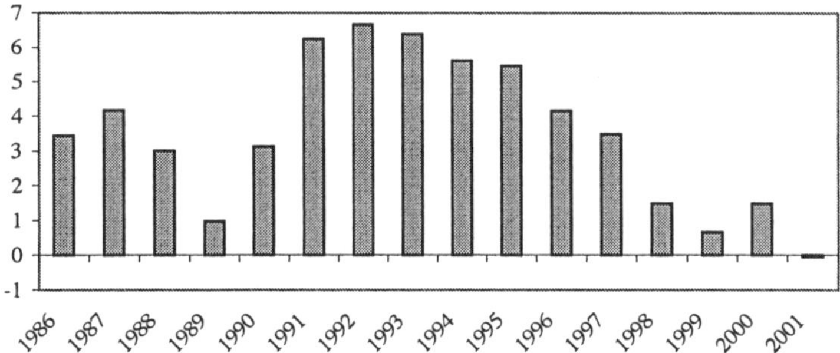

Sources: European Commission and National Statistical Institute.

Figure 6.10 Real interest rate

It turned out that the growth rate for the Portuguese economy was always above the EU average by more than 1 percentage point during 1996–2001. This might suggest the importance of Monetary Union for Portugal, but it is too early to estimate the lasting economic impact of the adoption of the euro. As to the demand-side effects, the decrease of nominal interest rates relaxed the liquidity constraints faced by households and firms, since it reduced the weight of the debt service. More importantly, the decrease of the real interest rates also created a sudden positive wealth effect for households. For a given time path of real earnings, the decrease in the real interest rates led to a higher present value of future incomes. Namely, the market value of human wealth increased significantly: people felt richer and they were richer. The market value of the wealth of firms also rose. Consequently, the banking sector regarded the optimal level of indebtedness to wealth as too low, for both firms as well as households.[15]

As a result, total credit to households and firms saw a strong rise for several years (see Figure 6.11), reflecting the adjustment in the levels of credit. Total credit to households (as a per cent of disposable income) and to non-financial firms (as a per cent of GDP) increased from 46.4 and 53.7 per cent in 1996 to 103.7 and 92.1 per cent in 2002 respectively. As a result of the increase in credit, the solvency of households has been questioned by some. However, the interest rate service of the debt has remained basically unchanged throughout the period (see Figure 6.12). Furthermore, since the credit was mainly used for investment in housing (see Figure 6.13) the net value of households' balance sheets has remained by and large unchanged. Thus, household solvency should not be a major source of concern, even though families are more vulnerable to shocks than otherwise, and in particular, to a sudden increase in unemployment rates.

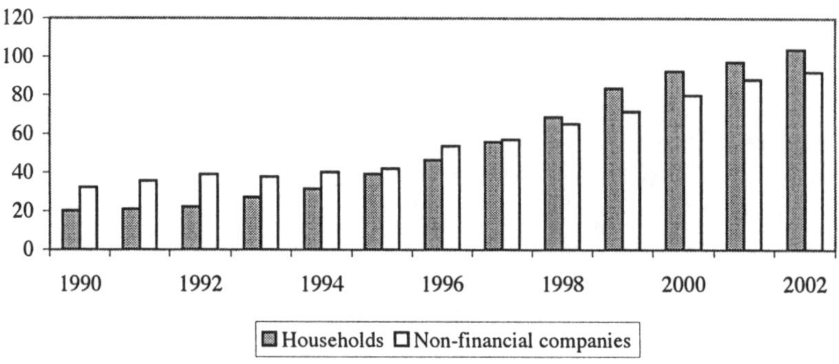

Note: (1) Up to 1994 credits from non-monetary institutions and from abroad are not included.

Source: Banco de Portugal.

Figure 6.11 Credit to households and non-financial companies[1] *(percentage of households' disposable income and of GDP respectively)*

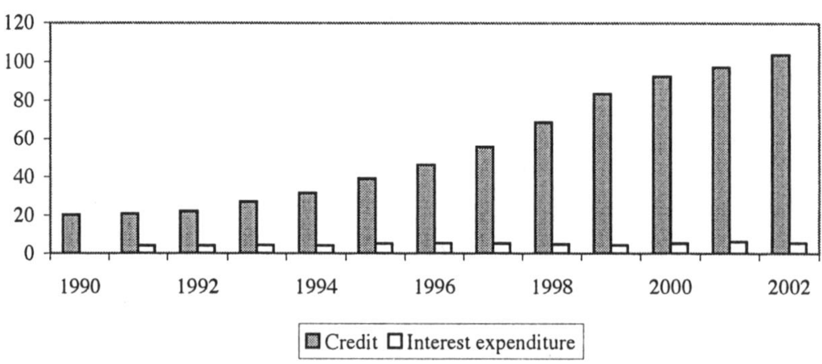

Note: (1) Up to 1994 credits from non-monetary institutions and from abroad are not included.

Source: Banco de Portugal.

Figure 6. 12 Credit to households and interest expenditure[1] *(percentage of households' disposable income)*

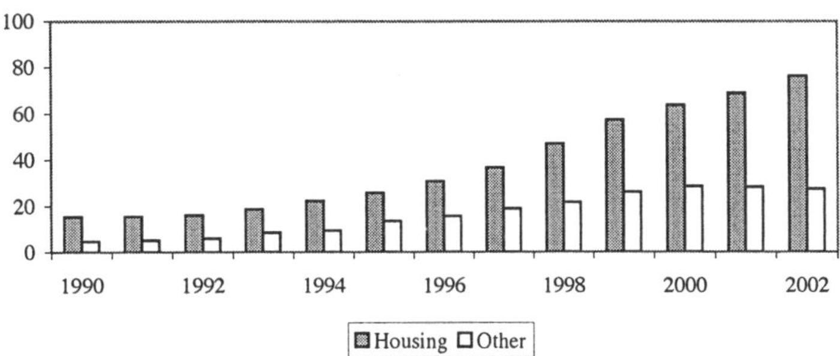

Note: (1) Up to 1994 credits from non-monetary institutions and from abroad are not included.

Source: Banco de Portugal.

Figure 6.13 Structure of credit to households[1] *(percentage of households' disposable income)*

In a segmented money market economy, such an increase in the demand for credit would have implied an increase in interest rates. However, in a small economy in a monetary union, the supply of credit is only limited by the creditworthiness of each agent. Hence, the increase in demand did not result in an increase in prices (i.e. interest rates): supply has actually been perfectly elastic for this period. As the domestic banking sector was able to intermediate this stock adjustment of households and to some extent of firms, the banking sector significantly increased its exposure to the euro money market in order to supply the credit demanded. Reflecting these developments, the external current account deficit widened by 7.0 percentage points of GDP between 1996 and 2001 (see Figure 6.14).

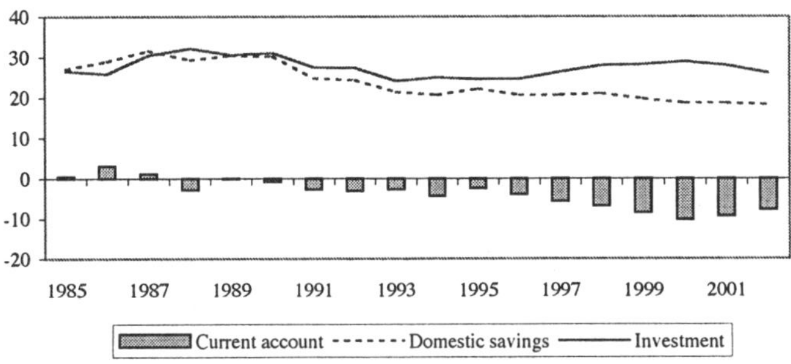

Source: Banco de Portugal.

Figure 6.14 Saving, investment and current account (percentage of GDP)

Simultaneously, there was an increase in foreign direct investment (FDI) outflows, since large Portuguese firms began to gain access to international financing and, without becoming short on hard currency, they were able to expand to new markets abroad. Portugal thus became a net foreign investor (see Figure 6.15), despite the simultaneous increase of FDI inflows to Portugal. This is an instance of the vanishing *original sin* of a more mature economy, as described in Hausmann (2002).[16] The maturity or currency mismatch was significantly reduced for a Portuguese investor. Furthermore, not only did the original sin vanish for small economies of the euro area, but also in these economies it became possible to separate households' and firms' decisions to borrow from decisions to invest in the NER. For those economies it meant the end of the Feldstein-Horioka Puzzle, as described in Blanchard and Giavazzi (2002) or Alesina et al. (2001).

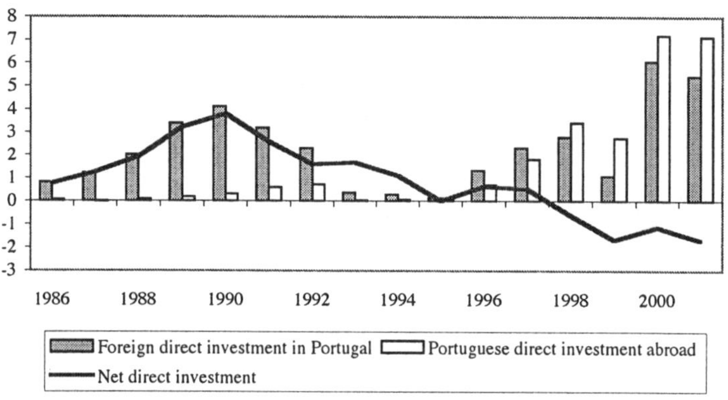

Source: Banco de Portugal.

Figure 6.15 Foreign direct investment flows (percentage of GDP)

6.2 Overheating?

An interesting question is whether the recent past in Portugal should be characterized as a case of overheating. We consider this to be so, but let us argue that many other transitory effects took place leading to a more complex situation than a traditional overheating problem. As mentioned above, the increase in investment, with a somewhat lower savings rate, led to a CA deficit, which is a sign of overheating for a region like Portugal. It could also be argued that a higher-than-EU-average inflation rate is another instance of that phenomenon. In fact, the Portuguese HICP inflation has been on average

1.2 percentage points above euro area inflation since 1999. Lastly, the fiscal policy since 1998 has been pro-cyclical as will be discussed later on.

However, against this view one should recognize that there has been no asset price bubble typical of overheating situations. Lower interest rates naturally contributed to a rise in nominal and real asset prices. Inasmuch as the decline in real interest rates is permanent and inherent to the NER, a real appreciation of assets is not surprising and should not be viewed as a sign of overheating. Furthermore, the stock market in Portugal did follow rather closely the evolution of other markets, leaving little room for any specifically domestic bubble (see Figure 6.16). Lastly, the real estate price index did increase more than the HCPI (see Figure 6.17), but rather moderately when compared with previous boom periods or with other countries for these years.

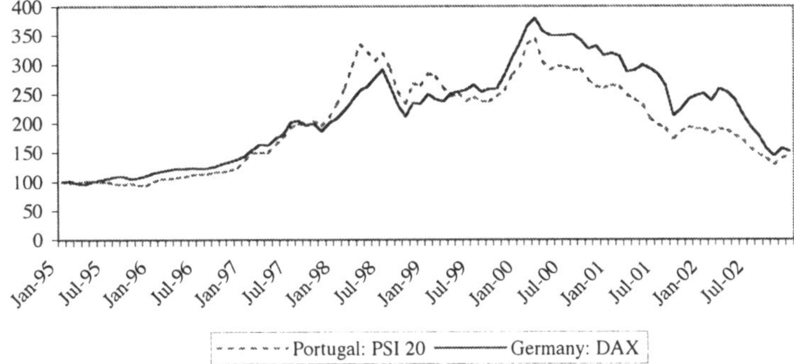

Source: Bloomberg Database.

Figure 6.16 Stock market index in Portugal and Germany

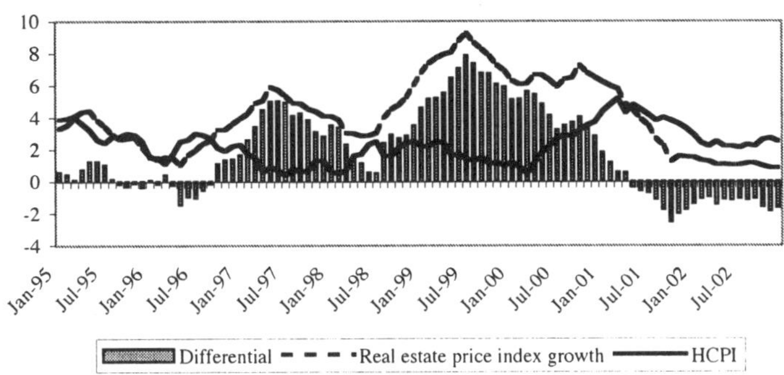

Sources: Confidencial Imobiliário and European Commission.

Figure 6.17 Real estate price index growth and HCPI

In short, there are signs of overheating for the period under consideration, but not all of the characteristic elements are there.[17] A second issue is related to the fact that most of the above signs of overheating are market-driven and not fundamentally related to expansionary public policies. It is an equilibrium response towards the new regime. As argued in Alesina et al. (2001), the CA deficit should not be a source of concern, and stopping it would amount to unduly closing an important source of financing for investment. In other words, the overheating, including the CA deficit, was fundamentally market-led, driven by the transition to the NER, and in that way the market would naturally self-correct the imbalances. Besides the widening of the CA, special attention should be given to inflation and to fiscal policy for a full assessment of the overheating problem for the period under consideration.

6.2.1 Inflation

For a long time the determinants of the inflationary process have been studied for the Portuguese case[18] and one could argue that (i) the traditional causes of inflation — namely, money and fiscal variables — are not present and, (ii) the simple version of Purchasing Power Parity (PPP) does not fit the facts for all periods, leaving room for some sort of Balassa-Samuelson effect.[19]

As shown in Cunha and Machado (1994), fiscal policies and monetary aggregates were not found to have a significant impact on inflation. Now in a monetary union it is even less likely that fiscal variables could lead to enduring impacts on domestic inflation. What seems plausible is for the Portuguese inflation rate to be anchored to the euro area average inflation plus some form of Balassa effect.

Regional inflation differences are to be expected, as in the case of the USA,[20] but no local policy explanation is to be found. These differences are *relative* (among regions) price differences, i.e. they are due to real causes. A Balassa technological explanation is one possible real cause, but other somewhat similar stories should not be precluded.[21] The simple fact that markets become more integrated due to less formal and informal barriers to trade, financial integration, vanishing exchange rate risk, better means of communication, etc. lessens price level differences; all in all, cheaper countries become more expensive and that implies prolonged periods of equilibrium real appreciation that cannot — and should not — be avoided by policy activism.[22]

In this vein, an alternative story is presented in the Annex, tested for the Portuguese case, and paving the way for a real explanation for inflation differences with respect to the euro area average. There we show that the increasing integration and competition, as well as the general increase in productivity, should lower inflation. The Balassa effect, to the contrary, through the services inflation differential, leads to a real appreciation. Depending on the periods under consideration, the first effect may dominate.

6.2.2 Fiscal policy

What could and should be done by the fiscal authorities is subject to heated debate in Portuguese public opinion and among economists. We have been trying to show that most of the imbalances experienced by the Portuguese economy, namely the CA deficit and the inflation surge, are mainly market-driven by the adoption of the NER, and are unavoidable. In Blanchard and Giavazzi (2002) the same sort of point is made, showing that most of the CA deficit is explained in Portugal (and other small euro area economies) by a lower private savings rate and an increase in investment, while public savings play a minor role. In Hoeller et al. (2002), a conclusion along the same lines is reached when it is argued that

> higher inflation in the overheating euro area countries is not related to loosening of the fiscal stance. ... On a cumulative basis, [in terms of structural balance budget] Finland tightened the most, by 3.8 per cent of GDP and Portugal the least, by 1.4 per cent of GDP between 1997 and 2001, which is considerably more than the change in the fiscal stance of France and Germany (both tightened by 0.3 per cent of GDP). (p. 15)

Therefore, it is evident that by and large most of the imbalances were unavoidable and broadly determined by market conditions, 'so, while benign neglect may not be optimal, it appears, at least for those [CA] deficits, to be a reasonable course of action' (Blanchard and Giavazzi, 2002, p. 43).

It is necessary to clarify some of these conclusions, however. The Portuguese fiscal stance has been pro-cyclical at least since 1998 and there are other reasons that would justify a more restrictive policy. Under such a policy it is clear that the course of inflation and the CA deficit would be largely unaltered. Nevertheless, a pro-cyclical fiscal policy is wrong because it raises credibility issues that are important to consider. On the one hand, Portugal's voluntary commitment to SGP should be honoured. On the other hand, the cost of financing may increase through higher interest rate spreads, which would be a pure loss. Lastly, it is also vital that the Portuguese authorities continue to be able to invest at the rates they have been doing in order to make full use of EU funds. For these reasons, a more conservative fiscal stance is long overdue.

7 FINAL REMARKS

This chapter has shown that the impact of the new economic regime entails changes that are desirable and long-lasting. However, in the medium term, some apparently unpleasant consequences are to be expected, due namely to wealth effects and loosening of liquidity constraints as a consequence of permanently lower interest rates.

The chapter has further demonstrated that most of these consequences could not, and for the most part, should not be avoided. As shown in Azevedo (2002), the synchronization of the Portuguese cycle with that of the EU is so close (and becoming more so) that we may argue that a different fiscal policy would not have led to a different outcome. However, as we emphatically assert, this is not to be read as an excuse to have a pro-cyclical fiscal policy and to breach the Stability Programme targets. It was, nevertheless, possible to avoid a real-estate bubble that would have created major financial problems today.

Before stressing the role of the NER, the chapter described at some length some of the structural reforms undertaken in Portugal. While studying the inflation process, the relevance of those reforms in countervailing the Balassa effect are mentioned and even estimated. Several other reforms, however, were not mentioned, or were referred to only in passing. Fiscal issues such as the tax reform of 1989 or the tax cut of 2000/1, for instance, were not given their proper due.

The road to the single currency followed by the Portuguese economy was also analysed. First, it should be stressed that stability starts at home. Only later will international markets follow. In this respect, it must be observed that for long periods before 1998, markets signalled in many ways that Portugal was the front runner among the Southern European countries for the single currency. Second, this was possible also because on all fronts the euro was accepted as a national target, made clear by the wide party support it received. This was the case in all areas of government, and was evident in all of the Maastricht criteria.

It is difficult to assess the relevance the Portuguese experience may have for the accession countries. For instance, when compared with Ireland, Portugal or Spain, the problems of former East Germany apparently are more difficult and more resilient than anyone could have anticipated just a few years ago.

A relevant footnote is that *so far* Portugal, as well as other catching-up countries, has been able to escape the mezzogiorno syndrome. As analysed in Sinn and Westerman (2001), this is something that cannot be taken for granted for any country, from the former East Germany to Portugal, in the years to come. It is not clear how it is politically possible to avoid the mezzogiorno syndrome if that is at least partially due to some form of Dutch disease resulting from an excess of EU transfers. Furthermore, in an EU that is undergoing a radical enlargement process, it is difficult to visualize the path that the EU economy will follow as a new economic space; its economic geography will make unforeseeable adjustments and changes in the near future. The institutional reforms both at the country level and at the EU level are a source of hope as well as of concern. It is our belief that the challenges ahead of us are to be seen as opportunities, and the problems are to be collectively solved at the European Union level through greater political unity.

ANNEX: EQUILIBRIUM REAL APPRECIATION[23]

The Balassa approach divides consumer goods into tradables and non-tradables. Let us consider instead that all goods are non-tradable at the consumer level and tradable at the producer level. Between the producer and the retailer several services are added to the good, transforming it into a non-tradable consumer commodity. This means that at the producer level goods are subject to the PPP, but not at the consumer level. In short, let us take the following descriptive model:

$$P = P_p^{\,a} S^{(1-a)} \qquad (1)$$

$$P^* = P^{*\,a}_{p} S^{*(1-a)} \qquad (2)$$

$$P_p = B.E.P^*_p \qquad (3)$$

where P stands for the consumer price level, P_p the producer price level, E the exchange rate, S the services price level and '*' labels the foreign variables. Equations (1) and (2) define the relationship described above between consumer prices, services and producer prices, where 'a' is a technological coefficient. For the sake of simplicity, it is assumed to be identical in both countries. Equation (3) – with B=1 – translates the PPP hypothesis at the producer level, where all goods are assumed to be internationally tradable.

Our estimation period — 1990–2002 — is relatively short and includes a period of strong liberalization and openness in the Portuguese economy as mentioned in Sections 2 and 3. Therefore, it is natural to expect the parameter B to be initially greater than one and more importantly, falling throughout the period.[24] This last remark — falling B — is likely to account for several factors. On the one hand, it reflects the fact that the Portuguese economy has enjoyed an increase in overall productivity above euro area countries; on the other hand, it may also reflect the increasing integration of the Portuguese economy in the EU economy, due to the single market, capital integration and the single currency, leading to a reduction of formal and informal barriers to trade. This gives voice to the often-repeated argument that liberalization is a way out of real appreciation.

Taking log differences, (1)–(3) become

$$\pi = a.\pi_p + (1-a).\vartheta \qquad (1')$$
$$\pi^* = a.\pi^*_p + (1-a).\vartheta^* \qquad (2')$$
$$\pi_p = \pi^*_p + \varepsilon + \beta \qquad (3')$$

where all variables are self-explanatory and β is the rate of change of B. After simple manipulation one gets to

$$\pi = \pi^* + \varepsilon + a\beta + (1-a)(\vartheta - \vartheta^* - \varepsilon) \qquad (4)$$

Alternatively, one may rewrite (4) as

$$APR = a\beta + (1-a)(SERV) \qquad (5)$$

where real appreciation (APR) is determined by the difference in services price inflation denominated in the home currency (SERV) and the liberalization factor β. This is the equation that was tested for the Portuguese case, taking the '*' country as the euro area.

Several estimations were performed giving basically the same strong results. Looking at the formulation as in Table 6.1 below, the long-term estimated equation is[25]

$$APR = -0.7 + 0.7SERV. \qquad (6)$$

This gives support to the approach described above where a = 0.3, which is a reasonable value. Note that 'a' is by definition a positive number. Also mentioned above, β will be negative, which also makes the term aβ negative.[26]

To sum up, as suggested by equation (6), the econometric results suggest that the differential between the Portuguese inflation and the euro-area average inflation stemming from the Balassa effect — asymmetric productivity growth between sectors — is somehow mitigated by the reduction of barriers to trade, market liberalization, overall productivity growth differentials between the two regions and so on.

Details of the Econometric Procedure

Three measures for the inflation rate were used: year-on-year (yoy) rate, monthly rate and a yoy rate based on a three-month moving average of the price index. With this, we define three measures of real appreciation rate all based on the same general expression, both for the total consumption bundle (APRH, APRM, APR3) and for the service sector only (APRH_SERV, APRM_SERV, APR3_SERV). All series are stationary at a 5 per cent significance level. Given that the estimation results for the three alternative specifications of inflation were quite similar, only the results obtained with the yoy inflation rate are presented (see Table 6.1).

Table 6.1 Estimation results

Dependent Variable: APRH
Method: Least Squares
Date: 02/04/03 Time: 14:26
Sample (adjusted): 1991:02 2002:12
Included observations: 143 after adjusting endpoints
Convergence achieved after 9 iterations
Newey-West HAC Standard Errors & Covariance (lag truncation = 4)
Backcast: OFF

Variable	Coefficient	Std. Error	t-Statistic	Prob.
C	−0.048842	0.019595	−2.492608	0.0139
APRH_SERV	0.856378	0.070080	12.22006	0.0000
APRH(−1)	0.934755	0.018834	49.63190	0.0000
APRH_SERV(−1)	−0.807614	0.061005	−13.23858	0.0000
MA(2)	−0.342550	0.063875	−5.362795	0.0000
MA(10)	−0.333448	0.104090	−3.203453	0.0017
MA(12)	−0.322953	0.109074	−2.960856	0.0036
R-squared	0.990624	Mean dependent var		1.166012
Adjusted R-squared	0.990210	S.D. dependent var		4.390448
S.E. of regression	0.434400	Akaike info criterion		1.218009
Sum squared resid	25.66362	Schwarz criterion		1.363043
Log likelihood	−80.08764	F-statistic		2394.885
Durbin-Watson stat	1.919258	Prob (F-statistic)		0.000000
Inverted MA Roots	1.00	0.83	0.83	0.40
		−0.49i	+0.49i	+0.78i
	0.40	0.00	−0.00	−0.40
	−0.78i	+0.80i	−0.80i	+0.78i
	−0.40	−0.83	−0.83	−1.00
	−0.78i	−0.49i	+0.49i	

Source: Eurostat, Harmonized Index of Consumer Price (HICP), Portugal and EU-12, monthly data for 1990–2002.

NOTES

* Special thanks are due to A. Morgado for special assistance. P. De Grauwe, M. Sebastião and G. Szapáry, made important comments on early drafts of the chapter which are gratefully acknowledged. The usual disclaimer applies.

1. The crawling-peg exchange rate regime had been adopted in 1977.
2. Actually, neither the limits of fluctuation nor the time span for allowing major deviations were spelled out. And despite announcements of a 3 per cent depreciation rate over the medium term, in fact there was a small — but clear — appreciation during the first year.

3. For a more complete description of this period, see Macedo et al. (2003).
4. For a discussion of the interactions between sustainability of currency bands, interest rates and credibility see Beleza et al. (1996).
5. The British situation concerning the Monetary Union is *a contrario sensu* another instance of this problem. This point was also raised in Cunha and Abreu (1999).
6. These are centre-left and centre-right parties respectively. The other two parties were one from the right wing (CDS/PP) and another from the left (the Communist Party).
7. There were also some coalitions, but in every case they were led by these two main parties.
8. In the elections held in 1991, 1995, 1999 and 2002, the voting shares were respectively, 79.7, 77.9, 76.4 and 77.8 per cent.
9. For a discussion of the Maastricht criteria and the accession countries see Szapáry (2002).
10. For further discussion on the disinflation process see Abreu (2001).
11. The SGP rule is ill-defined and the actual interpretation of this rule has recently been subject to some debate, as is well known.
12. In fact, the distinction between the domestic market and the foreign (euro area) market is basically semantic.
13. The change of nature of the external constraint has nothing to do with the solvency of the State, e.g. New York City went bankrupt without any *external* imbalance consideration.
14. Alternatively, in Barbosa (1998) it is estimated that a higher cumulative real GDP growth of 0.5 percentage point after one year and of 1 percentage point after ten years would have resulted against an alternative scenario under which Portugal would have adopted credible monetary and fiscal policies but outside the euro area. This result is obtained using an endogenous growth model for the Portuguese economy and assuming that, with credible policies but outside the Monetary Union, the long-run interest rates would have been higher by 350 basis points in the first and second years, by 200 basis points in the third year, by 150 in the fourth and, finally, by 50 basis points from the fifth year onwards.
15. Back-of-the-envelope calculations estimate the change in human capital wealth valuation above 60 per cent in just a few years.
16. This term was coined in Eichengreen and Hausmann (1999). Developing countries' investors either borrow short term in domestic currency or borrow long term in a foreign currency for a long-term domestic investment. In either case this creates (maturity or currency) mismatches as described in Hausmann (2002). This point was stressed by Governor V. Constâncio in a recent speech (Constâncio, 2002).
17. A comprehensive discussion of this issue can be found in Hoeller et al. (2002).
18. To the best of our knowledge the first econometric enquiry into the causes of inflation is Cunha and Barosa (1987).
19. See Cunha and Machado (1993a,b, 1994), Cunha and Barosa (1990) and Costa (2000).
20. For an interesting evaluation of this issue see Cecchetti et al. (1998).
21. As argued in Bhagwati (1984) the Balassa technological explanation is not very plausible. In the same vein see also Cunha and Esteves (2002).
22. Real appreciation may be caused by other factors than the Balassa ones. In other words, not all actually observed real appreciation is to be taken as equilibrium real appreciation.
23. This section draws heavily on Cunha and Silva (2003).
24. In fact, B can be at any level, since all variables in (3) are index numbers. It is only relevant for B to be falling.
25. That is $MA(.) = 0$; $SERV_t = SERV_{t-1}$; $APR_t = APR_{t-1}$.
26. This equation shows a large weight for the services sector, which should not be expected to be above 0.45. This is explained by the fact that the equation not only captures the services sector but also the services included in the goods sector production process, like retail or transportation services, for instance. In total and according to our estimation this amounts to 0.70.

REFERENCES

Abreu, Marta (2001), 'From EU accession to EMU participation: the Portuguese disinflation experience in the period of 1984–1998', *Economic Bulletin*, Banco de Portugal, December 2001.

Alesina, Alberto, J. Gali, H. Uhlig, O. Blanchard and F. Giavazzi (2001), 'Should large CA imbalances within the euro area be a source of concern?', in MECB Update, September, CEPR.

Azevedo, J. Valle (2002), 'Business cycles: cyclical comovement within the EU in the period 1960–1999', Banco de Portugal, WP 5-02.

Beleza, M., V. Gaspar and Maximiano Pinheiro (1996), 'Credibility, interest rates and the exchange policy sustainability', *Economic Bulletin*, Banco de Portugal, March 1996.

Banco de Portugal, *Annual Report*, several issues.

Barbosa, António P. (1998), *O Impacto do Euro na Economia Portuguesa*, Publicações Dom Quixote.

Bhagwati, J. (1984), 'Why services are cheaper in poor countries', *Economic Journal*, **94**, 279–86.

Blanchard, Olivier and Francesco Giavazzi (2002) 'Current account deficits in the euro area. The end of the Feldstein Horioka puzzle?', mimeo.

Carvalho, Irene (1999), 'Impacto das privatizações no mercado de capitais: 1996 – 1° Semestre de 1999', Bolsa de Valores de Lisboa.

Cecchetti, S., N. Mark and R. Sonora (1998), 'Price level convergence among US cities: lessons for the ECB', Oesterreichische Nationalbank, WP 32.

Constâncio, Vitor (2002), 'Política monetária comum e a economia portuguesa', FEUNL Symposium, 11 December.

Costa, Sónia (2000), 'Inflation differential between Portugal and Germany', *Economic Bulletin*, Banco de Portugal, June 2000.

Cunha, Luís C. and Marta Abreu (1999), 'Monetary policy in a monetary union: what do small countries stand to gain and to lose?', in F. Monteiro, J. Tavares, M. Glatzer and A. Cardoso (eds), *Portugal: Strategic Options in a European Context*, Lanham: Lexington Books.

Cunha, Luís C. and J. P. Barosa (1987) 'Short-run dynamics of inflation: the Portuguese case', in *Nova Economia em Portugal*, UNL, 1989.

Cunha, Luís C. and J. P. Barosa (1990), 'A inflação em Portugal: uma abordagem não estrutural', *Economia*.

Cunha, Luís C. and P. S. Esteves (2002), 'Lower prices in poor countries: technology, exchange rate risk and capital mobility', *Boletim de Ciências Económicas*, vol. XVL-A.

Cunha, Luís C. and J. F. Machado (1993a), 'A PPP model of real appreciation', FEUNL, Working Paper 210, 1993.

Cunha, Luís C. and J. F. Machado (1993b), 'Real convergence and real appreciation: the Iberian case', with J. F. Machado, FEUNL, Working Paper 211, 1993.

Cunha, Luís C. and J. F. Machado (1994), 'Theoretical irregularities on the Spanish and Portuguese Inflations', in *Ensaios de Homenagem a Manuel Jacinto Nunes* ISEG, 1996.

Cunha, Luís C. and P. Silva (2003), 'Cost of living and real convergence', mimeo.

Eichengreen, Barry and Ricardo Hausmann (1999), 'Exchange rates and financial fragility', NBER, Working Paper No. 7418.

European Commission (2002), *Statistical Annex of European Economy*, Directorate General for Economic and Financial Affairs, Autumn 2002.

European Monetary Institute (1998), *Convergence Report*, March 1998.

Hausmann, Ricardo (2002), 'Unrewarded good fiscal behavior: the role of debt structure', Harvard University, mimeo.

Hoeller, P., C. Giorno and C. de la Maisonneuve (2002) 'Overheating in small euro area economies: should fiscal policy react?', OECD, WP 323.

Macedo, J. B., L. C. Nunes and L. Pereira (2003), 'Central bank intervention under target zones: the Portuguese escudo in the ERM', mimeo.

OECD, *Economic Surveys – Portugal*, several issues.

Pereira, A. M. (1999), 'The impact of the euro on long-term growth in Portugal', *Economic Bulletin*, Banco de Portugal, June 1999.

Sinn, Hans-Werner and F. Westerman (2001), 'Two Mezzogiornos', NBER, WP 8125.

Szapáry, György (2002), 'Is Maastricht too tough?', *Central Banking*, **XIII** (1), pp. 75-91.

COMMENTS

Paul De Grauwe

I liked the chapter by Luís Campos e Cunha and Patrícia Silva which is full of interesting observations about the Portuguese economy, but I will use this occasion essentially to ask the question: what can we actually learn from the Portuguese experience about entry into the European Monetary Union of the new member states? The first thing that I learned from the Portuguese experience, but not only the Portuguese experience, is that convergence is easy. When we look at what happened in Portugal, the speed with which interest rates and inflation rates declined was remarkable. The budget deficit dropped very quickly, mainly as a result of a decline in long-term interest rates. Then the question is why it was so easy to have this nominal convergence in Portugal, and I would claim also in countries like Italy, for example. The main reason is that convergence came about not only because of the efforts of the authorities, but because of some self-fulfilling nature of nominal convergence, once the market expects that the countries will enter into the Monetary Union. Let me go into this virtuous circle of convergence. When markets expect convergence to occur, then convergence will be easy. We know why: long-term interest rates will quickly decline, countries that have relatively high government debts will experience a quick decline in their budget deficits, and the prospect of an irrevocably fixed exchange rate also anchors expectations and allows for lower inflation rates. So here we have the existence of a virtuous circle of convergence which very much depends on expectations of the market on the question whether or not countries will enter into the Monetary Union. If the political will is there to allow countries into the Monetary Union, convergence becomes easier. I think this virtuous circle occurred prior to the start of EMU in a number of mainly Southern European countries. There was a strong perception at a certain moment that, for political reasons, EMU could not start without the Southern European countries, including Italy, being part of the Monetary Union. Therefore, one can say that it is not because countries like Portugal and also Italy converged that it was decided that they should enter. It is probably the other way round: convergence was made easy because it was decided that these countries should be in the Monetary Union.

The question is: can we expect a similar virtuous convergence circle for the new member states? And here I have some doubts that are based on two possible reasons. One is political. I argue that in the case of the convergence prior to EMU, there was the political will that the whole group, including Italy, Portugal, Spain and Belgium, should embark on it. There was a clear political will to do this with these countries. It is unclear today whether the same strong political will exists to let the new member states enter EMU quickly. I do not doubt that there is a political will to let them enter at some point in time, but to let them enter quickly, I am not sure that the same strong political will exists. So that is one reason that allows me to have some doubts whether this virtuous circle will occur. I am not saying that countries may not converge, but it will just be harder if the virtuous circle is not there. Another reason for some doubt, although less strong than the previous one, is the fact that most of the new member states have lower levels of government debt, and much of the convergence dynamics, the virtuous circle, is based on having high initial debts, like Italy and Belgium had, for example. Then this virtuous circle can play its full role via the decline in interest rates. And here I will just show the difference in government debt levels (Figure 6.18). I take 1994, that is five years prior to the start of EMU, and 2000, which is five or six years before the new member states could potentially enter. One can see the difference there; at least the original members had much higher government debts than the new member states had at a comparable period of time. That is one point I wanted to make. If the political will is there, it is easier to have nominal convergence.

The second point I would like to make relates to the Balassa-Samuelson syndrome. Is that going to be important in the transition? What I have learnt from the chapter is that this problem played practically no role in the case of Portugal, nor did it in other high-productivity-growth countries at that time, like Ireland, for example. So these countries lowered their inflation rates very easily prior to entry. However, once in EMU, significant differences appeared in inflation rates, indicating that maybe there is something relating to the Balassa-Samuelson, but that has appeared later. Figure 6.19 shows the average yearly inflation rates within the member countries during the three years of existence of the eurozone. One can see relatively large differences. Of course, a lot could be due to other reasons than Balassa-Samuelson effects, but still it has been surprising to most of us that these differentials could be this large. Why is this? I think we should be aware that the Balassa-Samuelson phenomenon is a long-run phenomenon, very much as the quantity theory of money is a long-run phenomenon. It will typically not be observed in the short run. So during transition periods, if these are short enough, these problems of high-productivity-growth countries leading to high inflation may be of relatively little importance. Figure 6.20 and 6.21 show that inflation and long-term interest rates in the accession countries are similar to those in the EMU members at a comparable period of entry.

Let me conclude by saying that the new member states are in a position that is very much comparable to the position of the eurozone countries at a comparable period prior to entry. The question is: will the new member states be able to profit from the virtuous circle in the convergence dynamics?

My conclusion is that it will depend very much on the perceptions of the financial markets on the political will to let the new member states enter quickly into EMU. If there is some doubt about this, then the convergence process may not be as smooth as the one that we have experienced in the current EMU member countries.

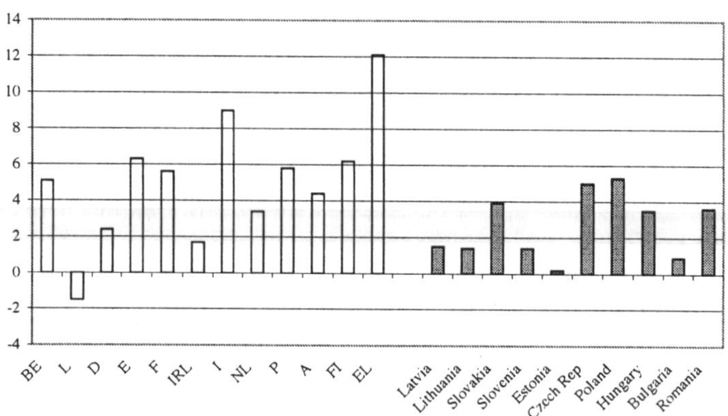

Figure 6.18 Government budget deficits (% GDP) of EMU members (1994) and CEECs (2001)

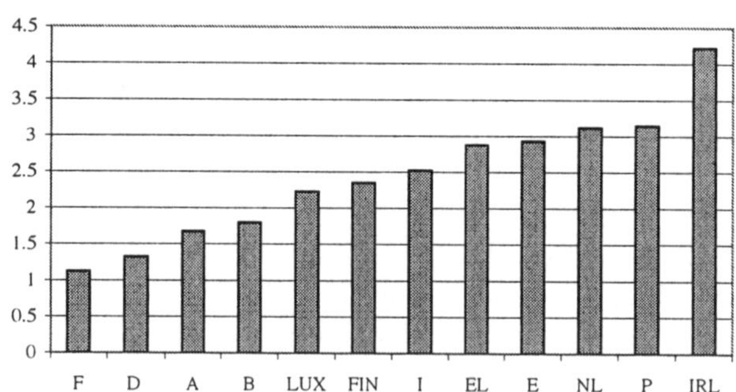

Figure 6.19 Average yearly inflation in eurozone countries during 1999–2002 (in %)

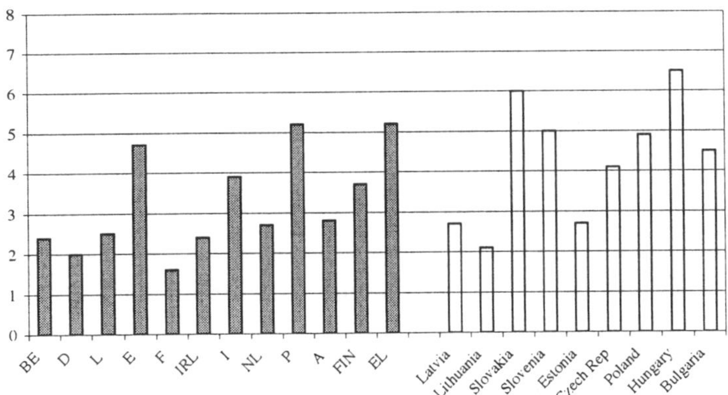

Figure 6.20 *Inflation rates of EMU members (1994) and accession countries (2001)*

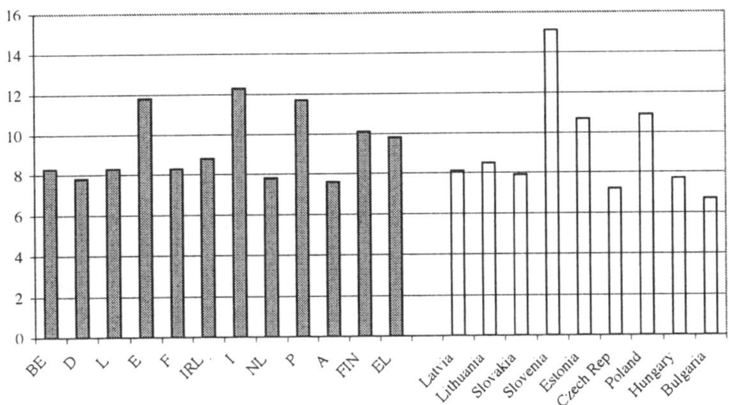

Figure 6.21 *Long-term interest rates of EMU members (1994) and accession countries (2001)*

7. Macroeconomic adjustment to structural change

Gabriel Fagan, Vítor Gaspar and Alfredo Pereira

1 INTRODUCTION

Ten countries — Cyprus, Czech Republic, Estonia, Hungary, Latvia, Lithuania, Malta, Poland, Slovakia and Slovenia — were accepted to become new members of the European Union on 1 May 2004. The historical agreement on EU enlargement was reached at the European Council, held in Copenhagen, on 12–13 December 2002. The Accession Treaty was signed, in Athens, on 16 April 2003. Subsequently, the ten accession countries and the fifteen current members of the EU will ratify the treaty. From 1 May 2004 on, the new members will be 'member states with a derogation' in the sense of article 122, paragraph 1, of the European Union Treaty.

According to the *acquis communautaire,* price stability should be the primary goal of monetary policy, in all member states. Article 4 of the treaty establishing the European Community stipulates that, when conducting their economic policies, the member states and the Community must follow the guiding principles of 'stable prices, sound public finances and monetary conditions and a sustainable balance of payments'. Gradual and sustainable disinflation towards low and stable inflation, as in the euro area, is normally referred to as nominal convergence. Such a process of nominal convergence is accompanied by a downward adjustment in nominal long-term interest rates, to levels approaching those prevailing in the euro area, reflecting both declining inflation expectations and a diminution of risk premia. Moreover, the new member states will become, eventually, and in accordance with the timetables and procedures in the treaty, members of the euro area.

All of these ten countries have GDP per capita well below the EU average. Specifically, in 2001, they ranged from about one third (Latvia) to about three quarters (Cyprus) of the EU average, measured in terms of GDP per capita, valued in accordance with purchasing power parity standards. Successful integration of the new entrants into the EU will be associated with a catching-up process, defined as convergence in the levels of output per capita and productivity, reflecting a number of structural changes.

In the summary of the ECB Seminar on the Accession Process, held in Helsinki, on 12 November 1999, one of the key points underlined was that 'nominal and real convergence' should be pursued in parallel. By modifying their economic structures in line with those prevailing within the EU and by implementing appropriate structural reforms, accession countries will speed up the process of 'catching up', whereby their living standards will progressively evolve towards levels closer to those of the EU (real convergence). Historical experience shows that this process should go hand in hand with the achievement and maintenance of price stability and sound public finances (nominal convergence). Progress towards fulfilling the Maastricht criteria as a condition for adoption of the euro is therefore fully compatible with structural reform.

The desired parallelism between nominal convergence and real convergence makes macroeconomic adjustment and structural change critical issues in the context of European integration. The ten accession countries have made considerable progress in terms of disinflation and most of them have experienced growth rates above the EU average. Furthermore, most of these countries have also experienced a significant real appreciation of their currencies vis-à-vis the euro. Their monetary and exchange rate policy regimes cover the full range of possibilities: from inflation targeting *cum* floating adopted in the Czech Republic and Poland, for example, to currency boards, followed, for example, in Estonia and Lithuania. Hungary, in turn, allows the exchange rate of the forint to float inside ±15% fluctuation bands against the euro.

Structural change and real convergence in these countries will be associated with adjustments in relative prices. One relative price, which is particularly relevant in the context, is the real exchange rate, defined as the price of non-tradable goods relative to the price of tradable goods. The real exchange rate, as a relative price, adjusts to changes in relevant variables including conditions in the rest of the world, productivity trends, trade barriers, taxation, migration flows, financial flows, international transfers, institutional and behavioural characteristics of product and labour markets and much else. In fact, the list of factors potentially affecting the equilibrium real exchange rate and its adjustment path towards equilibrium coincides with the list of factors, which may affect relative prices in a dynamic general equilibrium context, for an open economy. It includes all factors influencing the relative supply and demand for non-tradable goods. Therefore, the real exchange rate is unlikely to be constant over time (see, for example, Neary, 1988 and Edwards, 1989).

For the countries joining the EU, many of the above factors are likely to play a relevant role in determining the real exchange rate and its evolution over time. One popular explanation of trend real exchange rate appreciation is inspired in the Balassa-Samuelson effect (Balassa, 1964 and Samuelson, 1964). The basic idea is very simple. Catching-up implies convergence in productivity levels. The scope for productivity increases is much greater in the production of traded goods (e.g. manufacturing goods) than non-traded goods (e.g. services). Therefore, countries catching up will experience stronger relative productivity gains in the production of traded goods. With the interest rate determined in the world capital market and a competitive domestic labour market, this implies an increase in the relative price of non-traded goods. There are many estimates available of the actual and likely magnitudes of Balassa-Samuelson effects both for the euro area and for accession countries (see, for example, Pelkmans, Gros and Nunez Ferrer, 2000; Bundesbank, 2001; Coricelli and Jazbec, 2001; Halpern and Wyplosz, 2001; Sinn and Reutter, 2001; Egert, 2002; Fisher, 2002; Mihaljek, 2002; and MacDonald and Wojcik, 2002).

In this chapter we develop a two-sector dynamic general equilibrium model with price and wage stickiness. We consider an overlapping generation set-up on the household side (see, for example, Blanchard, 1985, and Yaari, 1965). In the literature on open economies, this set-up is usually preferred to the infinite horizon Ramsey approach, since it leads to a well-defined steady-state level of foreign debt. The production side of the economy consists of two final goods sectors: traded and non-traded goods sectors. The non-traded goods sector and the labour market are characterized by monopolistic competition (see, for example, Dixit and Stiglitz, 1977). Furthermore, the accumulation of capital is subject to real adjustment costs while the price of the non-traded good and the wage rate are subject to nominal adjustment costs (see, for example, Kim, 2000).

We calibrate and numerically simulate this model using a stylized data and parameter set inspired in the cases of two of the euro area countries, which have undergone significant catching-up, Ireland and Portugal. We do so to capture the main features of a typical country engaged in the process of catching up to the EU standards of living. Our reading of the experiences of Portugal and Ireland leads us to focus on productivity growth, financial integration and unilateral public transfers associated with EU structural policies. This is clearly a simplification. Nevertheless, it allows us to capture some main features of the structural changes associated with a catching-up process in the EU.

In the context of the dynamic general equilibrium model, the equilibrium real exchange rate will be one of the relative prices to be determined in equilibrium. It will be shown that trend productivity differentials lead to trend relative price changes. However, in the short run the adjustment in relative prices is unlikely to follow productivity differentials closely and we find that there is a sizeable 'front-loading' of the impacts on the real exchange rate.

Structural change and macroeconomic adjustment are likely to interact in complex ways. It may be that price and wage stickiness will make adjustment towards equilibrium very slow as argued by Blanchard and Muet (1993). Their focus was on the length of time it would take for the real exchange rate to return to its equilibrium following a process of disinflation based on a fixed exchange rate regime. However, since they were focusing on the German mark versus the French franc, they, quite reasonably, assumed that the equilibrium real exchange rate was constant over time. For accession countries the behaviour of the economy under alternative price norms, when the real exchange rate changes endogenously, seems to be a more relevant case to look at. An alternative view is that, in the context of a model with forward-looking agents, the impacts of anticipated structural changes on the real exchange rate and other macroeconomic variables will be 'front-loaded' as a result of immediate wealth effects on consumption and labour supply.

This chapter is organized as follows. In the second section, we describe the dynamic general equilibrium model and we briefly address parameterization and calibration issues, while leaving the full details for an Annex. In the third section, we simulate the model under specific structural changes and determine, in particular, the long-term response of the real exchange rate as well as its transitional path. We also examine the sensitivity of the results to the presence of price and wage stickiness. In this section, the impact of two highly stylized 'policy regimes' on the adjustment of the economy is explored — one focused on stabilizing the nominal exchange rate ('exchange rate stability') and the other focused on stabilization of the domestic consumer price level ('price stability'). Finally, in the fourth section, we summarize the main results of the chapter and highlight their policy implications.

2 THE DYNAMIC GENERAL-EQUILIBRIUM MODEL

Details of the model are provided in Table 7.1. Tables 7.2 and 7.3 provide numerical values for parameters and variables respectively, obtained through the process of calibration described in the Annex (see also section 2.7). We consider a decentralized economy in a dynamic general-equilibrium framework. All private sector agents maximize utility or profits, taking, unless otherwise indicated, goods and factor prices as given. In addition, all agents have perfect foresight. This means that agents fully anticipate future prices and other variables. Therefore, their planned future actions are determined and implemented without the need for any changes.

The economy is inhabited by households, firms producing in two different sectors and a government. The two production sectors are a traded goods sector and a non-traded goods sector. The traded goods sector is competitive. The price of traded goods is the exogenous world price, adjusted for the nominal exchange rate, which, under a 'small open economy' assumption, is independent of domestic traded goods output. In contrast, the non-traded sector is characterized by monopolistic competition with firms acting as price setters. Regarding the households, we follow the conventional overlapping-generations specification of Yaari (1965), Blanchard (1985), Buiter (1988) and Weil (1989). Households, faced with a finite probability of death, maximize a utility function, which depends on consumption of both traded and non-traded goods and leisure. As regards the labour market, we introduce imperfect competition and a set of wage-setting institutions (unions) into the framework.

The model also incorporates a highly simplified government sector. Regarding links to the rest of the world, we assume a high, but not perfect, degree of capital mobility where the domestic interest rate equals the foreign rate plus exogenous and endogenous risk premiums, the latter depending on the stock of net foreign assets relative to output. In cases where the nominal exchange rate is allowed to float, we assume that a standard uncovered interest parity (UIP) condition applies.

A notable feature of our framework, in contrast to much of the earlier literature exploring the impacts of long-run structural changes, is that we incorporate a number of important frictions into the model. We assume price stickiness in a context of monopolistic competition in the market for non-traded goods and in the labour market. With regard to the labour markets this is achieved by including in the model a set of agents which act as wage setters, specifically trade unions. Our set-up means that the price of non-traded goods and the wage rate are both subject to price mark-ups and to nominal adjustment costs. Nominal stickiness in these markets is modelled in terms of quadratic adjustment costs, following Kim (2000) rather than the Calvo (1983) scheme, mainly for reasons of analytical convenience. Moreover, as shown by Rotemberg (1987), the two approaches yield equivalent price equations. An additional friction in both the traded and the non-traded goods sectors stems from investment adjustment costs which are again modelled by means of a quadratic adjustment cost term. The general equilibrium is defined as paths for the endogenous variables such that budget constraints and the first-order conditions of firms and households are satisfied simultaneously and at all points in time given the paths of the exogenous variables.

2.1 The Traded Goods Sector

The traded goods sector comprises a set of identical firms, each of which acts in a competitive manner in output and factor markets. On the basis of a 'small open economy assumption', the price of traded goods is determined by the exogenous world price — which is independent of the levels of traded output of the individual firms and the economy as a whole — along with the nominal exchange rate. Output, YT_t, is produced with a Cobb-Douglas technology as in equation (T.1) in Table 7.1, exhibiting constant returns to scale in labour, LT_t^d, and private capital, KT_t, where θ_{LT} is the labour share and AT is total factor productivity in the traded sector. Capital accumulation is characterized by (T.2) where physical capital depreciates at a rate of δ_{KT}. Investment is subject to adjustment costs as in Christiano et al. (2001). These costs comprise learning and installation costs and are meant to reflect rigidities in the accumulation of capital towards its optimal level. These adjustment costs are internal to the firm and are modelled as a loss in capital accumulation and are, therefore, included in equation (T.2). Adjustment costs are assumed to be non-negative, monotonically increasing and strictly convex. Specifically, we assume adjustment costs to be quadratic in investment per unit of installed capital. The investment good in the traded sector comprises a Cobb-Douglas aggregation of traded and non-traded goods (as shown in T.7). At time t, the firms' net cash flow, $NCFT_t$ (see equation T.3), represents revenues from sales net of wage payments and investment spending.

Table 7.1 The dynamic general-equilibrium model

Traded goods sector: Output, factor demands and pricing	
$YT_t = AT\,(LT_t^d)^{\theta_{LT}}\,KT_t^{1-\theta_{LT}}$	(T.1)
$KT_{t+1} = (1-\delta_{KT})KT_t + IT_t - \mu_{IT}\dfrac{IT_t^2}{KT_t}$	(T.2)
$NCFT_t = pt_t YT_t - w_t LT_t^d - pit_t IT_t$	(T.3)
$\theta_{LT}\,pt_t YT_t = w_t LT_t^d$	(T.4)
$\dfrac{q_{t+1}^{KT}}{1+r_{t+1}}(1-2\mu_{IT}\dfrac{IT_t}{KT_t}) = pit_t$	(T.5)
$q_t^{KT} = (1-\theta_{LT})\,pt_t\dfrac{YT_t}{KT_t} + \dfrac{q_{t+1}^{KT}}{1+r_{t+1}}\left[1-\delta_{KT}+\mu_{IT}\left(\dfrac{IT_t}{KT_t}\right)^2\right]$	(T.6)
$IT_t = stITT_t^{it}\,ITN_t^{(1-it)}$	(T.7)

Table 7.1 The dynamic general-equilibrium model (cont.)

Traded goods sector: Output, factor demands and pricing

$$pit_t = \left(\frac{1}{st}\right)\left(\frac{pt_t}{it}\right)^{it}\left(\frac{pn_t}{(1-it)}\right)^{(1-it)} \tag{T.8}$$

$$pt_t AT(LT_t^d)^{\theta_{LT}} KT_t^{1-\theta_{LT}} - q_t^{KT}\{KT_t - (1-\delta_{KT})KT_{t-1} - IT_t + \mu_{IT}\frac{IT_t^2}{KT_t}\} + \tag{T.8a}$$

$$\frac{q_{t+1}^{KT}}{1+r_{t+1}}\{KT_{t+1} - (1-\delta_{KT})KT_t - IT_{t+1} + \mu_{IT}\frac{IT_{T+1}^2}{KT_{t+1}}\} + \ldots$$

Non-traded goods sector: Output, factor demands and pricing

$$YN_t = AN(LN_t^d)^{\theta_{LN}} KN_t^{1-\theta_{LN}} \tag{T.9}$$

$$KN_{t+1} = (1-\delta_{KN})KN_t + IN_t - \mu_{IN}\frac{IT_t^2}{KT_t} \tag{T.10}$$

$$NCFN_t = (pn_t - \mu_p\left(\frac{pn_t}{pn_{t-1}} - 1\right)^2)YN_t - w_t LN_t^d - pin_t IN_t \tag{T.11}$$

$$\Psi_t = (pn_t - \mu_p\left(\frac{pn_t}{pn_{t-1}} - 1\right)^2)YN_t + (pn_{t+1} - \mu_p\left(\frac{pn_{t+1}}{pn_t} - 1\right)^2)\frac{YN_{t+1}}{1+r_{t+1}} \tag{T.12}$$

$$w_t = \frac{\partial\Psi_t}{\partial LN_t} \tag{T.13}$$

$$\frac{\partial\Psi_t}{\partial LN_t} = \left\{-\frac{1}{\varepsilon_{pn}}\frac{pn_t}{pn_{t-1}}\left[1 - 2\mu_p\left(\frac{pn_t}{pn_{t-1}} - 1\right)\right] + \left[pn_t - \mu_p\left(\frac{pn_t}{pn_{t-1}} - 1\right)^2\right]\right. \tag{T.14}$$

$$\left. - \frac{2}{\varepsilon_{pn}}\frac{1}{1+r_{t+1}}\frac{YN_{t+1}}{YN_t}\frac{pn_{t+1}}{pn_t}\mu_p\left(\frac{pn_{t+1}}{pn_t} - 1\right)\right\}\theta_{LN}\frac{YN_1}{LN_t}$$

$$\frac{\partial\Psi_t}{\partial KN_t} = \left\{-\frac{1}{\varepsilon_{pn}}\frac{pn_t}{pn_{t-1}}\left[1 - 2\mu_p\left(\frac{pn_t}{pn_{t-1}} - 1\right)\right] + \left[pn_t - \mu_p\left(\frac{pn_t}{pn_{t-1}} - 1\right)^2\right]\right. \tag{T.15}$$

$$\left. - \frac{2}{\varepsilon_{pn}}\frac{1}{1+r_{t+1}}\frac{YN_{t+1}}{YN_t}\frac{pn_{t+1}}{pn_t}\mu_p\left(\frac{pn_{t+1}}{pn_t} - 1\right)\right\}(1-\theta_{LN})\frac{YN_1}{KN_t}$$

$$\frac{q_{t+1}^{KN}}{1+r_{t+1}}(1 - 2\mu_{IN}\frac{IN_t}{KN_t}) = pin_t \tag{T.16}$$

$$q_t^{KN} = \frac{\partial\Psi_t}{\partial KN_t} + \frac{q_{t+1}^{KN}}{1+r_{t+1}}\left[1 - \delta_{KN} + \mu_{IN}\left(\frac{IN_t}{KN_t}\right)^2\right] \tag{T.17}$$

Table 7.1 The dynamic general-equilibrium model (cont.)

Non-traded goods sector: Output, factor demands and pricing

$$IN_t = snINT_t^{in}INN_t^{(1-in)} \quad (T.18)$$

$$pin_t = \left(\frac{1}{sn}\right)\left(\frac{pt_t}{in}\right)^{in}\left(\frac{pn_t}{(1-in)}\right)^{(1-in)} \quad (T.19)$$

Wage setting

$$(\varepsilon_w - 1)\left(\frac{w_t(\bar{L}-\ell_t)}{pc_tC_t}\right) = \quad (T.20)$$

$$\varepsilon_w\left(\frac{(\bar{L}-\ell_t)}{\ell_t}\right) + \mu_w\left(\frac{w_{t+1}}{(1+r_t)w_t}\right)\left(\frac{w_{t+1}}{w_t}-1\right) - \mu_w\left(\frac{w_t}{w_{t-1}}\right)\left(\frac{w_t}{w_{t-1}}-1\right)$$

The household sector

$$U_{a,t} = \sum_{v=0}^{\infty}\gamma^v\beta^v \tfrac{\sigma-1}{\sigma}\left(c_{a+v,t+v}^{\frac{\sigma-1}{\sigma}} + B\ell_{a+v,t+v}^{\frac{\sigma-1}{\sigma}}\right)^{\frac{\sigma}{\sigma-1}} \quad (T.21)$$

$$\sum_{v=0}^{\infty}\gamma^v\left[1+r_{t+v}\right]^{-v}pc_tc_{a+v,t+v} \le TW_{a,t} \quad (T.22)$$

$$TW_{a,t} \equiv HW_{a,t} + FW_{a,t} + PVF_{a,t} \quad (T.23)$$

$$HW_{a,t} = \sum_{m=0}^{\infty}\left(\tfrac{\gamma}{1+r_{t+m}}\right)\cdot\left[W_{t+m}(\bar{L}-\ell_{a+m,t+m}) - LST_t\right] \quad (T.24)$$

$$FW_{a,t} = (1+r_{t-1})FW_{t-1} + NCFT_{t-1} + NCFN_{t-1} + \left[W_{t-1}\cdot(\bar{L}-\ell_{a-1,t-1})\right] \quad (T.25)$$

$$+TR_{t-1} + R_{t-1} - pc_tC_{a-1,t-1} - LST_{t-1}$$

$$PVF_{a,t} = \sum_{m=0}^{\infty}\left(\tfrac{1}{1+r_{t+m}}\right)(NCFT_{a,t} + NCFN_{a,t}) \quad (T.26)$$

$$pc_tC_t = \left(1-\left[1+r\right]^{\sigma-1}\gamma\beta^{\sigma}\right)\left[HW_t + FW_t + PVF_t\right] \quad (T.27)$$

$$C_t = scCT_t^cCN_t^{(1-c)} \quad (T.28)$$

$$pc_t = \left(\frac{1}{sc}\right)\left(\frac{pt_t}{c}\right)^{c}\left(\frac{pn_t}{(1-c)}\right)^{(1-c)} \quad (T.29)$$

The public sector

$$pt_tCGT_t + pn_tCGN_t + rPD_t + TR_t + ner_tFT_t = LST_t + ner_tFT_t \quad (T.30)$$

Conditions for market equilibrium and price determination

$$FD_{t+1} = (1+r_t)FD_t + pt_t(CT_t + CGT_t + ITT_t + INT_t - YT_t) \quad (T.31)$$

$$-ner_t(FT_t + R_t)$$

$$YN_t = CN_t + CGN_t + ITN_t + INN_t + ner_tFT_t / pn_t \quad (T.32)$$

$$LT_t^d + LN_t^d = L_t \quad (T.33)$$

$$FW_t = PD_t - FD_t \quad (T.34)$$

Table 7.1 The dynamic general-equilibrium model (cont.)

Conditions for market equilibrium and price determination	
$pt_t = ner_t ptw_t$	(T.35)
$r_t = rf_t + rp_t + rp\left(\dfrac{FD_t}{pt_t YT_t + pn_t YN_t}\right) + \log\left(\dfrac{ner_{t+1}}{ner_t}\right)$	(T.36)

Traded goods firms are assumed to maximize the discounted value of net cash flow by choosing paths for labour input and investment (broken down into traded and non-traded goods), subject to the production function and the capital accumulation equation. The first-order condition for labour is given by equation (T.4), a standard condition whereby the marginal product of labour is equal to the real product wage. Because of capital adjustment costs the first order conditions for capital and investment are more complex. The relevant terms of the Lagrangian are:

$$pt_t AT(LT_t^d)^{\theta_{LT}} KT_t^{1-\theta_{LT}} - w_t LT_t^d - pit_t IT_t + q_t^{KT}\{KT_t - (1-\delta_{KT})KT_{t-1} - IT_{t-1}$$

$$+\mu_{IT}\frac{IT_{t-1}^2}{KT_{t-1}}\} + \frac{q_{t+1}^{KT}}{1+r_{t+1}}\{KT_{t+1} - (1-\delta_{KT})KT_t - IT_t + \mu_{IT}\frac{IT_t^2}{KT_t}\} + \ldots$$

where q_t^{KT} is the shadow price of the installed private capital stock, which evolves according to (T.6), while r_t is the domestic nominal interest rate. Differentiating this expression with respect to IT and KT yields equations (T.5) and (T.6), the first of which expresses investment as a function of the shadow price (q ratio) while the second gives the law of motion for the shadow price.

Finally, the investment good in the traded sector is a Cobb-Douglas composite of traded and non-traded goods, ITT_t and ITN_t respectively, given by equation (T.7), where *it* is the share of investment expenditures in traded goods and *st* is a scale factor. Accordingly, the firm faces a dual investment price index, pit_t, which is given by equation (T.8). The optimal choice of *ITT* and *ITN* yields the standard condition by which the nominal expenditure share for traded goods in total traded-sector investment expenditure is equal to *it*.

2.2 The Non-Traded Goods Sector

The set-up in the non-traded goods sector differs in a number of respects from that of the traded goods sector. In particular, the non-traded goods sector is embedded in a monopolistic competition framework and the price of non-traded goods is subject to nominal adjustment costs. These features mean that the first-order conditions differ from those of the traded sector by incorporating terms in mark-ups and also terms reflecting costly price adjustment.

2.2.1 Firms in the non-traded goods sector and the aggregator

The model set-up we employ for the non-traded sector has now become standard in the 'New Neoclassical Synthesis' literature (see, for example, Christiano et al., 2001; Erceg et al., 1999; and Smets and Wouters, 2002). Specifically, we assume that the composite non-traded good is produced by a single firm, the non-traded goods aggregator. This single firm uses inputs supplied by an infinite number of firms located along a continuum in [0,1]. The introduction of the aggregator, which behaves in a competitive manner, into the set-up is for ease of exposition. Each intermediate goods firm produces and supplies to the aggregator a differentiated good. In a context of monopolistic competition these intermediate goods firms are price setters in the market for their output but are price takers in the factor markets.

The intermediate goods supplied by the different firms, $YN(s)$, where s ε [0,1], are assumed to be imperfect substitutes. The composite non-traded good is produced by the aggregator using the following Dixit-Stiglitz technology:

$$YN_t = \left[\int_0^1 YN_t(s)^{(\varepsilon_n - 1)/\varepsilon_n} ds\right]^{\varepsilon_n/(\varepsilon - 1)} \tag{1}$$

where ε_n is the absolute value of the elasticity of demand for the intermediate good produced by firm s, this elasticity being equal for all s.

Letting $pn(s)$ denote the price of the output of firm s, the aggregator's profit function is:

$$pn_t YN_t - \int_0^1 pn(s) YN(s) ds \tag{2}$$

Assuming that the aggregator behaves competitively, i.e. acts as a price taker on both the purchasing and selling side, maximization of this expression with respect to each YN_t yields the aggregator's demand for each intermediate good:

$$YN_t(s) = \left[pn_t(s) / pn_t\right]^{-\varepsilon_n} YN_t \tag{3}$$

Simple manipulations of the previous expressions and using the zero profit condition for the aggregator, yield the following expression for the price of the composite non-traded good supplied by the aggregator:

$$pn = \left[\int_0^1 pn(s)^{1-\varepsilon_n}\right]^{1/(1-\varepsilon_n)} \quad (4)$$

2.2.2 Intermediate goods firms

Each intermediate goods producer s aims to maximize discounted cash flow by choosing a level of its output price and labour and investment subject to three constraints: (1) the production function (T.9), (2) the capital accumulation equation incorporating quadratic adjustment costs as in the traded sector (T.10) and (3) the demand function for their specific good (equation (3), above).

An important feature of our model is that intermediate goods firms' price setting is subject to nominal adjustment costs. This means that it is costly for the firm to adjust prices to the otherwise ideal level. Nominal adjustment costs for firm s are given, following Kim (2000), by a quadratic function of the percentage price change:

$$\mu(s)_p\left(\frac{pn(s)_t}{pn(s)_{t-1}} - 1\right)^2 YN(s)_t \quad (5)$$

where $\mu(s)_p$ reflects the degree of price stickiness for firm s or the cost of changing prices from the previous levels (a value of zero for this parameter would correspond to perfect price flexibility). Notice that nominal adjustment costs incurred by the firm depend on the amount of output which is actually supplied, which is in itself a function of the prevailing price. We have, therefore, modelled nominal adjustment costs as per unit costs.

Intermediate goods firms are therefore assumed to choose paths for $pn(s)$, $KN(s)$, $IN(s)$ and $LN(s)$ so as to maximize the expected discounted value of the firm:

$$\sum_{t=T}^{\infty} R(t)\{(pn_t - \mu_p\left(\frac{pn_t}{pn_{t-1}} - 1\right)^2)YN_t - w_t LN_t^d - pin_t IN_t\} \quad (6)$$

where R(t) is a discount factor defined in the usual way, e.g. R(t) = 1, R(t + 1) = $1/(1/1 + r_t)$, R(t + 2) = $1/((1 + r_t)(1 + r_{t+1}))$ etc. The maximization is subject to three constraints: the demand for the firms' output from the aggregator given by equation (3) above; the production function (T.9); the capital accumulation equation (T.10). The latter two equations are defined in an analogous way to the traded sector.

The first-order conditions for this problem can be derived in a straightforward, if tedious, manner. To move from individual to aggregate behaviour, we note that firms are assumed to have identical technologies, budget constraints and demand functions for their output. Therefore, the equilibrium in this monopolistically competitive set-up will be symmetric. Thus, output levels, prices, investment, capital and labour inputs will be identical across firms. Imposing these conditions, using (1) and (4), yields a set of aggregate first-order conditions for the non-traded sector which are shown in equations (T.13) to (T.17).

Equations (T.13) and (T.14) show the aggregate first-order conditions for labour input. These differ from the standard case (e.g. as in the traded sector) in two key respects. First, there is a mark-up term, reflecting the monopolistic nature of the market. Second, there are terms in current and discounted future price changes, reflecting the impact of costly price output adjustment. Note that this would collapse to the standard marginal productivity condition for labour as $\in_n \rightarrow \infty$ and $\mu_p \rightarrow 0$ (i.e. in the absence of market power and price adjustment costs). The same features apply to the marginal condition for capital (T.15). The investment equation (T.16) and the law of motion for the shadow price of non-traded capital stock (T.17) are, apart from the different definition of the marginal productivity of capital, the same as in the traded goods sector. Finally, given the definition of the composite investment good in the non-traded sector (T.18) and its dual price index (T.19), the intratemporal choice of traded and non-traded goods in investment is determined by conditions identical to those in the traded sector.

2.3 The Household Sector

Population is normalized to be equal to 1 and assumed to be constant. Each household/generation faces the same utility function with identical intertemporal discount rates and survivor rates. Households are price takers in all markets. In addition, for reasons that will become apparent in the next section, we assume that each generation comprises an infinite number of workers distributed uniformly along a continuum [0,1] of skills or 'professions'. This implies that each generation comprises workers of different skills/professions with the 'proportions' of each profession equal across generations and that, further, the distribution of workers in each skill class s across generations is equal across skill classes.

A conventional overlapping-generations specification following Yaari (1965), Blanchard (1985), Buiter (1988) and Weil (1989) was adopted here. See Frenkel and Razin (1996) for a detailed discussion of this type of household model. In this framework, the planning horizon is finite but in a non-deterministic fashion. A large number of identical agents are faced with a probability, $\gamma \in (0,1)$, of surviving through to the next period. The assumption that γ is constant over time and across age cohorts yields the perpetual youth specification by which all agents face a life expectancy of

$\gamma \in (0,1)$, and the probability of being alive j periods ahead is simply γ^j. Since population is normalized to unity, per capita and aggregate values are equal. In addition, given an assumed constant population, the birth rate is equal to the death rate $(1 - \gamma)$.

The household, aged a at time t, has to choose present and future consumption and leisure streams that maximize utility, equation (T.21), subject to the consolidated budget constraint, equation (T.22). The objective function is lifetime expected instantaneous utility subjectively discounted at the rate of β. Preferences, $u_{a+v,t+v}$, are additive separable in private consumption and leisure, and take on the CES form where B is a size parameter and σ is the constant elasticity of substitution. As a simplifying assumption, we will consider a Cobb-Douglas utility function ($\sigma = 1$). The effective subjective discount factor can be written as $\gamma\beta$ meaning that a lower probability of survival reduces the effective discount factor making the household relatively more impatient.

The budget constraint, equation (T.22), reflects the fact that the households' expected consumption expenditure stream discounted at the market interest rate should not exceed the households' total wealth, $TW_{a,t}$, evaluated at time t. The market interest rate is $1 + r_{t+v}$, but the one-period loan rate at which households borrow and lend among themselves in a perfectly competitive market is $1/\gamma$ times greater. In effect, the probability of dying, $1-\gamma$, acts as a perceived default rate. To ensure a before-tax return of $1 + r_{t+v}$ with certainty, creditors charge $(1 + r_{t+v})/\gamma > 1 + r_{t+v}$.

For the household of age a at time t, total wealth, $TW_{a,t}$, equation (T.23), is age-specific and is composed of human wealth, $HW_{a,t}$, net financial worth, $FW_{a,t}$, and the present market value of the firms, PVF_t. Human wealth, equation (T.24), represents the present discounted value of the household's future labour income minus lump sum taxes (LST) stream. Financial wealth comprises government debt minus foreign debt (T.25). Note that future labour earnings have to be discounted at a higher rate reflecting the probability of survival, since human wealth is household-specific and cannot be transferred at the time of death.

Income net of spending adds to net financial wealth, as in equation (T.25). Household income is augmented by profits distributed by corporations, $NCFT_t$, and $NCFN_t$, international transfers such as emigrants' remittances, R_t, and public transfers such as old-age pensions, TR_t. Loans among households cancel out upon the consolidation of households' financial assets and are thus omitted. On the spending side, debts to foreigners are serviced, taxes are paid and consumption expenditures are made. Under the assumption that no bequests are made, households are born without any financial wealth. Note also that total wealth is age-specific on account of age-specific labour supplies and consumption streams.

Solving the household's intertemporal problem yields an expression for consumption in which, under our simplifying assumptions, the marginal propensity to consume out of total wealth is age-independent and aggregation over age cohorts is greatly simplified. Aggregate consumption demand as a function of the aggregate stock of total wealth is given by equation (T.27). In our set-up, as explained in the next section, employment will be demand-determined given the wage rates set by unions.

Finally, aggregate consumption spending is a Cobb-Douglas composite of expenditure in traded and non-traded goods, CT_t and CN_t respectively, and is given by equation (T.28), where c is the share of investment expenditures in traded goods and sc is a scale factor. Accordingly, the households face a dual consumer price index, pc_t, which is given in equation (T.29).

2.4 Wage Stickiness and the Labour Market

The now standard way of introducing wage stickiness into dynamic general equilibrium models is to use a set-up where representative households themselves face a downward demand for their labour and act as wage setters (see Erceg et al., 1999). In the current set-up, this approach cannot be applied directly since households in the present model are not homogeneous. They are differentiated by levels of wealth (due to age effects) and accordingly differ with regard to their consumption. Labour-market decisions, such as the setting of wages, would not, therefore, be identical across households if households themselves were wage setters. In addition, problems would arise in dealing with newly arrived households who previously would not have set a wage.

In order to incorporate wage stickiness in our set-up while overcoming this problem, the approach taken is to add an additional set of agents to the labour market. These additional agents — called for convenience 'unions' — act as agents for the labour-market decisions of households and set the wage rate charged to firms by their members so as to maximize the utility of a 'representative' union member. Given this wage, 'the right to manage model' applies and the level of employment is determined by the firms' labour-demand functions. A labour aggregator purchases labour inputs of different skill classes from unions/households and supplies a single composite labour to the traded and non-traded goods firms.

2.4.1 The labour aggregator

The specification of the behaviour of the aggregator is now relatively standard (see Erceg et al., 1999). It is assumed that a representative aggregator supplies a composite labour input L_t to firms by combining differentiated types of labour input, differentiated by professions/skills. The different labour inputs are supplied by unions located along a continuum, with unions representing household members of a specific skill type. The labour services supplied by the different unions, $L(s)$, where $s \varepsilon [0,1]$, are assumed to be imperfect substitutes. The composite labour supplied to firms is produced by using the following Dixit-Stiglitz technology:

$$L_t = \left[\int_0^1 L_t(s)^{(\varepsilon_w-1)/\varepsilon_w} ds\right]^{\varepsilon_w/(\varepsilon_w-1)} \tag{7}$$

Letting $W(s)$ denote the wage rate for labour of type s and w the wage rate charged by the aggregator to the firms in the traded and non-traded sectors, the aggregator's profit function is:

$$w_t L_t - \int_0^1 w(s)L(s)ds \tag{8}$$

Assuming that the aggregator behaves competitively, i.e. acts as a price taker on both the purchasing and selling side, maximization of this expression with respect to each $L(s)$, yields the aggregator's demand for each type of labour input:

$$L_t(s) = \left[w_t(s)/w_t\right]^{-\varepsilon_w} L_t \tag{9}$$

ε_w is the (absolute value of) the elasticity of demand for labour for the members of union s, this elasticity being equal for all s by virtue of (7). Substituting (9) for (8) and imposing the zero profit condition for the aggregator, yields the following expression for the wage rate for the composite labour supplied to firms:

$$w_t = \left[\int_0^1 w_t(s)^{1-\varepsilon_w}\right]^{1/(1-\varepsilon_w)} \tag{10}$$

2.4.2 Unions

Each type of labour, $L(s)$, is supplied exclusively to the aggregator by a union located along the continuum of unions. Unions act as agents for their members, setting a wage rate for their specific type of labour so as to maximize the utility of a representative member. Given this wage rate, the union (s) supplies as much labour of type (s) as is demanded by the aggregator. On the other side, members of the union agree that, in return for receiving the union wage, they will supply as much labour as required, with each member of the union working the same hours and receiving the same wage for their type of labour. Facing the downward sloping demand curve (9), each union chooses a wage rate for its type of labour so as to maximize the following representative member welfare function:

$$\left[\sum_{t=0}^{\infty} R(t)\begin{pmatrix} U\{C_t(s),(L-L_t(s))\} - \frac{1}{2}\mu_w[\ \frac{w_t(s)}{w_{t-1}(s)} - 1]^2 \\ +\lambda(pc_t C_t(s) - w_t(s)L_t(s)....) \end{pmatrix}\right] \tag{11}$$

where $R(t)$ is a discount factor defined in the usual way, e.g. $R(t) = 1$, $R(t + 1)=1/(1 + r_t)$, $R(t + 2) = 1/((1 + r_t)(1 + r_{t+1}))$ etc. The functional form of $U(C,1 - L)$ is the same as for the individual household.

The consumption term entering the union's objective function ($C(s)$) is the average consumption of members. Given our earlier assumption that the distribution of union members across generations is identical, average consumption of the members of union s, $C(s)$, will in fact be equal to average consumption in the economy as a whole. It is interesting to note that in basing its choice on average consumption, the union is implicitly assigning a higher weight to older (and therefore richer) members, a type of seniority principle. In setting the wage, the union also takes into account the fact that hours worked by members will be determined by the labour-demand function of the aggregator (9). The quadratic term in the change of the union wage rate in the welfare function reflects an assumed disutility of changing nominal wages. This term, reflecting 'psychic adjustment costs', can be motivated by the idea that changing nominal wages involves considerable negotiating efforts in the union, reducing members' utility. Finally, in choosing the wage rate, the union takes into account the budget constraint of its members and their decisions regarding the choice of consumption level. This is shown in the final term in the objective function above. Given the households first-order condition for consumption, λ will equal the marginal utility of consumption of the representative member divided by the consumer price index. This term is taken as given in the union's optimization problem.

Substituting the labour-demand function (11), differentiating with respect to $w_t(s)$ and substituting the marginal utility condition for consumption for λ, yields the following Euler equation for the wage rate of union (s):

$$\left[\begin{array}{l} \left(\frac{L_t}{pc_t}\right)(1-\varepsilon_w)U_C - \varepsilon_w\left(\frac{L_t}{w_t(s)}\right)U_{1-L} + \left\{\frac{\mu_w w_{t+1}(s)}{(1+r_t)w_t^2(s)}\right\}\left\{\frac{w_{t+1}(s)}{w_t(s)} - 1\right\} \\ -\left\{\frac{\mu_w}{w_{t-1}(s)}\right\}\left\{\frac{w_t(s)}{w_{t-1}(s)} - 1\right\} = 0 \end{array}\right] \tag{12}$$

In order to interpret this equation, note that along a zero wage growth steady state, the last two terms in the above expression will be zero. This implies that the steady state real wage rate of the union will be given by:

$$\left(\frac{w_t(s)}{pc_t}\right) = \left(\frac{\varepsilon_w}{\varepsilon_w - 1}\right)\left(\frac{U_{1-L}}{U_C}\right) \quad (13)$$

The second term on the right of this equation is an expression for the real wage that would be satisfied under perfectly competitive labour-market conditions. The real wage charged by the union in the long run is thus a mark-up on the wage that would have prevailed if the labour market had been operating under perfect competition, with the size of the mark-up depending on the elasticity of demand for the union's labour services. With this in mind, the first two terms of the Euler equation therefore represent a non-linear 'error-correction' term in the deviation of the current union wage from its long-run equilibrium level. The remaining terms reflect a (forward-looking) adjustment to this long-run level resulting from the quadratic term in the utility function. The Euler equation therefore has the usual interpretation, where the union balances the costs of being away from its 'equilibrium' against the costs of adjustment which arise when changing nominal wages.

To move from the wage rate of individual unions to the aggregate wage rate, we note that under our assumptions, a symmetric equilibrium will apply. Specifically, the elasticity of the aggregator's demand for each type of labour ($\in_w$) and all of the other parameters and functional form of the union's objective function are equal across unions. By our assumptions on the distribution of union members across generations, average consumption will also be equal across unions. This implies that the solution to the first-order condition will be identical across unions. The equilibrium in the labour market will therefore be symmetric, implying that $w(i) = w(j)$ and $L(j) = L(i)$ for all i,j. This implies that the aggregate wage rate must satisfy an economy-wide Euler equation given by (T.20). From the aggregator's demand for labour function (9), hours worked per member will also be equal across unions. Since union membership is equally distributed across generations, this implies, in turn, that hours worked will also be the same across generations. Given the wage rates set by the unions, and the resulting aggregate wage rate (equation (10)), total labour input will be determined by firms' labour demand functions (equations T.4 and T.13).

2.5 Public Sector

The model includes a simplified public sector. We assume that in all periods, a balanced budget rule is followed. Accordingly, the budget for the public sector is given by equation (T.30). In this equation, CGT_t and CGN_t are public consumption of traded and non-traded goods respectively, rPD_t are interest payments on existing public debt, LST_t are lump sum axes levied on the households and TR_t are public transfers to the households. Finally, FT_t are foreign transfers to the government in foreign currency (e.g. EU transfers), which are converted into domestic currency using the nominal exchange rate of ner_t. The proceeds are spent immediately on additional non-traded goods, accounting for the appearance of this term on both sides of the budget constraint.

Government consumption is assumed to be exogenous in real terms. In particular, public consumption of traded and non-traded goods both grow at a given rate. Naturally, to the extent that there are changes in the nominal exchange rates or in the price of the non-traded goods, government consumption changes in nominal terms. Lump sum taxes adjust according to the balanced budget condition above.

2.6 Further Equilibrium Conditions and the Determination of Prices and Interest Rates

In addition to the first-order conditions and budget constraints discussed earlier, a number of whole-economy constraints are satisfied. The intertemporal budget constraint for our open economy is given by equation (T.31). This states the balance of payments condition that the change in foreign debt (the financial account) is equal to the current account deficit (nominal spending on traded goods and interest payments on the foreign debt minus domestic production of traded goods and international transfers). In turn, the equilibrium in the non-traded goods market is given by equation (T.32). Here the only relevant point is that it is assumed that international transfers are, as mentioned in the previous section, exclusively spent on non-traded goods. Equation (T.33) shows that total labour input is the sum of labour inputs in the traded and non-traded sectors. Finally, the definition of household financial wealth is given by equation (T.34). In this model, we assume that the domestic economy is a small open economy, i.e. a price taker in the traded goods markets as well as the financial markets. This means that domestic agents take the price of the traded good and the interest rate as exogenous.

In the determination of the domestic price of traded goods we start by assuming a regime of fixed exchange rates. In this case, the nominal exchange rate and the international price of non-traded goods, ptw_t, are exogenous. The domestic price of traded goods, pt_t, is given by (T.35). Alternatively, we assume a regime of flexible exchange rates in which the authorities target consumer price stability. In this case the nominal exchange rate will evolve so as to ensure a path for traded goods prices which generates a stable overall consumer price level. Via an uncovered interest parity (UIP) term, this path will in turn determine the path of the domestic interets rate vis-à-vis the world risk-free rate, ir_t, which is assumed to be constant over time.

Apart from UIP considerations, we assume that the domestic interest rate also contains both exogenous and endogenous risk premia. The exogenous risk premium, rp_t, is assumed to reflect a lack of integration into global financial markets and is a parameter which we change in some simulations. The endogenous risk premium is a function of the foreign debt to GDP ratio. The purpose of including this rather arbitrary element is to dampen down fluctuations in net foreign assets. Putting all these elements together, the domestic interest rate is given by equation (T.36).

We define the steady-state growth path as an intertemporal equilibrium trajectory for the economy in which all the flow and stock variables grow at the same rate while market prices and shadow prices are constant. There are three major types of restrictions imposed by the existence of a steady-state growth path. First, the existence of a steady state determines the value of critical production parameters, like adjustment costs and depreciation rates given the initial stocks of physical and human capital. These stocks, in turn, are determined by assuming that the observed levels of investment of the respective types are such that the capital to GDP ratios do not change in the steady state. Second, the need for constant ratios of public and foreign debt to GDP implies that the steady-state public account deficit and the current account deficit are a constant fraction of the respective stocks of debt that coincides with the growth rate of the economy. Finally, the exogenous variables, such as public transfers or international unilateral transfers, etc., have to grow at the steady-state growth rate.

2.7 Calibration

The data and parameters that are used in simulating the model are presented in Tables 7.2 and 7.3, respectively, and the details of the calibration procedure are given in the Annex . The calibration approach is to choose a set of model parameters so as to match a steady-state data set which broadly corresponds to the stylized facts of the Irish and Portuguese economies. These features mainly relate to shares of traded and non-traded goods in output, employment and demand components. In addition, we take into account information about the functional distribution of income. The basic information sources are input-output tables and national accounts for both countries. On the basis of this information, a baseline data set was constructed and is shown in Table 7.3, where for convenience GDP and all prices are normalized to unity. In deriving this data set from the raw data, we have assumed that the traded sector basically comprises agriculture and manufacturing while the non-traded sector comprises the remainder of GDP.

Table 7.2 Parameter set

Parameters	Value	Type
Household parameters		
Discount factor	0.03581	calibrated
Probability of survival	0.97500	data
Savings rate out of total wealth	0.94129	calibrated
Production scalars in traded goods sector		
Scale parameter	8.77966	scale
Labour share	0.55000	data
Capital share	0.45000	data
Depreciation rate	0.09596	calibrated
Adjustment cost as a percentage of investment	0.20000	assumed
Adjustment cost parameter	1.66733	calibrated
Production scalars in non-traded goods sector		
Scale parameter	12.12338	scale
Labour share	0.60000	data
Capital share	0.40000	data
Depreciation rate	0.08150	calibrated
Adjustment cost as % of investment	0.20000	assumed
Adjustment cost parameter	1.96320	calibrated
Expenditure shares of traded goods		
In private consumption	0.50000	data
Scale parameter for private consumption	2.00000	scale
In investment in traded goods sector	0.40000	data
Scale parameter for investment in the traded goods sector	1.96013	scale
In investment in the non-traded goods sector	0.35000	data
Scale parameter for investment in the non-traded goods sector	1.91066	scale
In public consumption	0.05000	data
Monopolistic competition and nominal adjustment costs		
Mark-up in non-traded goods sector	0.10000	assumed
Nominal adjustment costs for the price of the non-traded good	50.00	data
Mark-up in the labour market	0.10000	assumed

Table 7.2 Parameter set (cont.)

Monopolistic competition and nominal adjustment costs		
Nominal adjustment costs for the nominal wage rate	50.00	data
Interest rate parameters		
Responsiveness of the endogenous risk premium to foreign debt	0.4000	data

Table 7.3 Data set

Data	Value	Type
Domestic spending data		
GDP growth rate	0.00000	normalized
GDP	1.00000	normalized
GDP — traded sector	0.38000	data
GDP — non-traded sector	0.62000	data
Private consumption	0.57500	data
Private investment in the traded goods sector	0.10125	data
Private investment in the non-traded goods sector	0.12375	data
Public consumption	0.20000	data
Foreign account data		
Trade deficit	0.00000	normalized
Interest payments	0.00000	normalized
Unilateral public transfers	0.00000	normalized
Current account deficit (+)	0.00000	normalized
Public account data		
Public consumption	0.20000	data
Government transfers	0.15000	data
Interest payments on public debt	0.02500	data
Lump sum tax revenues	0.37500	data
Public deficit (+)	0.00000	normalized
Population		
Population/labour force	1.00000	normalized
Population growth rate	0.00000	normalized
Labour force in the traded goods sector	0.38327	calibrated
Labour force in the non-traded goods sector	0.61673	calibrated
Leisure	0.20000	assumed
Leisure scale parameter	–0.17320	scale
Stock variables		
Private capital in the traded goods sector	0.84409	calibrated

Table 7.3 Data set (cont.)

Stock variables		
Private capital in the non-traded goods sector	1.21473	calibrated
Foreign debt	0.00000	normalized
Public debt	0.50000	data
Human wealth	4.51063	calibrated
Value of the firms	4.78406	calibrated
Prices		
Nominal exchange rate	1.00000	normalized
International price of traded goods	1.00000	normalized
Domestic price of traded goods	1.00000	normalized
Price of non-traded goods	1.00000	normalized
Price of private consumption	1.00000	normalized
Price of investment in the traded goods sector	1.00000	normalized
Price of investment in the non-traded goods sector	1.00000	normalized
Wage rate	0.54719	calibrated
Risk-free interest rate	0.03500	data
Interest rate — exogenous risk premium	0.01500	data
Interest rate — endogenous risk premium	0.00000	normalized
Shadow price of capital in the traded goods sector	1.75000	calibrated
Shadow price of capital in the non-traded goods sector	1.75000	calibrated

We choose the parameters of the model in a way such that the model, when run on the baseline, reproduces this data set. This comprises four steps. First, some parameter values are assumed on the basis of available literature or educated guesses. These include investment adjustment costs as a percentage of investment and mark-up parameters. Second, the values of the share parameters (production function parameters, shares of traded and non-traded goods in investment and consumption) can be determined straightforwardly from the respective shares in the data. Third, some parameters, specifically the parameters for nominal stickiness and wages and non-traded prices, are chosen to match empirical evidence from other studies. A final subset of parameters, namely the discount rate, the depreciation rates in both sectors and the investment adjustment cost parameters are chosen so that the model reproduces the baseline data set.

We solve the model numerically using the stacked-time algorithm of Juillard and Laxton (1996). This involves stacking the equations for all periods (in our case 200 years) and solving them simultaneously, subject to given initial and terminal conditions, the latter being set to the steady-state values. As is well-known in highly non-linear models, such as the one used in this chapter, the existence of multiple equilibrium steady states cannot be excluded, in general. Such a possibility is very disturbing for the research strategy we follow since our solution method relies on the existence of a unique long-term equilibrium. Clearly, our use of simple functional forms and the choice of parameters implying strong convexity makes the problem of multiplicity of equilibria less likely to occur. In order to rule out the relevance of multiple equilibria we performed extensive numerical investigations. We searched a large grid of initial conditions for the model variables and non-calibration parameters. Systematically and without exceptions, the model converged to the same steady-state equilibrium or in the context of the calibration exercises we systematically and without exceptions obtained the same calibration parameters consistent with the steady-state conditions. This systematic search has assured us that indeed our model, for the range of functional forms and parameters considered, exhibits a unique steady-state equilibrium.

3 MACROECONOMIC ADJUSTMENT TO STRUCTURAL CHANGE: SIMULATION RESULTS

In this section we seek to characterize macroeconomic adjustment to structural changes using the model outlined in earlier sections. We examine the response of standard macroeconomic aggregates — prices, output and employment — as well as the allocation of resources between the two sectors. We focus especially on the long-term impact on the real exchange rate as well as on its dynamics of adjustment towards its long-run equilibrium. We explore the extent to which the presence or absence of price and wage stickiness impacts on these adjustment processes. Finally, we consider how different exchange rate regimes affect the macroeconomic adjustment. In particular, we examine the implications for macroeconomic adjustment of a policy of fixed nominal exchange rate regime compared to a policy orientated to domestic price stability under floating rates.

3. 1 Simulation Design

In our simulation experiments we consider the effects of three stylized structural changes, which, as emphasized in the introduction, are seen as the principal structural changes associated with integration into the EU on the basis of the experience of Portugal and Ireland. The *first structural change* corresponds to a protracted increase of productivity growth in the traded goods sector. It is meant to reflect a standard source of real convergence connected with increased trade integration. The magnitude of the change is such that the shock in total factor productivity growth in the traded goods sector when combined with the other two shocks (see below) accumulates to a level effect on total output of about 30% in 50 years. This implies an increase in the traded sector TFP growth rate of about one percentage point a year for a period of 30 years. The *second structural change* reflects the process of financial integration. It corresponds to a reduction in the interest rate the domestic economy faces in the international markets. We consider a reduction of the exogenous risk premium of 150 basis points spread over 10. The *third structural change* is associated with the Community's structural policies. It is modelled as a pure demand shock. We consider an increase in international transfers, reflecting access to EU structural funds, corresponding to 3% of GDP. This change lasts for a 15-year period, after which transfers return to baseline.

In terms of the different sets of simulations to be considered, we start by considering the effects of structural changes under price stickiness and a fixed nominal exchange rate and proceed to determine the role of both assumptions. In the *first set of simulation results* our objective is to establish that a plausible package of structural changes leads in our model to reasonable results which are not in contradiction with known stylized facts. In the *second set of simulation experiments* we consider the effects of the same structural changes in the absence of price and wage stickiness but still with a fixed nominal exchange rate to determine how the macroeconomic adjustment would change in absence of such stickiness. The point is to establish that in the context of monopolistic competition nominal price rigidities are important to produce the plausible results introduced before. Finally, in the *third set of simulation results*, we consider the effects of structural changes under price and wage stickiness but with a policy orientated to domestic price stability under a flexible nominal exchange rate. The idea is to show the effects of the choice of monetary policy regime, associated with nominal exchange rate floating, on the macroeconomic adjustment process.

For the sake of brevity we will refer to short-term effects as effects happening within a ten-year period, medium-term effects as those occurring between ten and twenty years, and long-term the effects thereafter. Furthermore, all the references to baseline refer to the model outcomes before the structural shocks are imposed and, therefore, refer to the values for our stylized economy that reflect the long-term trends for the economy in the absence of such structural shocks.

3.2 Effects of Structural Changes under Market Rigidities and Fixed Nominal Exchange Rate

How does our stylized economy adjust to the structural shocks considered under price and wage stickiness when the nominal exchange rate is fixed? What are the effects on the long-term allocation of resources and real exchange rate? What are the properties of the adjustment to the new equilibrium allocation of resources and real exchange rate? These are some of the questions we address in this section. The simulation results for this case are presented in Figure 7.1.

The structural changes under consideration lead to a sharp increase of the real exchange rate in the short term to 25% above the baseline level followed by a relatively slow convergence to a new long-term steady-state level which is about 30% above the baseline. The nominal wage rate and the consumption price index follow a similar pattern with a sharp increase in the short term followed by smooth convergence to a level about 45% and 15% above the baseline levels respectively. As a corollary, the effects of structural changes on consumer price inflation are front-loaded. Indeed they virtually disappear after a ten-year period.

The effects of the structural changes on nominal wages and consumption prices suggest that real wages increase sharply within the first five years and then converge slowly to a long-term increase of about 22%. The long-term evolution of employment follows a corresponding pattern. It shows a long-term increase of about 12.5%, but in the short term the structural changes lead to increased employment on impact. This increase, however, shrinks until it eventually turns into a decrease. The recovery towards the long-term increase starts around 15 years into the structural changes.

It is interesting to understand this short-term response pattern of employment to the structural changes under consideration. Although the real wage rate increases in the short term, this is just one of the determinants of labour supply and, ultimately, employment. Indeed, these structural changes — because they are fully anticipated by forward-looking households — lead to a substantial increase in the total wealth of households. Recall that total wealth includes, in addition to financial wealth (the foreign debt position), the forward-looking stocks of human wealth and the value of the firms. The structural changes represent a substantial gain in the profitability of the production sectors as well as on the discounted wage income of households. This being the case, the structural changes induce on impact a major increase in the wealth position of the households. They respond, in a standard fashion, by increasing consumption (more on this below) and leisure. Hence, a short-term reduction in desired labour supply. As will be discussed in more detail below, however, the impacts are offset in the very short run by wage stickiness which prevents an immediate adjustment of wages to desired levels, resulting initially in a rise in employment due to a shift in labour demand.

This evolution in the supply of labour hides a very different evolution of employment in the traded and non-traded goods sectors. In fact, the structural changes lead to a substantial positive but declining effect on employment in the non-traded goods sector and a negative short-term effect in the traded goods sector, which however turns into a substantial long-term gain. This suggests that the structural changes induce a shift in the composition of employment to the non-traded goods sector in the short term but decisively to the traded goods sector in the medium and long term.

In terms of the capital accumulation we see that the structural changes lead to a long-term increase in the shadow price of capital for both sectors of about 20% in both the traded and non-traded goods sectors. The transitional patterns, however, are very different between the two sectors. In the short and medium term the shadow price of capital in the traded goods sector increases smoothly to a level of 35% above the baseline thereby overshooting the new long-term level. In turn, the shadow price in the non-traded goods sector increases on impact to about 40% over its baseline level and then declines smoothly to the new steady-state level.

The effects of the structural changes on the two stocks of capital follow a corresponding pattern. The stock of capital in the traded sector increases strongly initially and then smoothly converges to a new steady state level about 70% above the baseline. The stock of capital in the non-traded sector increases at a smooth but decreasing rate to the new steady-state level, which is about 22.5% above the baseline level. Again the structural changes induce a shift in the sectoral composition of capital. In the short run the composition shifts to the non-traded sector while in the long term it shifts decisively to the traded sector. It should be pointed out that this pattern of results is consistent with the fact that investment in the non-traded goods sector is more dependent on non-traded goods and the price of these goods increases substantially in the long term.

Naturally, the evolution of output, both at the aggregate and the sector level, closely follows the evolution of employment and capital accumulation. In the short term aggregate output is only very marginally affected. The increase in capital formation is matched by a decline in employment. In the longer term, however, as both employment and capital accumulation increase, so does aggregate output. Indeed, aggregate output ultimately increases to a level that is about 35% above the baseline. At the sector level, the decline in employment in the traded sector in the short term induces a decline in output in this sector. In the long term, however, output increases by up to 100% over its baseline level. In turn, output in the non-traded sector increases significantly in the short term but the long-term gains are less impressive, i.e. just about 8%. This means that the structural changes induce a major shift in the output composition towards the traded goods sector in the long run.

Let us consider now the evolution of private consumption. The evolution of private consumption is conditioned by two main factors. The first is the evolution of the consumer price index. The structural changes under consideration induce on impact an increase of about 5% on the consumption price index. This increase continues and becomes more accentuated as the consumption price index reaches a new steady state about 15% above the baseline level. The corresponding inflation rate increases sharply on impact but the bulk of the effects are in place after a ten-year transition period.

A second factor affecting private consumption is the evolution of total wealth, including human wealth, financial wealth and the value of firms. The positive impact of structural changes on long-term wages leads to an increase in human wealth while an increase of the profitability of firms leads to an increased present value of firms. Finally we observe that financial wealth (mostly reflected in foreign financing) declines, but only slightly. Overall, therefore, consumers experience an increase in total wealth. Reflecting this increase of total wealth, private consumption increases sharply on impact also by about 25%. Then it progressively declines to a gain of about 14% as the build-up in foreign debt diminishes total wealth. Finally, it rebounds somewhat to reach a long-term gain of about 18% versus the baseline.

We can therefore summarize these results as follows. The structural changes lead to a marked increase in the real exchange rate in the long term. In the long term, there is an increase in output and both employment and capital formation, as well as in private consumption, but the composition of output, employment and capital as well as consumption shift markedly to the traded goods sector. In the short term, however, the shift is towards the non-traded sector. So far we have considered all the structural shocks simultaneously and we have just summarized their combined effects. It is useful, however, to consider briefly the differential effects of the different shocks in the perspective of determining which ones seem to be more important for either the observed long-term effects or the macroeconomic adjustment leading to such effects.

In terms of the effects on the real exchange rate, the short-term effects seem to be induced mostly by financial integration and to a lesser extent by structural transfers while the long-term effects are exclusively due to the total factor productivity shock in the traded goods sector. Indeed, the effects of financial integration are very small after a ten-year period while the effects of structural funds are always very small. In terms of the intertemporal patterns of employment and capital accumulation, all shocks seem to contribute to the short- and medium-term reallocation towards the non-traded goods sector. Financial integration alone seems to be behind the long-term level and composition effects in terms of employment, while both the total factor productivity shock in the traded goods sector and financial integration seem to underlie the long-term effects on the level and allocation of capital accumulation. Finally, in terms of the evolution of private consumption, the productivity shock leads to a progressively increasing positive effect that clearly dominates in the long term, while financial integration and structural transfers have important short-term effects that become of only marginal relevance in the long term.

3.3 Effects of Structural Changes in the Absence of Market Rigidities

The central feature of our model set-up is the presence of nominal rigidities in both the market for non-traded goods and the labour market in a context of monopolistic competition. This feature, while standard in most current macroeconomic models which are used to assess the effects of persistent but temporary shocks, is rarely included in growth models such as ours, which are used to study the impacts of permanent changes. Therefore, it is worthwhile highlighting how the features of price and wage stickiness, which we have incorporated into the model, affect the macroeconomic adjustment to structural change.

Clearly, we do not expect nominal rigidities to have any material impacts on the long-term effects of the structural changes and this is confirmed by our results. This being the case, we concentrate on the short- to medium-term differences between the macroeconomic adjustment to structural changes in the presence and in the absence of nominal price rigidities. The simulation results are presented in Figure 7.2. The presence of nominal rigidities changes the short-term price dynamics in a very substantial way. In the absence of nominal rigidities, the wage rate would respond to the structural changes by jumping immediately to a level rather close to, but just below, its new long-term steady-state level and then gradually converge to this level. In contrast, the price of non-traded goods exhibits an overshooting pattern, jumping initially to a level above its new long-run equilibrium before gradually converging to this value. As a consequence the real exchange rate also shows a similar overshooting pattern.

The effects of structural changes in the labour markets are also greatly affected by the presence of nominal rigidities. The greater short-term increase in the real wage in the absence of nominal rigidities leads to a much greater reduction of employment in the traded sector and a much lower increase in the non-traded sector. Overall employment actually declines in the short-term while it increases in the case of sticky prices. The reduction in short-term employment under flexible prices/wages, in contrast to the short-term rise which occurs under sticky wages, is easily explained. In the absence of wage stickiness, the increase in consumer wealth leads to a decline in labour supply, driving up the wage and lowering employment. Under sticky wages, in contrast, this process is muted. Wages do not exhibit the same marked jump pattern since they can, under wage stickiness, only gradually adjust to the long-run level. With employment demand determined in this case, employment actually rises in the short run as a result of a shift in the labour demand curve.

The effects of nominal rigidities on the pattern of capital accumulation are also important. This is because a significant part of the investment activities in both sectors involves purchases of non-traded goods. Therefore, the fact that the price of the non-traded goods increases immediately in response to the shocks under price flexibility implies that investment demand shows a much lower short-term response to the shocks in this case. In fact, investment in the traded goods sector decreases significantly in the short term while investment in the non-traded goods sector increases by much less than under price rigidities. Accordingly, the short-term reduction in capital accumulation in the traded sector is much more marked while the increase in capital accumulation in the non-traded sector is less marked.

The differences in the equilibrium in the input markets reflects itself clearly in the differences in the short-term pattern of response of output to the structural shocks with and without nominal price rigidities. Reflecting a reduction in employment and a lower capital accumulation in the short term under price flexibility, total output actually declines in the short term. This is unlike the case of price stickiness, in which output actually increases on impact. In terms of the sector composition of output, the pattern of response changes also in the expected manner. Output in the traded sector actually decreases more sharply in the short term in the absence of price stickiness while output in the non-trade sector actually increases less sharply. Hence the combined effect is a reduction in aggregate output.

Finally, the increase in consumption in the flexible price case is less sharp than in the case of sticky wages/prices. This primarily reflects the lower increase in real human wealth in the former case, since the effect of higher real wages (a difference of 6 percentage points) is offset by lower employment in this case (20 percentage points). An interesting corollary of these results is that the main effect of wage and price stickiness is to greatly diminish the short-run effects of wealth on labour supply, with the result that output is higher in the short run.

3.4 Effects of Structural Changes under Flexible Nominal Exchange Rate

In the previous sections we have considered the effects of the structural changes on the assumption of a fixed exchange rate regime. In this section, we analyse the effects of the structural changes on the assumption that the exchange rate is allowed to adjust in order to maintain domestic consumer price stability. In this stylized policy regime, we abstract from the specific issue of how the domestic price level could in fact be stabilized by the authorities. For example, we do not specify a policy rule for interest rates or the money stock. Instead, we adopt an approach whereby a stable domestic price level is imposed as a given unit of account on the economy and allow the nominal exchange rate and nominal interest rates to endogenously adjust so as to ensure this outcome. In addition, the regime under consideration involves stabilizing the domestic price *level* at some target level rather than stabilizing the domestic inflation *rate* at some non-zero rate. In our set-up, which involves only one-off permanent shocks, this simplifying assumption should not significantly affect the results. The simulation results are presented in Figure 7.3.

Since we have observed that the effects of the structural changes on consumer price inflation under a fixed exchange rate regime are front-loaded, we would expect the efforts towards nominal exchange rate management to be relevant mostly in the very short term. Indeed, the increase in the price of the non-traded goods induced by the structural changes is now matched by an offsetting reduction in the domestic price of traded goods through the nominal exchange rate appreciation. While these changes in the price levels are permanent, the changes in the relative price of non-traded to traded goods, relative to the corresponding path under fixed nominal exchange rates, are small and temporary. Indeed, the paths of the real exchange rate are indistinguishable across both cases.

Accordingly, and because the nominal changes do not have a substantial impact on the relative prices, the intertemporal allocation of resources does not change significantly with flexible nominal exchange rates. The reduction in overall employment in the short term is slightly stronger in this case while the effects on capital accumulation are only visible in the non-traded sector where a marginally lower path is observed. Therefore, the short-term change in aggregate output is slightly less pronounced under price stabilization. This is due almost exclusively to a lower increase of output in the non-traded goods sector.

More interesting is the change in consumption patterns. Since the short-term consumer price inflation effects observed in the fixed exchange rate case are now eliminated, private consumption actually increases by more in the very short term, i.e. the first five years, under flexible nominal exchange rates. After this, however, the trajectory of consumption is slightly reduced compared to the fixed exchange rate case. The general point of this discussion is that the change from a regime of fixed exchange rates to a regime of flexible exchange rates oriented to price stability does not seem to yield substantial changes in the macroeconomic adjustment. Ultimately even the effects on private consumption are relatively small and short-lived.

In comparing the impact of different policy regimes, it is more interesting to examine the implications on the welfare of agents rather than simply comparing the paths of individual macroeconomic variables. Figure 7.4 shows the impact of the three structural shocks on the utility of the representative agent in the economy. As can be seen, utility is higher in the earlier period under domestic price stabilization, reflecting the higher consumption mentioned in the previous paragraph, while being somewhat lower later on. Discounting this flow of utility yields a conclusion that the improvement in welfare from the package of structural changes is not significantly different across the two policy regimes considered. We take these results as indicating that, in the model, there is no trade-off between exploiting the full benefits of the real convergence process and maintaining domestic price stability.

4 SUMMARY AND POLICY IMPLICATIONS

This chapter addressed the issue of macroeconomic adjustment to structural change for a small open economy catching up in the EU. The issue is relevant for the ten countries set to become new members of the EU on 1 May 2004: Cyprus, Czech Republic, Estonia, Hungary, Latvia, Lithuania, Malta, Poland, Slovakia and Slovenia. Successful integration of these countries will require both nominal convergence, i.e. macroeconomic adjustment, and real convergence, i.e. structural change. To analyse macroeconomic adjustment to structural change we considered a two-sector, imperfect competition, dynamic general-equilibrium model allowing for price setting in the non-traded goods sector and wage setting. We made use of a set-up including overlapping generations, real adjustment costs to capital accumulation and costs to nominal price and wage adjustment. The model is calibrated with data and parameter sets inspired by the cases of Ireland and Portugal, two euro area countries that have undergone a process of significant catching up.

The structural changes considered included an increase in total factor productivity growth in the traded goods sector, financial integration (a reduction in the interest rate faced by the domestic economy) and international public transfers from the EU. Under a regime of fixed exchange rates these structural changes induce a long-term increase in the real exchange rate which goes with a substantial increase in aggregate output and private consumption and a reallocation of resources from the non-traded sector to the traded sector. This means that the source of increase in aggregate output and consumption is the increase in the traded goods output and consumption.

The short-term effects of the structural changes, however, are markedly different from the long-term effects. In the short term, the allocation of resources tends to shift towards the non-traded goods sector and one may even witness an absolute reduction in employment and aggregate output. Moreover, under fixed exchange rates, real appreciation implies an increase in domestic inflation. Domestic inflation converges to the level prevailing in the rest of the world only as real appreciation fades.

An important point we bring out is that the pattern of short-term macroeconomic adjustments to structural changes is strongly affected by the presence of nominal rigidities in the labour and non-traded goods markets. Indeed, in the absence of price stickiness the short-term effects of the structural changes on the real exchange rate and, therefore, on the real wages and the consumption price index, would be much greater and, indeed, much closer to the long-lasting steady-state effects. This changes the dynamics of real adjustment in that both employment and output may even decline in the short term as a result of the structural changes while consumption would increase by substantially less. In our example, the presence of nominal rigidities seems to smooth the effects of the structural changes over time.

Finally, when the nominal exchange rate is allowed to adjust in order to guarantee consumer price stability there are no significant impacts on the response of real variables to the process of structural change and the welfare of the representative agent is basically unaffected by this choice. The patterns of resource allocation across sectors, overall economic activity, employment and consumption are not significantly affected. In other words, the quantitative features of macroeconomic adjustment to structural change stay the same. We interpret this finding as illustrating the absence of any significant trade-off between nominal and real convergence.

REFERENCES

Balassa, Bela (1964), 'The Purchasing Power doctrine: a reappraisal', *Journal of Political Economy*, **72** (6), pp. 584–96.

Blanchard, Olivier (1985), 'Debt, deficits and finite horizons', *Journal of Political Economy*, **93**, pp. 223–47.

Blanchard, Olivier and Alain Muet (1993), 'Competitiveness through disinflation: an assessment of the French macroeconomic strategy', *Economic Policy*, April 1993, **8** (16), pp. 11–56.

Buiter, Willem (1988), 'Death, birth, productivity growth and debt neutrality', *Economic Journal*, **98**, pp. 279–93.

Bundesbank (2001), 'Monetary aspects of the enlargement of the EU', *Monthly Report*, October.

Calvo, Guillermo (1983), 'Staggered prices in a utility-maximizing framework', *Journal of Monetary Economics*, **12** (3), pp. 383–98.

Christiano, Lawrence, Martin Eichenbaum and Charles Evans (2001), 'Nominal rigidities and the dynamic effects of a shock to monetary policy', mimeo, May 2001.

Coricelli, Fabrizio. and Bostjan Jazbec (2001), 'Real exchange rate dynamics in the transition economies', CEPR Discussion Paper 2869, London.

Dixit, Avinash and Joseph Stiglitz (1977), 'Monopolistic competition and optimum product diversity,' *American Economic Review*, **67**, pp. 297–308.

Edwards, Sebastian (1989), *Real Exchange Rates, Devaluation and Adjustment: Exchange Rate Policy in Developing Countries*, Cambridge, Massachusetts: The MIT Press.

Egert, Balazs (2002), 'Nominal and real convergence in Estonia: the Balassa-Samuelson (dis)connection', paper presented at the conference 'Exchange rate strategies during the EU enlargement', Budapest, 27–30 November 2002.

Erceg, Christopher, Dale Henderson and Andrew Levin (1999), 'Optimal monetary policy with staggered wage and price contracts', *Journal of Monetary Economics*, **46**, pp. 81–313.

Fisher, Christoph (2002), 'Real currency appreciation in accession countries: Balassa-Samuelson and investment demand', Deutsche Bundesbank Discussion Paper 19/02, July.

Frenkel, Jacob and Assaf Razin (1996), *Fiscal Policy and Growth in the World Economy*, Third Edition, Cambridge, Massachusetts: The MIT Press.

Gali, J., M. Gertler and D. Lopez-Salido (2001), 'European inflation dynamics', *European Economic Review*, **45** (7), pp. 1237–70.

Halpern, Laszlo and Charles Wyplosz (1997), 'Equilibrium exchange rates in transition economies', *IMF Staff Papers*, **44** (4), pp. 430–61.

Halpern, Laszlo and Charles Wyplosz (2001), 'Economic transformation and the real exchange rate in the 2000s: the Balassa-Samuelson connection', *Economic Surveys of Europe*, UNECE 2001/1, pp. 227–39.

Juillard, Michel and Douglas Laxton (1996), 'A robust and efficient method for solving non-linear rational expectations models', IMF Working Paper WP/96/106.

Kim, Jinill (2000), 'Constructing and estimating a realistic optimizing model of monetary policy,' *Journal of Monetary Economics*, **45**, pp. 329–59.

MacDonald, Ronald and Cezary Wojcik (2002), 'Catching up: the role of demand, supply and regulated price effects on the real exchange rate of four accession countries', in *Focus on Transition*, Oesterreichische Nationalbank.

Mihaljek, Dubravko (2002), 'The Balassa-Samuelson effect in Central Europe: a disaggregated analysis', paper presented at the conference 'Exchange rate strategies during the EU enlargement', Budapest, 27–30 November 2002.

Neary, J. Peter (1988), 'Determinants of the equilibrium real exchange rate', *American Economic Review*, **78** (1), pp. 210–15.

Pelkmans, Jacques, Daniel Gros and Jorge Nunez Ferrer (2000), 'Long-run economic aspects of the European Union's eastern enlargement', Scientific Council for Government Policy, WRR, Working Paper 109.

Rotemberg, Julio (1987), 'The new Keynesian microfoundations', in S. Fischer (ed), *NBER Macroeconomics Annual*, Cambridge, Massachusetts: The MIT Press, pp. 69–104.

Samuelson, Paul (1964), 'Theoretical notes on trade problems', *Review of Economics and Statistics*, **46**, May, pp. 145–54.

Sinn, Hans-Werner and Michael Reutter (2001), 'The minimum inflation rate for Euroland', NBER Working Paper No. 8085.

Smets, Frank and Raf Wouters (2002), 'An estimated dynamic general equilibrium model for the Euro Area', ECB Working Paper No. 171.

Weil, Philippe, (1989), 'Overlapping families of infinitely-lived agents', *Journal of Public Economics*, **38**, pp. 183–98.

Yaari, Menahem (1965), 'Uncertain lifetime, life insurance and the theory of the consumer', *Review of Economic Studies*, **32**, pp. 137–50.

ANNEX: CALIBRATION AND PARAMETERIZATION PROCEDURES

The data and parameters used to simulate the dynamic general equilibrium model are presented in Tables 7.2 and 7.3, respectively. These data and parameters were obtained in two fundamentally different ways. First, some data and parameters are obtained directly from or are directly implied by data sources or the literature (referred to in Tables 7.2 and 7.3 as Data). In this group we also include guesses for parameters for which there is no information (referred to as assumed in the tables), scale parameters (referred to as scale in the tables), and parameters and variables which, without loss of generality, we have normalized (referred to as normalized in the tables). Second, the remaining data and parameters were obtained by calibration of the model (referred to as calibrated in the tables). This means that they were obtained in such a way that the model replicates the observed data given the parameters obtained from the data sources, assumed or normalized. We turn now to a detailed discussion of both parameterization and calibration.

Parameterization

In this subsection we present the baseline data set which is used in the simulations and for which the model should, when suitably calibrate, match in the steady state. The overall objective is to produce data and parameter sets that broadly match the 'stylized facts' of the Irish and Portuguese economies. The sources are mostly input/output tables and national accounting information but educated guesses of some values are frequently also used. Whenever relevant we attempt to use information for a relatively large time span. This is because we want the base case of the model to capture the stylized long-term trends for these economies while minimizing the business cycle effects. This way the counterfactual simulations can be interpreted and pure deviations from the long-term trends.

We start by considering a zero growth steady state. For convenience, the baseline value of aggregate GDP is normalized at unity. Similarly, in the baseline all price indices are normalized to unity. Furthermore, we normalize the total time endowment to 3.0 and total hours worked in steady state to one-third of the total endowment, the standard value in the dynamic general-equilibrium literature. Finally, we normalize all international flows (0.00) including foreign debt (0.00). All data is presented as shares of the normalized GDP.

The decomposition of the GDP between traded and non-traded goods is always a difficult matter. To establish this decomposition we used input/output tables and ranked sectors of activity according to their share of exports in total final use (i.e. output minus intermediate sales). A cut-off point of 30% was used. On this basis, the non-traded sector comprises all services sectors plus building and construction. Manufacturing and agriculture are included in the traded goods sector. We determined that non-traded goods correspond to approximately 60% of total output in Ireland and about 63% in Portugal. We use a figure of 62% of the aggregate GDP in the simulations.

To determine the domestic composition of spending between the traded and non-traded sectors, we start from the aggregate private and public consumption and investment in both the traded and non-traded sectors from national accounting sources and re-scale their values to match the remaining assumptions. The values used for the simulations are 57.5%, 20%, 10.1% and 12.4% of the aggregate GDP respectively. These values together with the aggregate values for each expenditure category allow us immediately to obtain the scale parameters for the corresponding expenditure category.

The absence of a trade deficit in the baseline imposes restrictions on the values that can be assumed by the different types of domestic consumption and investment expenditure on both traded and non-traded goods. We assume that the shares of traded goods in private consumption, public consumption, private investment in the traded sector, and private investment in the non-traded sector are 50%, 5%, 40% and 30% respectively. These values are consistent with the zero trade balance assumption and some stylized facts about the composition of domestic expenditures based on input-output tables. Indeed, it is widely accepted that private consumption relies more heavily on traded goods than the other expenditure (the actual figures for Ireland and Portugal are between 45% and 50% of private consumption being purchases of non-traded goods). Also, public consumption spending is mostly on non-traded goods. Finally, the shares of traded goods in investment expenditures is greater in the traded goods sector than in the non-traded goods sector (the actual shares of traded goods in private investment in Ireland and Portugal are around 51% for the traded sector and 45% for the non-traded sector).

The public sector account assumes a balanced budget with a public debt of 50% of GDP. Government transfers are 15% of GDP and the total taxation consistent with the balanced budget assumption, and also accounting for interest payment on the public debt, is 37.5% of GDP.

In terms of the parameter set, we use the input/output tables for Ireland and Portugal to determine the labour shares in both the traded and non-traded goods sectors. The clear indication is that the labour shares in value added are greater in the non-traded goods sector, a fact reflected in the stylized figures used for the simulations, 55% for the traded sector and 60% for the non-traded sector which are somewhere between the real figures for Ireland and Portugal.

Given the labour shares and the assumption of wage equalization between the two sectors, we obtain the allocation of labour force between sectors using the first-order conditions for labour for both the tradable goods sector and the non-tradable goods sector. The values we obtain are that 38% of the labour force is employed in the traded sector and the remaining 62% in the non-traded goods sector. These values are very much in line with the data for both Ireland and Portugal, which suggests that the shares of employment in the traded goods sector are 36% and 38.5% respectively.

In turn the nominal wage rate is obtained using the first-order condition for labour for the tradable goods sector. It depends on the labour share parameters for both sectors directly and through the allocation of the labour force. We obtain a value of 0.55, which means that wage income amounts to 55% of GDP. This value is in line with the labour shares assumed for the two sectors and the fact that there is a mark-up in the non-traded sector. Finally, the scale parameter for leisure is obtained from the long-run version of the wage equation. It depends on the observed values for consumption, labour force participation and the value obtained for the wage rate. It depends directly on leisure as a fraction of the total labour force and on the mark-up in the labour market.

The probability of survival is set at 97.5%, which corresponds to an active life of 40 years. In turn, the interest rate faced by the domestic economy is assumed to be 5%. This includes the risk-free interest rate of 3.5% and the exogenous risk premium of 1.5%. The endogenous risk premium is normalized to 0.00 since it is a function of the foreign debt to GDP ratio which is itself normalized to 0.00. The responsiveness of this endogenous risk component to the foreign debt to output ratio is set at 0.4. This value is consistent with the estimates for the euro area that a one percentage point in the government debt to GDP ratio translates into an increase of 4 basis points in the government bond yield. As to the real adjustment costs we assume that they are the same for both sectors and correspond to 20% of the investment observed in the baseline. This means that 20% of the observed investment is lost in terms of capital accumulation. This value is in line with the assumptions in the literature.

Finally, we need to consider the values for the nominal adjustment costs in the non-traded and labour markets as well as the degree of monopolistic competition in both markets. We assume that the price mark-ups in both markets are 10%. As to the nominal adjustment cost parameters we choose these parameters to match available evidence on price and wage stickiness in the euro area. As noted earlier, there is a symmetric relationship between the price equations generated by Calvo contracting and our quadratic adjustment formulation. Using the Calvo approach, estimates of the average length of time over which prices remain fixed in the euro area range from 4 quarters (Gali et al., 2001) to 10 quarters (Smets and Wouters, 2002). These estimates, however, relate to the whole economy. In our framework, 40% of output is accounted for by the traded goods sector, which we assume to be a flexible price sector. These aggregate estimates would thus imply an average duration of prices in the non-traded sector of between 8 and 20 quarters. Taking as our starting point, the midpoint of this range, namely 14 quarters, would lead to a value of the nominal price adjustment cost of 50 in our baseline steady state. As to wage stickiness, the evidence for euro area countries is relatively thin. We calibrate our nominal wage adjustment cost parameter so that the dynamic response of wages to consumer prices of our equation matches that of the estimated wage equation of Smets and Wouters (2002). This leads to a value, at baseline steady state, of 50.

Model Calibration

We calibrate the model to capture long-term trends in the economy. In particular the calibrated values are such that the model replicates the long-term data and other information we presented above. This means that the calibration conditions are based on the model steady-state conditions, i.e. on the fact that in the long term the ratios of all the relevant variables to GDP are constant. In addition, the calibration procedures recognize that the steady-state restrictions imposed on the model depend on the presence of price and wage setting as well as on the effects of monopolistic competition in the non-traded sector as well as the labour market. By definition, the calibrated variables and parameters cannot be set independently in that they depend on the values assumed by the parameters and variables introduced in the previous section. The plausibility or lack thereof of the calibrated values is, accordingly, in itself an indication of the plausibility or lack thereof of the parameters and data presented in the previous section. The details of the calibration strategy are discussed below and are presented in a recursive manner, highlighting the dependency of the calibrated values on the parameters and data introduced in the previous section.

We start with the determination of human wealth. Human wealth is obtained from the corresponding equation of motion. It depends on the wage rate and therefore on the labour-share parameters for both sectors. In addition, it depends on the interest rate, the growth rate for the economy and on the survival probability. The calibrated value is 451% of the GDP. The steady-state profits for the firms for each sector are obtained from the corresponding equations in the model. They depend on the wage rate and therefore on the labour-share parameters for both sectors. The value of the firms in both sectors is obtained from the corresponding equation of motion. It depends on the wage rate and therefore on the labour-share parameters for both sectors. In addition, it depends on the interest rate and the growth rate for the economy. The calibrated value is 478% of GDP.

The subjective discount rate is obtained from the consumption equation given observed consumption, foreign debt and public debt, and the calibrated human wealth and value of the firms. It is, therefore, affected by all the parameters that enter into the calibration of human wealth and the value of the firms. In addition it depends on the probability of survival. The value calibrated is 3.6%, which is in line with the risk-free interest rate in the economy. The savings rate out of total wealth depends on the probability of survival and the subjective discount rate and indirectly on everything used to determine the subjective discount rate. The calibrated value is 94.1%.

The shadow price of capital in the traded goods sector is obtained from the corresponding variational condition and using the assumptions about the determination of adjustment costs (see below). It depends on the interest rate and adjustment costs as a share of observed investment in the sector. The calibrated values are 1.75 and are the same in both sectors since the real adjustment costs are assumed to be equal and the nominal rigidities in the non-traded sector are zero in the context of the calibration.

The depreciation rate in the tradable goods sector is obtained from equalizing the variational condition for the shadow price of capital and the equation of motion for the shadow price of capital as well as the assumptions about the determination of adjustment costs (see below). It depends on the observed values of output and investment in the sector as well as the calibrated value of the shadow price of capital. In addition it depends on adjustment costs as a share of observed investment in the sector, the share of capital in production and the growth rate of the economy. Indirectly it depends on the interest rate through the shadow price of capital. The calibrated value is 9.6%, which implies an average life of the capital assets of just over ten years.

The capital stock in the traded goods sector is obtained from the corresponding equation of motion. It depends on the observed level of investment in the sector as well as on the assumptions about the determination of adjustment costs (see below). In addition it depends on the rate of growth of the economy as well as the depreciation rate and everything implicit in its determination. The calibrated value is 84.4% of aggregate GDP. The adjustment cost parameter for investment is obtained from the definition of adjustment costs assuming that total adjustment costs are a given share of observed investment in the sector. It depends on observed investment in the sector as well as the calibrated stock of capital and all parameters involved in its determination. The calibrated value is 1.67. The scale parameter for the tradable goods sector is obtained from the production function given observed output, labour and capital shares in production, and the calibrated labour input and capital stock. The calibrated value is 8.8.

The calibration procedure to obtain the depreciation rate, the capital stock, the adjustment cost parameter, and the output scale parameter for the non-traded goods sector is similar to the procedure for the traded sector. In addition to the factors identified above for the tradable goods sector, the calibration for the non-traded goods sector depends also on the mark-up parameter. The calibrated value for the depreciation rate is 8.2%, which implies a life of about 12 years for the capital assets. The calibrated stock of capital is 121% of aggregate GDP. Finally, the calibrated values for the adjustment cost and the scale parameters are 1.96 and 12.1 respectively.

It is important to note that the calibrated values for the depreciation rates in both sectors are in line with the figures commonly used in the literature. Furthermore, they are consistent with the evidence for Ireland and Portugal that the depreciation rate in the traded goods sector is higher than in the non-traded goods sector. As to the values for the capital stocks, they imply an aggregate capital-output ratio of 2.1. Furthermore, consistent with the observed output and investment patterns in Ireland and Portugal, the capital stock is greater in the non-traded goods sector in absolute value but the capital intensity is greater in the traded goods sector, 2.2 versus 1.9.

A few final remarks are due on the role of nominal rigidities and monopolistic competition in the calibration procedure. Changes in the nominal rigidities do not affect the calibrated values since it is assumed that prices grow at the appropriate steady-state growth rate (in this case zero) and only deviations from this growth rate are subject to nominal adjustment costs. This implies that in the steady state by design there are no nominal adjustment costs in either the non-traded goods market or the labour market. In turn, changes in the degree of monopolistic competition in the labour markets only affect the scale parameter for leisure. The rest of the variables are not affected. Changes in the degree of monopolistic competition in the non-traded goods market affect many of the calibration values. This is because they affect the calibrated allocation of labour between the two sectors and therefore the calibrated wage rate and everything that depends on it in the calibration process.

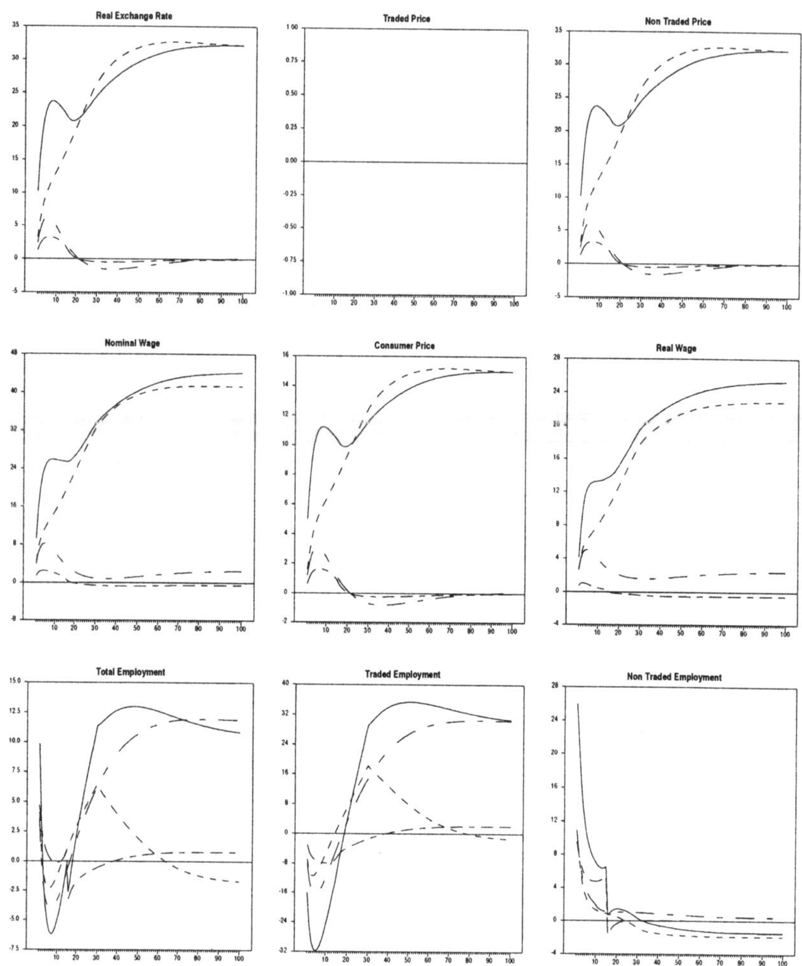

Notes:
Figure 7.1 shows percentage differences from base in the levels of the variables for all variables except:

- Output growth, inflation and interest rates (percentage point difference from base)
- Foreign debt (difference from base in GDP points).

The dashed line (———) shows the effect of the interest rate shock.
The dashed line (- - - -) shows the effect of the traded TFP shock.
The thin dashed line (– – –) shows the effect of the international transfers shock.
The solid line (——) shows the combined effect of all 3 shocks.

Figure 7.1 All 3 shocks – fixed exchange rate

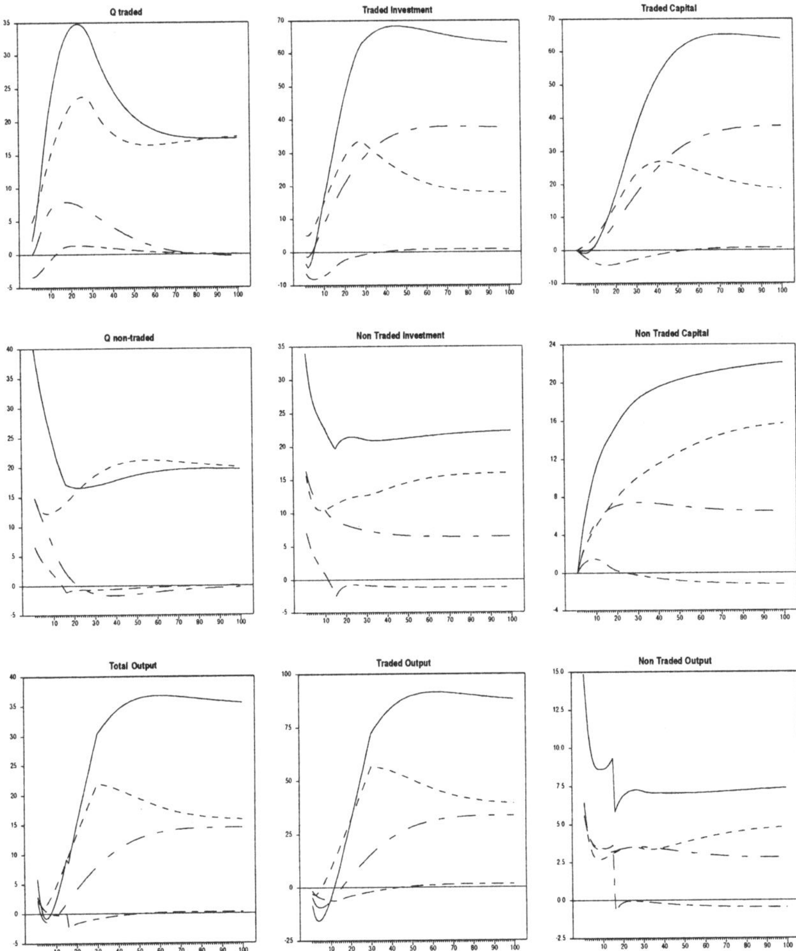

Notes:
Figure 7.1 shows percentage differences from base in the levels of the variables for all variables except:

- Output growth, inflation and interest rates (percentage point difference from base)
- Foreign debt (difference from base in GDP points).

The dashed line (———) shows the effect of the interest rate shock.
The dashed line (- - - -) shows the effect of the traded TFP shock.
The thin dashed line (---) shows the effect of the international transfers shock.
The solid line (——) shows the combined effect of all 3 shocks.

Figure 7.1 All 3 shocks – fixed exchange rate (cont.)

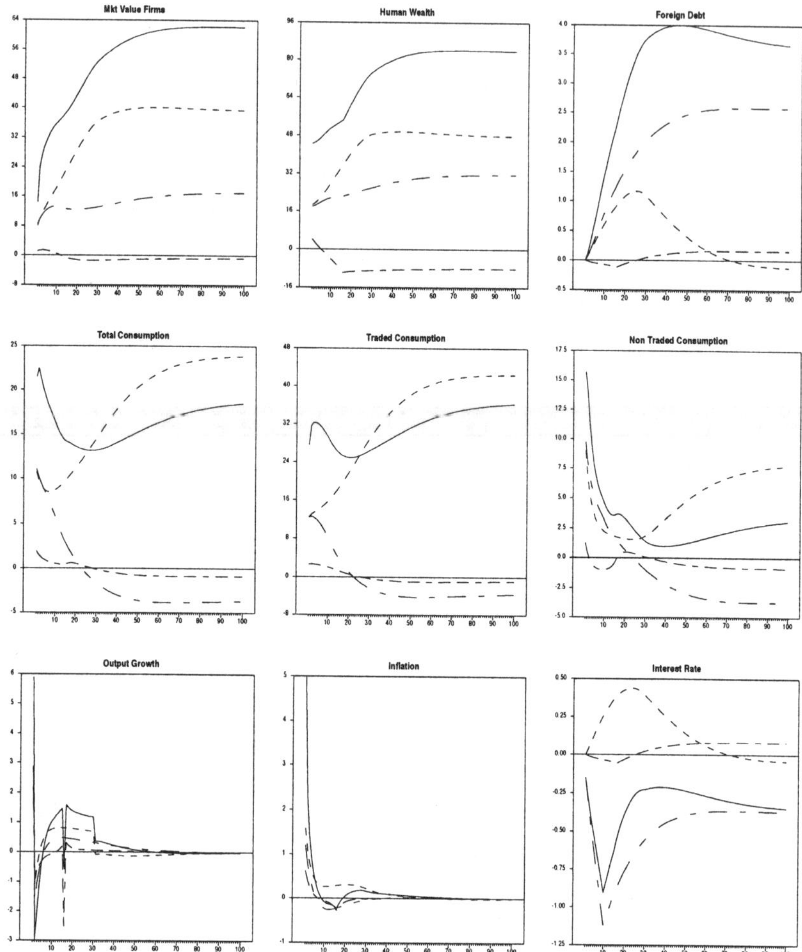

Notes:
Figure 7.1 shows percentage differences from base in the levels of the variables for all variables except:

- Output growth, inflation and interest rates (percentage point difference from base)
- Foreign debt (difference from base in GDP points).

The dashed line (———) shows the effect of the interest rate shock.
The dashed line (- - - -) shows the effect of the traded TFP shock.
The thin dashed line (---) shows the effect of the international transfers shock.
The solid line (——) shows the combined effect of all 3 shocks.

Figure 7.1 All 3 shocks – fixed exchange rate (cont.)

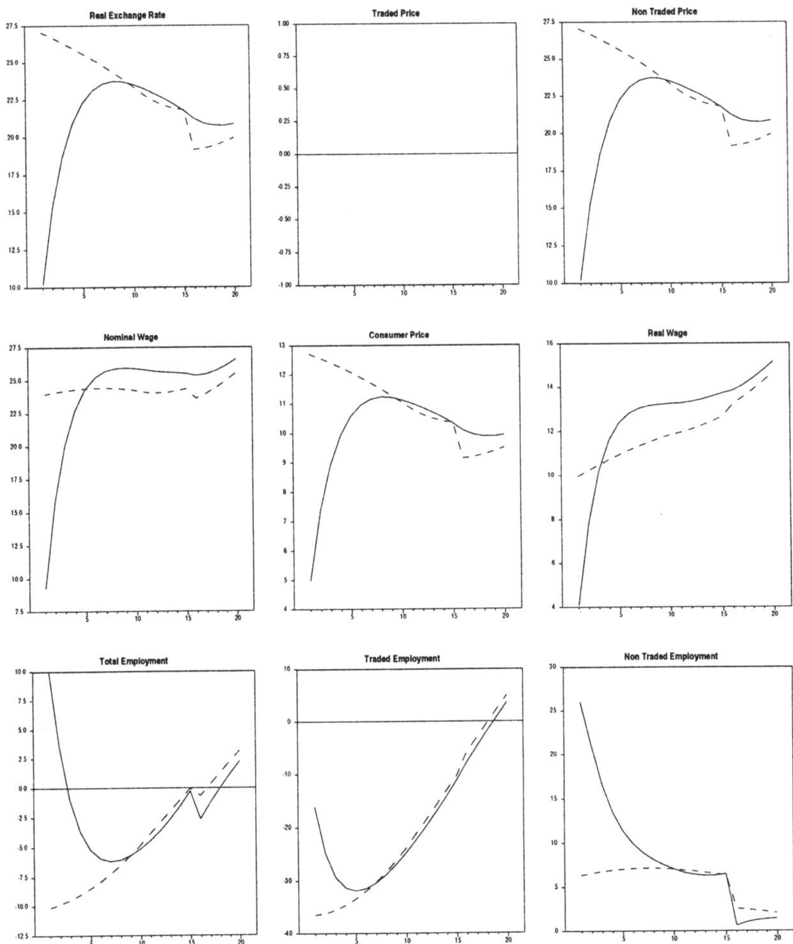

Notes:
Figure 7.2 shows percentage differences from base in the levels of the variables for all variables except:

- Output growth, inflation and interest rates (percentage point difference from base)
- Foreign debt (difference from base in GDP points).

The solid line shows the effect of all 3 shocks under sticky non-traded prices and wages.
The dashed line shows the effect in the absence of price and wage stickiness.

Figure 7.2 All 3 shocks — stickiness versus non-stickiness

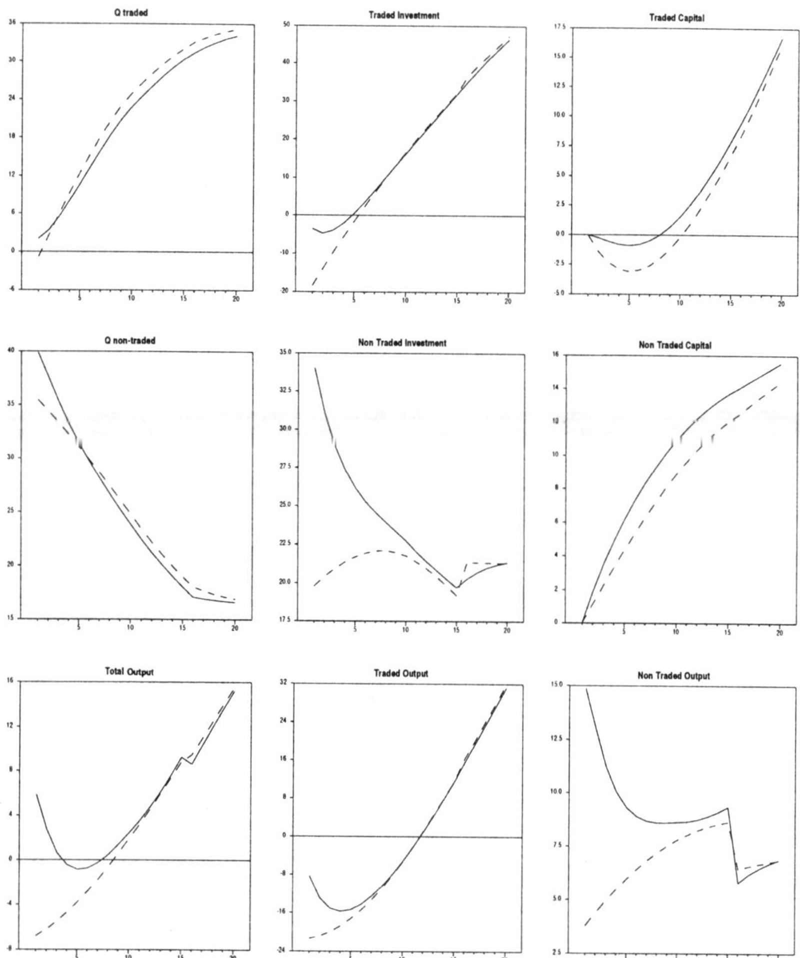

Notes:
Figure 7.2 shows percentage differences from base in the levels of the variables for all variables except:

- Output growth, inflation and interest rates (percentage point difference from base)
- Foreign debt (difference from base in GDP points).

The solid line shows the effect of all 3 shocks under sticky non-traded prices and wages.
The dashed line shows the effect in the absence of price and wage stickiness.

Figure 7.2 All 3 shocks – stickiness versus non-stickiness (cont.)

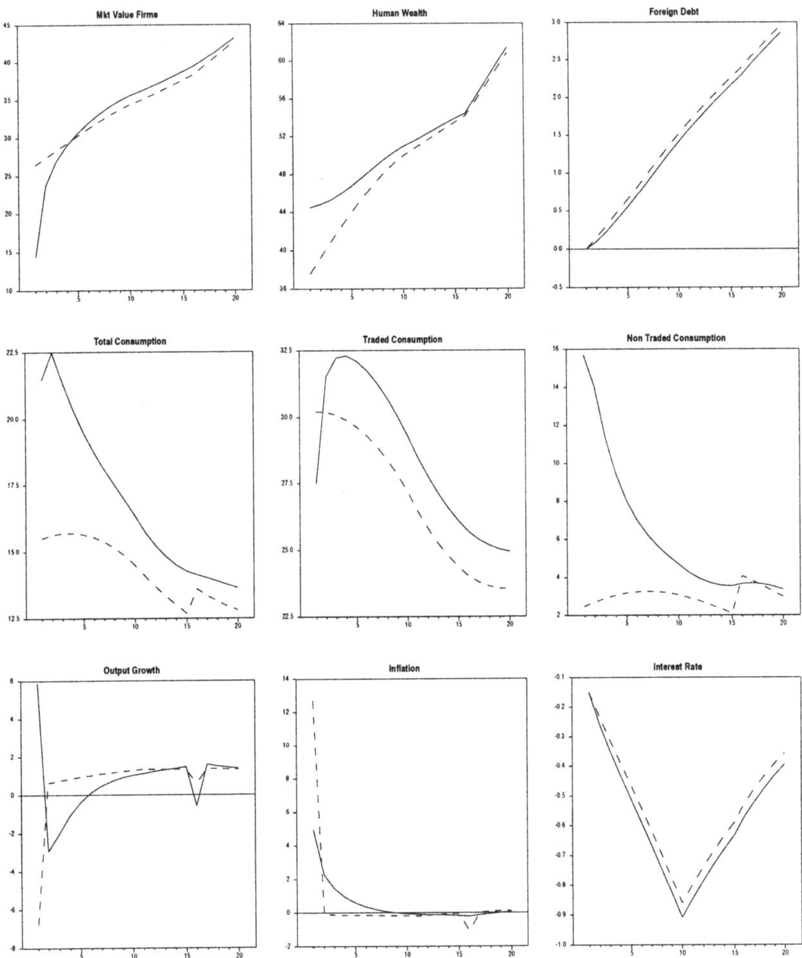

Notes:
Figure 7.2 shows percentage differences from base in the levels of the variables for all variables except:

- Output growth, inflation and interest rates (percentage point difference from base)
- Foreign debt (difference from base in GDP points).

The solid line shows the effect of all 3 shocks under sticky non-traded prices and wages.
The dashed line shows the effect in the absence of price and wage stickiness.

Figure 7.2 All 3 shocks – stickiness versus non-stickiness (cont.)

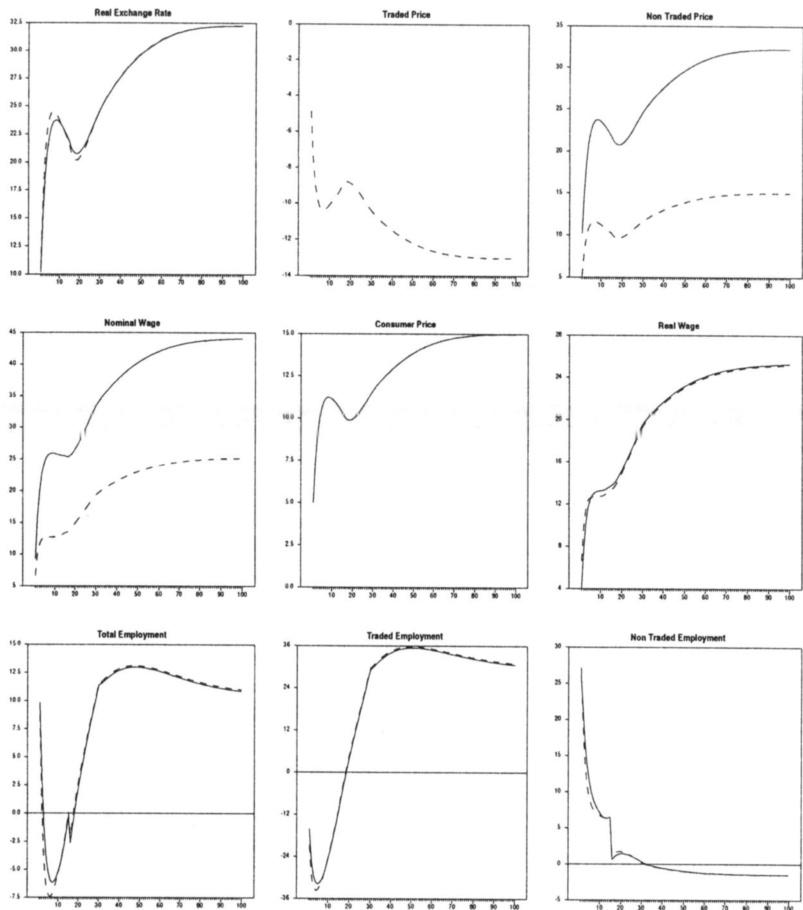

Notes:
Figure 7.3 shows percentage differences from base in the levels of the variables for all variables except:

- Output growth, inflation and interest rates (percentage point difference from base)
- Foreign debt (difference from base in GDP points).

The solid line shows the effects of the 3 shocks under a fixed exchange rate.
The dashed line shows the effects of the same shocks under floating exchange rates.

Figure 7.3 All 3 shocks – fixed versus floating exchange rate

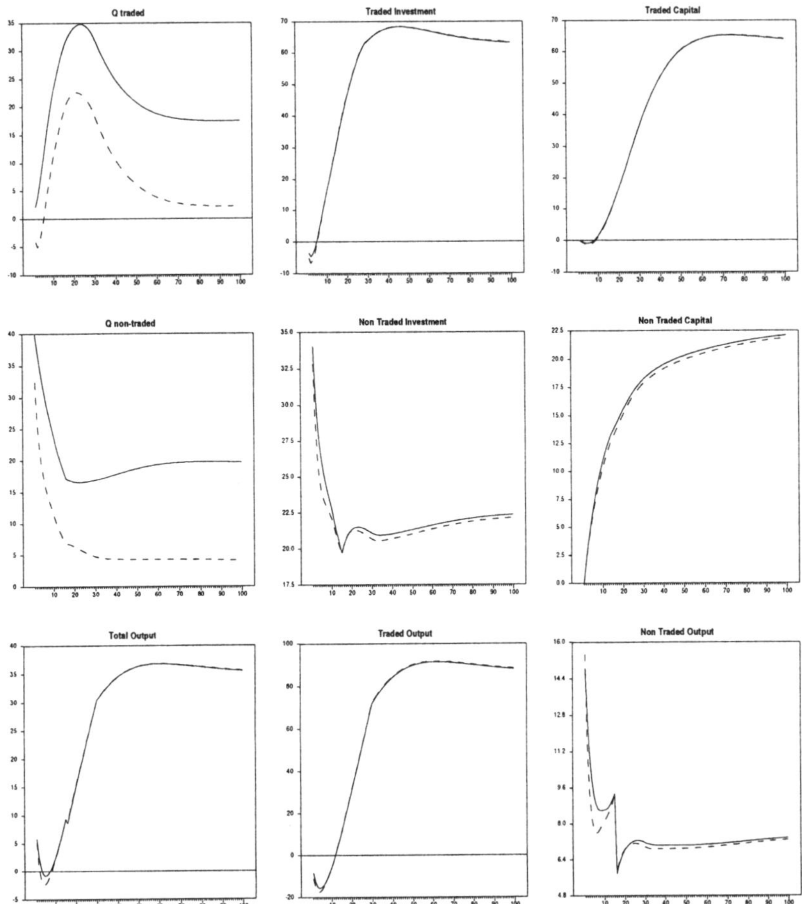

Notes:
Figure 7.3 shows percentage differences from base in the levels of the variables for all variables except:

- Output growth, inflation and interest rates (percentage point difference from base)
- Foreign debt (difference from base in GDP points).

The solid line shows the effects of the 3 shocks under a fixed exchange rate.
The dashed line shows the effects of the same shocks under floating exchange rates.

Figure 7.3 All 3 shocks – fixed versus floating exchange rate (cont.)

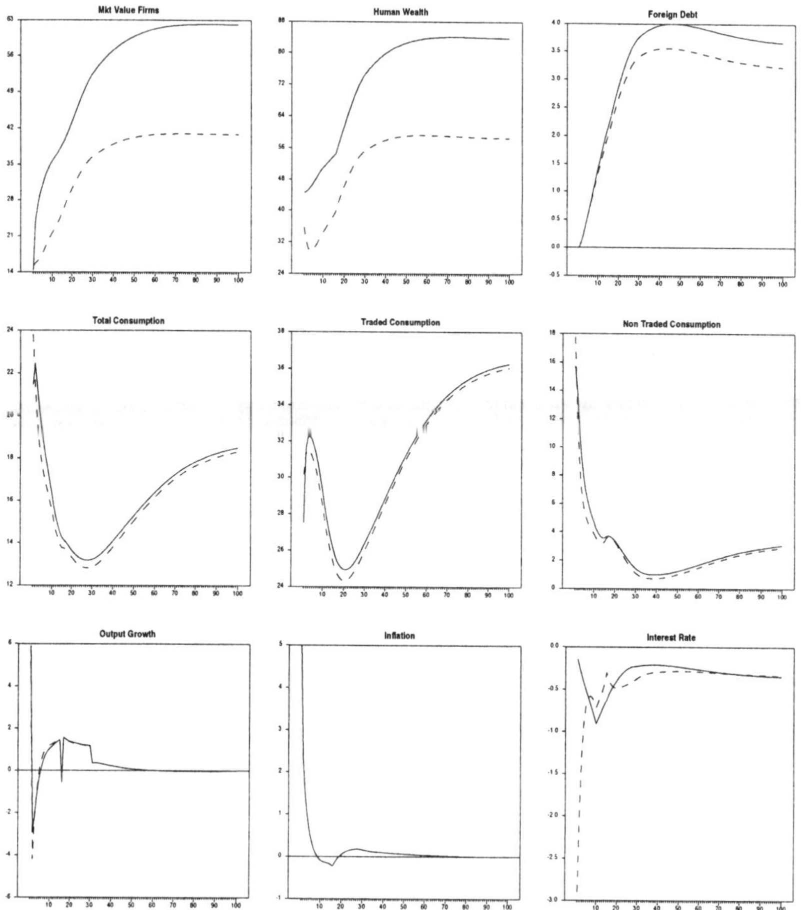

Notes:
Figure 7.3 shows percentage differences from base in the levels of the variables for all variables except:

- Output growth, inflation and interest rates (percentage point difference from base)
- Foreign debt (difference from base in GDP points).

The solid line shows the effects of the 3 shocks under a fixed exchange rate.
The dashed line shows the effects of the same shocks under floating exchange rates.

Figure 7.3 All 3 shocks – fixed versus floating exchange rate (cont.)

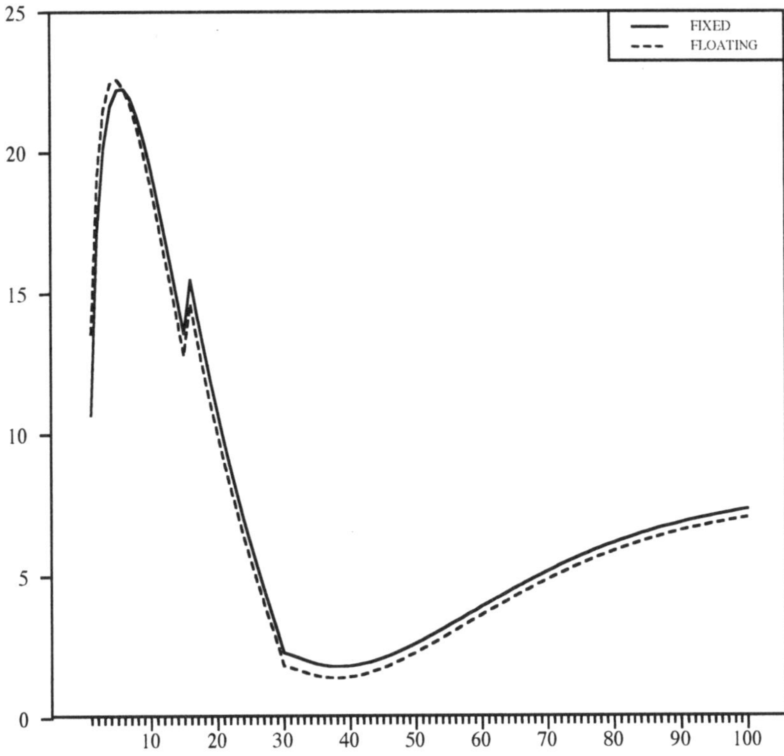

Notes:
The solid line shows the effects of the 3 shocks under a fixed exchange rate.
The dashed line shows the effects of the same shocks under floating exchange rates.

Figure 7.4 Consumer utility – percentage difference from baseline

COMMENTS

Willem Buiter

This chapter addresses an important topic, the response of a representative small accession country to a triad of shocks associated with the transition process: (1) a sustained increase in the rate of growth of total factor productivity in the traded goods sector; (2) an increase in the degree of international financial integration, modelled as a reduction in the exogenous component of the domestic-foreign interest rate differential; and (3) a sustained increase in external transfers, modelled as a 15-year increase in foreign currency transfers, which are then spent entirely on non-traded goods. The vehicle they use is a two-sector Yaari-Blanchard OLG model of a small open economy. The foreign price of traded goods and the foreign interest rate are taken to be exogenous. The model incorporates two sources of nominal rigidity: rigidities in the setting of nominal non-traded goods prices and rigidities in the setting of nominal wages. Numerical simulation is used to analyse the behaviour of the system in response to these shocks under a fixed nominal exchange rate regime and under a floating exchange rate regime.

Here are a few technical comments and reflections to start with. First, the infinite-horizon Ramsey approach with an exogenous rate of time preference does not lead to an *indeterminate* steady state level of foreign debt. When the two time preference rates are equal, the steady state net foreign asset position is *hysteretic*. It cannot be determined from the steady state conditions alone but requires knowledge of the initial conditions and of the behaviour of the exogenous variables during the transition to steady state. Given that information, however, the solution is unique. When the two time preference rates are not the same, the country with the lowest time preference rate will in the long run own all global wealth.

Second, future labour income is not discounted at a higher rate reflecting the probability of survival. That is true for the individual but not for the aggregate or population. While you may not be around to pay the postponed taxes, if you are, you pay more. In the 'Poisson' model of death the two effects cancel each other out. It is the birth rate that does the work (see Buiter, 1988, 1990/91).

Third, the model has a single firm producing the composite non-traded good — 'the non-traded goods aggregator'. This single firm, this monopolist par excellence, is, however, assumed to act competitively. This single aggregator uses inputs supplied by a continuum of firms located on the [0,1] interval. These infinitesimally small firms are price setters (monopolists) in the market for their output but price takers in the factor markets. One would have expected to see the roles of the monopolist and the perfect competitor reversed.

Fourth, the nominal rigidities in the adjustment of the nominal price of non-traded goods and in the money wage rate is ad hoc. Menu costs, if they are significant at all, are fixed costs (see Caplin and Spulber, 1987). The authors postulate quadratic real adjustment costs of price changes (and of wage changes, with unions experiencing quadratic adjustment costs to changing prices). Even though there may be a precedent for this, it represents an abuse of analogy with the familiar strictly convex adjustment costs of the real capital stock (see Rotemberg, 1982). We should be open about the fact that we do not have a theory of nominal rigidities and not hide behind spurious or pseudo microfoundations (see, for example, Buiter, 2003). The optimization of an arbitrary objective function subject to arbitrary constraints is not microfoundations. Also, in the discussion of nominal wage rigidity, the authors confuse monopolistic behaviour and nominal stickiness or rigidity. Monopolistic pricing is fully consistent with perfect nominal and real flexibility. We need price or wage setting 'in advance' for nominal rigidities to arise.

A surprising feature of the model is that it determines money prices, wages and nominal exchange rates but does not have money or official foreign exchange reserves appearing anywhere. Money does not appear in a household and/or firm transactions technology, nor in the household objective functional or in the household budget constraint. Money does not appear in the objective function of firms nor in their budget constraints. Money does not appear in the government's budget constraint. The same variable appears to do double duty as the domestic nominal and real interest rate.

There are circumstances under which it is technically possible (though never advisable) to do monetary theory without explicitly considering money. In the 'money in the utility function' class of models, a necessary condition is that money be separable in the period objective function from consumption of goods and leisure. In addition, the monetary instrument must be either the nominal exchange rate or the domestic nominal interest rate — never the nominal money stock. If the exchange rate or the nominal interest rate is the instrument, care must be taken to ensure that the other equations of the model, including the government's budget constraint and budget rule, are consistent with this choice of instruments.

Consider a typical money demand function. With the nominal interest rate as an instrument and the price level predetermined, the nominal money stock will have to vary endogenously to satisfy the monetary equilibrium conditions. The government's budgetary rule must accommodate the necessary endogeneity of the composition of the government's financial portfolio and of its net financial balance. In addition, with a nominal interest rate rule, care must be taken that the economy does not follow Wicksellian unstable trajectories, with too low a nominal interest rate boosting demand, raising inflation, which further reduces the real interest rate, etc. The Taylor rule is one example of a nominal interest rate rule that is stabilizing for a large class of models.

The following are recommended for future revisions and additional research:

- Introduce money explicitly in the utility function and in the government and household (and perhaps enterprise) budget constraints. Distinguish systematically between nominal and real prices and quantities.
- Be precise about what the monetary instrument is under a floating exchange rate. There really are only two candidates: the nominal stock of base money and the nominal interest rate.
- Simplify: one source of nominal rigidity is enough. You are not estimating an empirical model to be used for forecasting, you are calibrating a small, relatively simple model in order to use it to do qualitative economic theory with numerical methods. The model is highly non-linear, with its two-sector production structure, endogenous capital stock, overlapping-generations household behaviour and nominal rigidities. It is almost guaranteed to have multiple steady states, especially since the long-run domestic real interest rate is endogenous through the endogeneity of the long-run risk premium. The methods of Juillard and Laxton assume that there is a unique long-run equilibrium. It should be possible to determine whether, or under what restrictions, the model has a unique steady state.
- Do the analysis one shock at a time. It is hard to be intuitive when you are being perturbed from three different directions.
- Do not model greater financial integration as a lower domestic interest rate (through a lower exogenous component in the risk premium) for both borrowers and lenders. Increased international financial integration goes together with a more efficient, competitive domestic financial sector. Therefore, lower rates for borrowers might be achieved at the same time as higher rates for lenders.
- Take a look at Blanchard and Giavazzi (2002) and the discussion of their paper in Buiter (2002). They consider the implications of productivity catch-up, a higher degree of international financial integration and a higher degree of trade integration (parameterized as more elastic global demand curves for national outputs). It is argued

that all three shocks imply higher current account deficits. Lower interest rates reduce private saving. Higher productivity growth reduces private saving (for permanent income reasons) and stimulates private investment. Higher trade integration also increases current account deficits. While their model has some weaknesses (the results depend on a country being completely specialized in its ownership of real assets, that is, claims to domestic GDP are owned by domestic residents only), they provide an interesting alternative approach to a similar set of policy questions.

REFERENCES

Blanchard, Olivier and Francesco Giavazzi (2002), 'Current account deficits in the euro area. The end of the Feldstein-Horioka puzzle?', *Brooking Papers on Economic Activity*, 2002, **II**, pp. 147–86.

Buiter, Willem H. (1988), 'Death, birth, productivity growth and debt neutrality', *Economic Journal*, **98**, June, pp. 279–93.

Buiter, Willem H. (1990), 'Debt neutrality, redistribution and consumer heterogeneity: a survey and some extensions', in W. C. Brainard et al. (eds), *Money, Macroeconomics and Economic Policy; Essays in Honor of James Tobin*, The MIT Press, 1991, (re)printed in Willem H. Buiter, *Principles of Budgetary and Financial Policy*, Cambridge, Massachusetts: The MIT Press, pp. 183–222.

Buiter, Willem H. (2002), 'Comment on "Current account deficits in the euro area. The end of the Feldstein Horioka puzzle?"', by Olivier Blanchard and Francesco Giavazzi, *Brooking Papers on Economic Activity*, **II**, pp. 187–96.

Buiter, Willem H. (2003), 'James Tobin; an appreciation of his contribution to economics', NBER Working Paper No. 9753, June, forthcoming in *The Economic Journal*.

Caplin, Andrew S. and Daniel F. Spulber (1987), 'Menu costs and the neutrality of money', *Quarterly Journal of Economics*, **102**, November, pp. 703–25.

Rotemberg, J. (1982), 'Sticky prices in the United States', *Journal of Political Economy*, **90**, pp. 1187–211.

Index